PORTRAITS OF PAUL

PORTRAITS OF PAUL
An Archaeology of Ancient Personality

Bruce J. Malina
and
Jerome H. Neyrey

Westminster John Knox Press
Louisville, Kentucky

Chapter 3 was originally published as "The Forensic Defense Speech and Paul's Trial Speeches in Act 22–26: Form and Function," in *Luke-Acts New Perspectives from the Society of Biblical Literature Seminar,* ed. Charles H. Talbert (New York: Crossroad, 1984), pp. 210–24. It appears here in greatly revised form courtesy of Crossroad Publishing Company.

Chapter 4 was originally published as "Dealing with Biblical (Mediterranean) Characters: A Guide for U.S. Consumers," *Biblical Theology Bulletin* 19 (1989): 127–41; and "Is There a Circummediterranean Person? Looking for Stereotypes," *Biblical Theology Bulletin* 22 (1992): 66–87. They appear here in greatly revised form with permission from the editors of *Biblical Theology Bulletin.*

Book design by Jennifer K. Cox
Cover illustration: Saint Paul Preaching in Ephesus. Le Sueur, Eustache, 1616–1655. French. Musee Du. Louvre, Paris. *Courtesy of SuperStock.*

First edition

Published by Westminster John Knox Press
Louisville, Kentucky

This book is printed on acid-free paper that meets the American National Standards Institute Z39.48 standard. ∞

PRINTED IN THE UNITED STATES OF AMERICA

96 97 98 99 00 01 02 03 04 05 — 10 9 8 7 6 5 4 3 2 1

Library of Congress Cataloging-in-Publication Data

Malina, Bruce J.
    Portraits of Paul : an archaeology of ancient personality / Bruce
J. Malina and Jerome H. Neyrey — 1st ed.
        p.   cm.
    Includes bibliographical references and index.
    ISBN 0-664-25681-3
    1. Paul, the Apostle, Saint. 2. Rhetoric in the Bible.
3. Prosopography. 4. Biography—To 500. I. Neyrey, Jerome H.,
date.   II. Title.
BS2506.M355   1996
225.9′2—dc20   96-18497

For John J. Pilch,
long-time friend and supportive colleague,
creative scholar, vibrant teacher,
and talented musician on his sixtieth birthday.

Sto lat, niech żyje nam!

Contents

Introduction

This book is about the ways first-century Mediterranean persons understood one another. It is about the ancient Mediterranean meaning of the self, that is, the human person. Presumably, the task of interpreting a biblical book is to discover what the document's original author(s) said and meant to some original audience. Meanings derive from, and in their own way constitute, the social system of the author and the original audience. One of the problems of New Testament interpretation is the paucity of generalizations available to modern readers for understanding ancient Mediterranean social systems. For it is the social system of the first-century Mediterranean that served as framework of available meaning for the authors and audience under discussion. A social system, whether past or present, can only be presented at a level of abstraction that most would call "theoretical." And many historians are extremely allergic to explicit theory. As Mann has observed:

> If historians eschew theory of how societies operate, they imprison themselves in the commonsense notions of their own society.... There are more social and historical data than we can digest. A strong sense of theory enables us to decide what might be the key facts, what might be central and what marginal to an understanding of how a particular society works. We elect our data, see whether they confirm or reject our theoretical hunches, define the latter, collect more data, and continue zigzagging across between theory and data until we have established a plausible account of how this society, in this time and place, "works." (Mann 1986, vii)

Such zigzagging is what the U.S. philosopher C. S. Peirce called abduction or retroduction (Malina 1991a, 259–60). Triandis reflects such a procedure when he notes: "The meaning of a construct needs to be established by moving back and forth between theory and measurement"

(1990, 42), where measurement means some numerical assessment of observed behavior. Woodson (1979, 1) in turn describes the process as follows:

> *Abduction.* The process in the logic of the discovery procedure of working from evidence to hypothesis, involving a back-and-forth movement of suggestion checking. In this process two pieces of data could be explained by a hypothesis, the validity of which could be corroborated by the finding of another piece of data. If the third piece of data is true, then the hypothesis is probably true. Since the question remains of what suggested the hypothesis, abduction differs from deduction, which follows the pattern of asserted antecedent to consequence (italics added).

The problem in biblical studies, of course, has been the "Received View," a philosophy of science label for the way of understanding things in vogue among a large number of practitioners and in the popular mind (see Malina 1986b, 171–73). The Received View relative to biblical interpretation is the "sensate thinker's" profile, concerned with the amassing of "facts." The attitude and perspective revealed in the psychobabble of many Received View historians and their fears, cautions, worries, and concerns with using social science models for understanding the past reveals rather obsessive engagement with facts (see Judge 1980). "Facts" really refer to data, to individual and unique bits of information, without a thought given to how those facts were invented in the first place. If the "facts only" focus of interest of "objective" historians were anatomy rather than ancient history, for example, they would have one believe that we must start a concerted scholarly effort to have all the pictures in *Gray's Anatomy* duly labeled with the names of those persons who posed for the veins, heart, lungs, bones, and so forth. This would be part of their same effort to have the site, time, and precise situation of those particles out of which scientists make molecular Tinkertoy models. And soon they would insist on knowing whose DNA served for the original mock-up of the spiral cell now so popular in textbooks of biology. With their exclusive interest in the distinctive, particular, individual, and unique "fact," such historians obviously do not eat apples. Rather they eat the first red object on the lowest branch of the third tree in the fourth row of the northwest orchard of Smith's farm in the southwest corner of the Snake River valley near Walla Walla, Washington, of the United States of America in North America on the Earth in the Solar System and Galaxy X, that object having been picked on September 14, 1998, at 9 A.M. by George Smith, son of Henry Smith, son of Louis Smith, and so on (popularly, but unhistorically, called a big Delicious apple).

And yet without a historian's interest and ability in zigzagging between theory and data, there are no "facts." For a fact is some theory-based interpretation of some datum. And meanings derive from social system-based interpretations of experience. The problem, of course, is at what point is specificity overkill, and at what point is generalization not useful. For interpreters of behavioral scenarios depicted in ancient documents, perhaps generalizations are more useful than the red-object specificity described above. And for interpreters of ancient descriptions of stereotypical behavior, perhaps generalizations are the only proper mode of articulation.

Regarding ancient Mediterranean persons, for example, consider C. K. Barrett's (1994) recent perceptive introduction to the "thought" of Paul. This scholar has no need for a consideration of Paul's social moorings to understand the apostle:

> A life of Paul has no necessary place in a discussion of the apostle as a Christian thinker, and all that has been offered here is a sequence of glimpses of the man in various settings, chosen because they represent some of the major stages of his career and included because he was not an abstract thinker, given to speculation about abstract truth. (1994, 20)

Barrett obviously believes one can discuss a writer's meanings apart from the social system in which the writer is embedded. When he does allude to social context, we find that Paul's contemporaries are much like modern northern Europeans:

> "Let each one be fully convinced in his own mind" (Rom. 14:5). It is more important that each Christian should think matters through, reach his own conclusion, and at the same time recognize the right of his fellow Christian to reach a different conclusion, than that there should be an artificial uniformity, and Paul has no intention of imposing his own view on others. (1994, 51)

Similarly, Becker's magisterial study of Paul would have us believe that Paul, like our twentieth-century contemporaries, derived his theological insights from introspection on his own personal, individual, singular experience:

> On what basis does Paul make his theological statements? If we ask this, we can make an observation that is valid from 1 Thessalonians to Romans: Paul speaks out of the experience of his call and especially out of the experience gained by him and the churches through the effect of the gospel on the worldwide mission field. Thus the apostle expresses himself on the basis of the new being effected by the Spirit, the common experience of all Christians with the gospel that changes people.... In this sense the theology of Paul is the theology of experience under the influence of the gospel and of the Spirit connected with it ... [so that] if Paul designs his theological statements on the basis of his experience of the gospel, then the

content of the gospel must consequently be the measure and criterion of everything—in short, for the interpretation of all reality. (1993, 373–76)

Yet when one searches for information about Paul's life, presumably the foundation for his personal introspection, we find that

> Apparently even Paul's contemporaries did not know much more than we about his Jewish [*sic!*] life. For beyond Paul himself the few bits of information that Acts places at our disposal—and that Acts no doubt drew from the general Paul legend—are likewise quickly summarized. These indications are so scant that while they increase somewhat the number of biographical mosaic stones, they do not allow us to construct a satisfactory overall picture of Paul's life. . . . The scant biographical data can be easily gathered. (1993, 33–34)

Perhaps Paul did, in fact, supply us with what he and his contemporaries considered full, sufficient, and substantial information for a biography. Perhaps it is with our expectations of what constitutes a "full" biography that we commit an anachronistic injustice to Paul and his contemporaries. This is what we hope to demonstrate. While Becker is fully abreast of the rhetorical resources available to Paul, he does not seem to have a larger comparative, social-scientific framework in which to situate the wealth of information he does have to produce a first-century Mediterranean Paul (see Becker 1993, 51–56; 273–78).

Unfortunately, the Received View encourages an ideological indisposition to the type of abduction adopted in this book. Hence, our concern is for those foolhardy enough to actually want to understand persons of the past instead of merely to collect data about them and describe them as though they lived in our own society and were motivated by the same concerns as we are. As even Received View historians are aware, contemporary relevance continues to be purchased at the cost of historical accuracy.

This book deals with that dimension of the social system of the ancient Mediterranean called modal or typical personality. It is a type of regional character study. How does a typical Midwesterner think of success? What does a typical big-city, American old person think? A typical Southerner? What do New Yorkers expect others to be like? What about Westerners or Southerners? What did people in the Mediterranean social systems of antiquity expect other Mediterranean persons to be like? How did they describe themselves in ordinary social contexts? The purpose of this book is to examine how first-century Mediterranean persons typically referred to others and, by implication, to themselves. Simply put, what did first-century persons mean when they referred to others as "you," "she," "he," or "they"? By implication, what would they mean by the word "I"? This study is a probe into the ancient awareness of person, the awareness of self. The category "self" points to a fundamental value object. In every society, the selves, along with the group, nature, time, and space, are the bearers of meaning. This study looks essentially to the self.

The ancients themselves were much concerned with typical selves but not in any of the introspective, psychological ways characteristic of the age of Romanticism and subsequent eras. First of all, they were much concerned to have influence on other selves. To this end, they developed a well-articulated rhetoric. The rhetorical documents of antiquity indicate that ancient Mediterraneans thought much and hard about how to approach another self, how to have impact on other selves, and in the process they gave more than enough indication of what they thought those other selves were like. Similarly they not only sought to influence other selves; they sought to protect themselves from the influence of other selves. To this end they equally thought long and hard about ways of discerning, judging, evaluating another self, without any probing or conversation, without learning anything empirically or psychologically about what the other self was like. From the documents that have come down to us, we can see that the ancients would quite readily agree that you can indeed tell a book by its cover. So too you can tell another person by the way she or he looks and moves. Thus any intelligent person can tell what any other person is like by his or her "cover" as well. The burden of this book is to help a twentieth-century reader understand what the world of first-century persons was like in terms of our probes.

While our information comes from the general Hellenistic world, we intend to take the data deriving from ancient descriptions of persons and to apply them to our reading of the New Testament. After all, Jesus was from Hellenistic Galilee; Paul tramped around the Hellenistic world. By the first century of our era, this Hellenistic Galilee, as well as the rest of the Hellenistic Mediterranean, was under Roman political influence but remained culturally Hellenistic nonetheless. Romans sought to civilize, not conquer; and civilization in the idiom of this period was called *Hellenism.*

In sum, the persons with whom we are ultimately concerned are those who populate the pages of the New Testament, and so our interest lies with the first-century Mediterranean world. By "first-century Mediterranean," we mean those persons of "the Greco-Roman empire, with its three million and a half square kilometers [as] an island of civilization surrounded by barbarians" (Strabo, *Geography,* end of book 6 as cited in Veyne 1989, 388). We consider this region a culture area because, after the entry of Rome into Greek affairs and its victory over Hannibal, Italy and the eastern Mediterranean henceforth ceased to be two separate worlds.

In what follows, the first chapter provides a brief introduction to the problem addressed by our research. The fact is many investigators have inquired into the quality of personhood attested to by authors of biblical writing in general and to other documents from the New Testament period in particular. In the first chapter we present a short survey of recent attempts to describe ancient persons along with some reasons for considering these attempts as inadequate. We then briefly sketch those typical but stereotypical clues useful for perceiving and describing persons in antiquity.

The second chapter opens with the view of person that emerges from those styles of praising others called *encomia*. Mediterranean thinkers developed and employed formal norms for thinking about persons and describing them. These norms were set out in "how-to" documents called *progymnasmata*. With the progymnasmata, would-be public speakers were instructed on how to write speeches of praise (encomia) and blame about persons, as well as places and things. After exposing this native Mediterranean material, we will indicate how it basically formed the particular cultural perspective through which Paul and other first-century people described themselves and others. We will suggest how the rules of the encomium literature shaped and guided Paul's presentation in the so-called autobiographical parts of his letters. In conclusion, we shall summarize our presentation by sketching some bold strokes for a scenario of person offered in the encomia. This will mark a first stage in our development of an adequate anthropological model of how ancient Mediterraneans thought of and described persons, themselves and others.

The third chapter considers the legal defense speeches one might hear when citizens gather for purposes of dispute resolution. We would call such a gathering a "court." For such situations, native instruction on how to describe friends and enemies is to be found in rhetorical handbooks dealing with public defense speeches. In court speeches, formally called "forensic speeches," the citizen speaker seeking to defend his reputation is expected to attack another person or group or lay out his own defense, or both. Of course, a citizen might represent some other person in a given case and thus act like a modern lawyer. Both Cicero and Quintilian, as well as others, instruct orators on how to portray the character (ethos) of the persons in question. As we did with the encomium in the progymnasmata, here too we shall describe the ancient documents and indicate how they contribute to and illustrate the comparative model of person we are developing. Significantly, rhetorical public defense instructions serve as an excellent lens for interpreting the portrayal of Paul in the forensic defense speeches of Acts 22—26. This chapter provides further information about the model of person shared by ancient Mediterranean elite authors.

The fourth chapter discusses what the ancients called *physiognomics*. In a recent essay, Bruce Malina (1992) presents and assesses the ancient physiognomic materials with a view to understanding the way ancient

Mediterraneans stereotyped their fellows. Furthermore, several articles on the portrayal of Paul in that second-century document known as *The Acts of Paul* have likewise employed material from the physiognomic literature of antiquity. After describing physiognomic perspectives and principles, we will suggest how the perception and portrayal of Paul in that document was crafted in light of native Mediterranean stereotypes of persons. In this way we offer a further, fuller assessment of the model of person operative in the physiognomic literature.

The fifth chapter compares the results of our inquiry into the kinds and styles of scenarios available from the rhetorical and physiognomic writings with the evaluations of social psychologists such as Triandis and anthropologists such as Geertz. We find their cautions against utilizing modern Western perceptions of personality to assess non-Westerners equally appropriate in the case of ancient Mediterraneans. Nearly all modern views of ancient Mediterraneans are ethnocentric and anachronistic. For accuracy's sake, other models are required for our understanding of persons in the world of the New Testament. Here, then, we suggest a perspective for understanding ancient, eastern Mediterranean persons with the aid of cultural anthropology and cross-cultural social psychology. While it is true that ancient Mediterraneans were individual beings, born one at a time, they were not individualistic persons. Ancient Mediterranean persons were collectivists, dyadic, and group oriented, much like 70 percent of the inhabitants of the world today. Such persons take their identity from the social relations in which they are embedded, primarily from the family.

In the sixth and final chapter, we shall then use the information provided by ancient rhetorical and physiognomic documents as the touchstone for describing a general picture of Paul and his contemporaries. In this context we consider Paul's claim to be a prophet and the meanings of this claim within his own social setting. We conclude the chapter with a brief overview of our insights into Paul that this study has developed.

There are two appendices—the first presents a list of progymnasmata and the rhetorical treatises that figure in our study, along with a sampling of progymnastic documents; the second draws the implications of the comparative models sketched out in the previous chapters with a view to understanding self-centered and other-centered behavior. Appendix 2 concludes with a table comparing United States and Mediterranean traits relative to the areas covered in this book.

In conclusion, we would like to thank Professor K. C. Hanson of Creighton University for his care in reading the final draft of this book and for making a number of valuable suggestions.

BRUCE J. MALINA
JEROME H. NEYREY

1

The Problem of
Ancient Personality

ANECDOTAL CLUES

When soldiers of the United States army flew to Saudi Arabia for the
Bush-Hussein War in Iraq (1991), newspapers constantly reported on the
"culture shock" these soldiers experienced among the Saudis. Female
military personnel in particular found themselves out of place in public.
Cries were raised that Saudi Arabia totally lacks Western democracy.
Westerners did not understand the Saudis, who did not understand Westerners. Nor did Westerners comprehend Saddam Hussein's triumphal remarks in the fourth week of the bombardment of his countrymen:

> The resistance of our heroes to the warplanes and rockets of aggression
> and shame is the strongest indication of the steadfastness, faith and light in
> the hearts of the Iraqis and their great readiness not to give up the role
> willed them by God, the will to which they responded, faithfully and obedi-
> ently. . . . Bush lost his prestige when he lost conviction and lost the ability
> to convince through dialogue in order to avoid the course of using arms. He
> lost prestige when he brought in the arms which the West had intended
> against the Warsaw Pact, against one of the countries of the third world,
> which is an Arab country. (The Associated Press translation of
> Hussein's speech on February 10, 1992)

This man boasts of honor and respect in the midst of a ravaged civilian
population! He proclaims victory in terms of the suffering of a faithful people under cruel foreign oppression. Saddam declares that President Bush
lost his prestige by pulverizing Baghdad's people (some 225,000 Iraqis
were killed). These sentiments made excellent sense in the Middle East
and North Africa but no sense in the United States. Why? The issues were
always those of culture: People in the United States and the various Arab

nations seem to have quite different notions of what it means to be a person and what success and failure mean in those different cultural regions.

The baseball strike in the United States (1994) was largely motivated by capitalist concerns known as wages and profits. Every player and owner demands the right to pursue the baseball business to his or her own advantage. Baseball is also played in Japan, but it would be unthinkable that players would strike for individualistic benefits and so let down their team or city or followers. Again, the issue is one of culture. Japanese baseball players, workers, and citizens can be characterized as having *Wa,* that is, a strong sense of group loyalty that rewards faithfulness to group goals (Whiting 1979, 60–71).

> Despite talk of a new individualism among the younger generation of Japanese—that they are unwilling to sacrifice and toil for the corporation as their fathers did—it is still a country where social responsibilities generally come before individual rights. . . . Many players are driven by the need to belong. "Baseball is a world of duty and humanity," said Hiromichi Ishige, captain of the Seibu Lions. "To evaluate oneself just by money and sell oneself at the highest price, that's business." (Robert Whiting, "Japan's No-Strike Zone," *New York Times,* October 9, 1994)

They do not understand us, and we do not understand them. Obviously what it means to be a human being in Japan is different from the way Euro-Americans perceive it.

In another vein, several years ago it was reported that the "honor" killing of an adulterous wife would no longer be acquitted in Brazil. The Supreme Court there struck down the standard defense of men who had killed their wives on the grounds of a "legitimate defense of honor."

> According to a study in Sao Paulo State for the period 1980–1981, 722 men claimed defense of their honor as justification for killing women accused of adultery. (James Brooke, " 'Honor' Killing of Wives Is Outlawed in Brazil," *New York Times,* March 29, 1991)

Obviously some cultural understanding of male "honor" and female "shame" underpins this sort of behavior, which is utterly unintelligible to contemporary Euro-Americans. Such behavior implies different cultural notions about the family, gender, and values.

All three of these anecdotes serve to remind us that there are quite different ways of perceiving and describing what it means to be a human person in the world. Such anecdotes could be multiplied endlessly (Malina 1993c; Harris and Moran 1987, 466–78). They underscore the fact that we live in an age of multiculturalism. The awareness of multiculturalism would require us to be sensitive to differences among cultures, without lapsing into some sort of cultural imperialism. Yet it would seem to be rather insufficient simply to be aware of cultural differences. Perhaps the better approach would be to understand why such cultural differences exist at all.

Now consider three other anecdotes, this time from the ancient Mediterranean world. The first-century A.D. historian Josephus defended the excellence of Israelite piety by praising the way Israelite prayer focused on the good of the group. In some ways, this attitude replicates the Japanese *Wa* described above.

> Our sacrifices are not occasions for drunken self-indulgence—such practices are abhorrent to God—but for sobriety. At these sacrifices prayers for the welfare of the community must take precedence of those for ourselves; for we are born for fellowship, and he who sets its claims above his private interests is specially acceptable to God. (*Against Apion* 2.195–96, Loeb)

Josephus clearly gives high praise to self-restraint. Such behavior would be quite foreign to the crowds of baseball fans in United States ballparks. And while United States baseball fans root for their home team, the kind of group dedication Josephus praises is of a totally different order, for "setting aside private interests" is a paramount value—but not to contemporary Americans.

Plutarch, another first-century A.D. author (died ca. 120), commented that all people in his world were situated in some sort of hierarchical relationship, subject to some authority figure. He considers this normal and praiseworthy, not strange or unnatural.

> The nurse rules the infant, the teacher the boy, the gymnasiarch the youth, his admirer the young man who, when he comes of age, is ruled by law and his commanding general. No one is his own master, no one is unrestricted. (Plutarch, *Dialogue on Love* 754D, Loeb)

Modern Western psychology might describe this submission to others as a form of arrested development or even of codependency. Clearly, then, it would seem that ancients and moderns perceive and describe the human person in quite different ways.

Finally, we mention briefly that the defining characteristics of persons in antiquity were nearly always understood in terms of group of origin (generation) and place of origin (geography). In fact, the social classification of persons by generation, geography, and gender constituted the significant focal categories by which people understood each other. The author of Acts claims praise and status for Paul when he has Paul say: "I am a Judean, from Tarsus in Cilicia, a citizen of no low-status city" (Acts 21:39). This information, we will show, adequately presents the person of Paul to his Roman captors as a figure of status. Conversely, the author of the letter to Titus attacks troublemakers in Crete by recalling the old stereotype: "Cretans are always liars, evil beasts, lazy drunkards" (Titus 1:12).

Knowing that the troublemakers are from Crete provides sufficient information to identify them as having certain character traits. Vergil, a Latin,
unabashedly writes in his epic about the craftiness of Greeks, that "to
know one [Greek] is to know them all" (*Aen.* 2.65, Loeb). Then Philo, the
Hellenistic author from Alexandria, tells us that "the Egyptian disposition
is by nature a most jealous and envious one and inclined to look on the
good fortune of others as adversity of itself" (*Flaccus* 5.29, Hendrickson).

Luke, Josephus, Plutarch, Vergil, Philo, and the author of Titus all wrote
in the first century, lived in the eastern Mediterranean, and shared the same
set of cultural outlooks. They were nurtured on similar sets of values, judgments, and assumptions concerning human behavior. They are roughly contemporaries of Paul. Yet how strange to us are their evaluations of persons.
But, then, these writers are probably no stranger than the "honorable" husbands in Brazil, the Saudi Arabians, and the Japanese baseball players. It
would seem, perhaps, that it is North Americans who are abnormal,
strangers in the world, insisting that all others comply to U.S. norms.

Our point is simple—if we wish to come to understand the persons of
the ancient Mediterranean world, persons from the world of Jesus and
Paul, we should be prepared to learn entirely new ways of perceiving so
as to assess those persons on their own terms. Otherwise, we will be per-
petuating the long-standing problem of being "Ugly Americans," a phrase
coined to describe the utter failure of U.S. personnel at the beginning of
the Vietcong insurgency to understand the ways of that "mysterious" culture. This book, then, is written for North Americans who wish to practice the virtue of multiculturalism by attempting to learn how to perceive
ancient Mediterraneans such as Jesus and Paul in terms of the social sys-
tem(s) of the ancient Mediterranean culture area. It is intended to serve
as a guide to perceiving and describing human persons from the perspective of a world removed from us, not only in time, but in cultural values and social structures as well.

AIM AND STRUCTURE
OF THIS BOOK

This book aims to explain how ancient Mediterraneans perceived and
described each other. We believe that an intelligent and fair reading of the
New Testament documents requires such an understanding. Granted
that the ancient Mediterranean world is a thing of the past, our contention
is that witnesses from that period and region have provided considerable
evidence that can be mined to provide adequate data for our task. As we
systematically build up our data base, we also desire to organize and
structure these data to suggest the internal logic, values, and processes

whereby persons at the time were evaluated. Their mode of praising and blaming each other points to an underlying social system that contrasts sharply with our own. We shall attempt, then, to present a series of perspectives concerning how to perceive, evaluate, and describe one's fellow human beings. These perspectives both derive from ancient Mediterranean writers and speakers and served to instruct others in the skills of addressing and dealing with others. The outcome will be a scenario describing what and how ancient Mediterraneans thought of each other.

Native Informants

How can we be on methodically safe ground when we try to understand the natives of a world that is removed from us both by millennia and mileage? Like contemporary ethnographers who rely on local informants to provide them with native perspectives, we will employ the services of three groups of informants. In order to retrieve information from the past, we turn largely to the rhetorical writers of the ancient Mediterranean. Rhetoricians were the ancient experts in communication skills. They were very interested in persuasion techniques. Two different but related sets of rhetorical documents provided ancient writers and speakers with instruction in the culturally approved, formal rules about the proper evaluation and description of persons. The authors of these documents thus are eminently qualified to be our reliable guides to how Mediterraneans understood and assessed each other, for their writings were considered normative in their own cultures.

The first set of rhetorical documents were called *progymnasmata.* The authors of the progymnasmata regularly presented a fixed canon of rules to give beginning writers practice in certain exercises essential for public speaking. Among these exercises was the *encomium,* that is, a set of formal instructions on how to praise a person. The encomium contained a summary of all the information the ancients thought necessary to provide rather full knowledge of some person and to present him or her adequately to an audience. Likewise, the ancient rhetorical handbooks contained another set of directives for those who would draw up judicial or deliberative speeches for courtroom or public assembly. In the handbooks, speakers were instructed on how to create a person's *ethos,* that is, the expected, culturally acceptable description of another's character or "personality." Finally, a set of writings called *physiognomonia* indicates how one can learn all about a person's character or "nature" from a person's looks and place of origin. Such physiognomic handbooks served writers, such as historians and playwrights, as well as artists such as sculptors and mask-makers, who regularly used this material to describe and present ancient persons.

We have, then, valuable and trustworthy native informants from the ancient Mediterranean world. The very nature of these rhetorical writings as standard rules and exercises for describing persons qualifies them for the precise formal task we are undertaking. Our native informants knew that they were presenting the norms of perception common to their culture area. They expected others to recognize these norms as such and to follow the norms in their social interactions. The contents of these rhetorical documents, moreover, remained exceptionally constant over centuries, from Aristotle (fourth century B.C.) through Quintilian (first century A.D.).

We shall look to our ancient Mediterranean informants to provide us in each chapter of this book with successive formal models for how they perceived and described persons in their cultural world. As we take up the comments of each informant, we will attempt to compare them to draw out their similarities. Thus, by the end of our investigation, we shall be able to provide readers with a reliable and comprehensive set of rules and clues from the natives of the ancient world about how they understood and described persons.

Test Case: "Paul"

Yet this book focuses on the apostle Paul. Generalized theory about how to perceive ancient persons is valuable in itself. But we need a test case to bring these data into a meaningful and useful configuration and to evaluate their worth and accuracy. What better person than Paul to illustrate this?

We choose Paul because we have access to his own self-presentation in his letters. And Paul is described by the authors of the Acts of the Apostles and *The Acts of Paul.* Paul speaks about himself constantly. But in certain of his letters such as Galatians, Philippians, and 2 Corinthians, he formally presents pieces of his "autobiography" that are intended to impress his audience. We will analyze these Pauline letters through the lens of the encomium, which is presented in the progymnasmata. Inasmuch as the author of Acts has Paul deliver several forensic defense speeches (Acts 22—26), we turn to that set of rhetorical writings to examine its rules for describing a person and to indicate what can be known about Paul according to this canon of native literature. Finally, there is a remarkable physical description of Paul in *The Acts of Paul,* which we will view under the rubric of ancient physiognomic literature. The stylized features of Paul convey significant cultural information about him, which was deemed quite adequate by the ancient informants for understanding what sort of person Paul was.

Thus, we consider the "portrait" of Paul, his personality and character.

But we do so exclusively with the assistance of our native informants, whose categories and evaluations form the basis for our inquiry. We rely on them to guide our perceptions, so that we might learn to see as they saw and to evaluate as they evaluated. In short, in the first part of this study, we shall restrict ourselves to the ancient, native data for describing persons, illustrating those data by systematic interpretation of three ancient documents that contain information about "Paul." We do not attempt to harmonize these sources to present a more historical portrait of Paul. Ours is no "quest for the historical Paul." Rather, we wish to know what kind of person Paul was according to the cultural canons of antiquity. We seek to discover what information his contemporaries deemed essential for adequately knowing him and properly evaluating him.

Cultural Anthropology

Yet our task is hardly over after we mine the insights of our native informants for describing and perceiving ancient persons. As the anecdotes cited above suggest, when modern Euro-Americans attempt to understand persons from other cultures, we invariably perceive them according to our own ethnocentric and perhaps anachronistic way, that is, as typically individualist human beings. Is there another path we might take to imagine how people differ culturally and socially?

In the final chapters of this book, we will introduce materials and concepts from contemporary cultural anthropology. Cultural anthropologists are concerned with describing different cultures in a comparative way, and with understanding the respective ways in which persons in different cultures are perceived and evaluated. We shall not, however, abandon the historical information recovered in our exposition of the encomium, the forensic defense speech, and the physiognomic literature. Rather, we will integrate those data into a larger model based on an extensive cross-cultural data set and refined over many years of research and analysis.

In short, we shall attempt to describe rather constant cultural patterns of understanding persons in the Mediterranean world. In the past as well as in the present, the Mediterranean culture area has been described in anthropological literature as a collectivist or group-oriented society. Our investigation both of the "portrait" of Paul from three ancient rhetorical perspectives and the contributions of our ancient informants will serve as the reliable historical thread that will be seen to mesh very closely with the observations and perspectives of contemporary Mediterranean anthropologists. We shall attempt in the last chapters to integrate the native insights into a broader comparative perspective of utility for the modern New Testament reader. As comprehensive as the ancient rhetorical literature might seem, a further systematic view of personality is available to moderns. And it is the interface of ancient native and foreign modern systems that we offer as the concluding contribution of this study.

WHY ANOTHER BOOK?
PAST ATTEMPTS AND NEW PERSPECTIVES

One might ask at the beginning, Why another book on Paul? Why another book on ancient personality? Did this book have to be written? We answer simply that we have available to us at this time significantly better resources for reading the New Testament than at previous times. We do not mean that we necessarily know how to speak languages better than our ancestors, or that we have discovered some new cache of documents previously unavailable to others. But we have learned to ask a series of more relevant questions that directly pertain to the issues of cultural differences, social psychology, and the phenomenon of reading. We do not claim to have vanquished the "tyranny of chronology," but we do appreciate the resources available to modern persons who want to know in a more scientific manner what ancient persons were like.

How Do We Read?

The fundamental process by means of which New Testament writings become living witnesses is the process of reading. Most New Testament interpreters, professional and nonprofessional, take reading for granted. Yet reading poses a fundamental problem for persons wishing to be fair and respectful with the New Testament witnesses. For all readers (and we include those listening to some other reader) bring their own understanding of the world to their reading (or listening). This understanding includes, among other things, the following: (1) some sense of how society works with its family, government, economic, and religious systems; (2) an appreciation of values relative to persons, groups, and things; as well as (3) knowledge of how individuals actually behave and how they are expected to behave as they interact with other human beings. Every adult Bible reader has a rather full, adult understanding of how his or her own society with its groups and individuals works. Now reading always entails that readers bring their own understandings of the world to their reading in order to enable an author, who presumably shares the same understanding of the world, to rearrange what readers bring to the reading. Considerate authors always take their readership into account and presume to share identical scenarios of how the world works. When the readers and the author share the same perception of the world, then the readers can readily understand the author. However, if the readers have an understanding of the world very different from that of the author, then misunderstanding or "non-understanding" occurs (see Malina 1991b). To have modern readers reading ancient authors is an instant recipe for misunderstanding and "non-understanding" of those authors and their original audiences.

Similar processes occur when people interact with other persons, whether from their own society or from some foreign area. As a rule, people from the same society understand each other because they bring a shared, general understanding of how the world works. Even if they get angry with each other, they usually understand what is at issue in their dispute. But visitors to foreign countries often find themselves bemused, puzzled, and even irritated and hostile toward the "natives," who just do not know how to behave properly, that is, the way the visitor does at home. Mutual anger in such circumstances often involves radically differing understandings of the issue in question—a clash of cultures.

Whenever persons today read the New Testament, they should find themselves much like visitors in a foreign land. To imagine the scenarios depicted in the New Testament is much like having just arrived in modern Damascus or Baghdad with all the attendant confusion of customs, currency, and language. The New Testament was authored by persons with experiences radically different from those available to twentieth-century Euro-Americans. New Testament authors cannot be considerate authors for modern readers; they did not write for us, nor could they imagine our culture. But modern readers can learn to become considerate readers or sensitive visitors to the New Testament world. We believe that the easiest and most direct path to this end lies in the efforts of modern readers to learn what first-century Mediterranean authors believed about how the world worked. Even the Roman Catholic church recognized the need for moderns to be considerate readers when it instructed students and scholars of the New Testament to practice exquisite cultural sensitivity when reading those ancient documents:

> The interpreter must investigate what meaning the sacred writer intended to express and actually expressed in particular circumstances as he used contemporary literary forms in accordance with the situation of his own time and culture. For the correct understanding of what the sacred author wanted to assert, due attention must be paid to the customary and characteristic styles of perceiving, speaking, and narrating which prevailed at the time of the sacred writer, and to the customs men normally followed at that period in their everyday dealings with one another. (Vatican II 1966, 120)

Fair and considerate readers, then, if they wish to have a correct understanding of those ancient documents, must pay due attention to acquiring sets of first-century Mediterranean cultural scenarios that depict "the

customs men normally followed at that period in their everyday dealings."
A key feature in any scenario of how a society operates is an appreciation
of the human being, the acting person. This book is about the way persons
were perceived and described in the first-century Mediterranean world.

How Do We Know Persons?

Continued reflection on human behavior yields descriptions of human persons. But what reflections? Human behavior, social scientists
inform us, follows paths marked off by the major structures of the society in which persons have been socialized. Just as a computer has a disk
operating system, so human groups have social structures that serve as
a human group's operating system. What makes the human system
work at all, the electricity of the system, is human self-interest. The
goals, both proximate and ultimate, that social structures enable are values. There is close relationship among values, self-interests, and social
structures.

Of course, the subjects of the whole system in operation are human-
beings-in-society; that is, persons in groups, individuals in social environments, or selves in relations with other selves. Persons in society are studied sociologically, individuals in environments are studied biologically,
and selves in relations are studied psychologically (Harris 1989). Thus we
can know persons either sociologically or biologically or psychologically.
This book studies persons in society, and so its dominant perspective is
that of sociology and anthropology; the focus is what is called *social psychology*. Social psychology is in fact "about the mesh between the self and
society" (Gamson 1992, 53). The philosophical underpinnings of such a
perspective have been duly set out by Harré (1980, 1984, 1989).

Yet we must still raise the question, What is a "self"? We turn to social
psychologists for their input and cite what we consider to be an adequate
definition of "self."

> The self here is defined as all the statements a person makes that include
> the word "I," "me," "mine," and "myself." This definition means that all as-
> pects of social motivation are included in the self. Attitudes (e.g. I like . . .),
> beliefs (e.g. X has attribute X in my view), intentions (e.g. I plan to do . . .),
> norms (e.g. my ingroup expects me to do . . .), roles (e.g. my ingroup ex-
> pects people who hold this position to do . . .), and values (e.g. I feel that . . .
> is very important), are aspects of the self.
>   The self is coterminous with the body in individualist cultures and in
> some of the collectivist cultures. However, it can be related to a group the
> way a hand is related to the person whose hand it is. The latter conception
> is found in collectivist cultures, where the self overlaps with a group, such
> as family or tribe. (Triandis 1990, 77–78)

This social psychologist makes a critical distinction between two types of "selves," an "individualist self" and a "collectivist self." In individualist cultures, self-interests are proper to single persons who believe somehow that they stand alone, while in collectivist societies self-interests are proper to in-groups, that is, groups of people who believe they share a common fate. In fact, this distinction between individualist and collectivist cultures lies at the heart of this project. We have taken our clues on this point from the important body of empirical studies in social psychology expertly synthesized by Harry Triandis (1990). The individualist-collectivist continuum is regularly featured in journals such as *The Journal of Cross-Cultural Psychology* (see, for example, Hui and Triandis 1986; Hui and Villareale 1989; Schwartz 1990; Triandis et al. 1993).

Regarding the continuum that runs from individualism to collectivism or vice versa, "individualism" roughly speaking means individual goals precede group goals. "Collectivism" means that group goals naturally precede individual goals. This is what Triandis implied in the quote about "individualist cultures" and "collectivist cultures." There can be little doubt that our New Testament witnesses were collectivist persons living in collectivist cultures. And so were all of their contemporaries in the first-century Mediterranean, whether Egyptians or Romans or Greeks.

In order to develop some detailed scenarios of ancient Mediterranean selves, we utilize writings from the general Hellenistic *cultural* period. Yet to better focus our presentation, we concentrate for the most part on that quintessential first-century Mediterranean, Paul of Tarsus. In a recent discussion of "Paul's Theological Difficulties with the Law" (1986), the Finnish scholar Heikki Räisänen argues that Paul the theologian is a less coherent and less convincing thinker than is commonly assumed. But on the basis of what norms should one judge Paul's mental coherence or ability as a thinker? Räisänen further notes that Paul's conception of the law is inconsistent, unintelligible, and unarguable. Again, one might ask, On the basis of what standards? Räisänen surely does us a service by pointing out these aspects of Paul's writing, but he does not offer any suggestion as to whether Paul is typical or atypical in this regard.

Now granting that Räisänen is correct in his assessment of Paul from the viewpoint of a twentieth-century northern European (and we agree with that assessment), what sorts of criteria must one adopt to judge Paul in this way? On the other hand, to underscore how deviant Paul is in his thinking compared to contemporary Euro-Americans does not bring us any closer to understanding that first-century Mediterranean. Our basic question is this: What scenarios for understanding human beings both as individuals and as group members must contemporary Euro-Americans bring to their New Testament reading so that the authors of those documents might not simply be assessed as different, but actually be understood in a fair and equitable manner? What cultural scenarios must we learn to be fair and respectful visitors to that foreign world? For if we wish to know ancient persons, we must learn to know them in new ways.

Past Attempts at Characterizing Mediterranean Persons

This book is hardly the first to attempt to describe the people of the Bible or the inhabitants of the ancient Mediterranean. And it will be worth our while to sample some of the more cogent attempts of other scholars as we begin our own path of discovery.

Corporate Personality: The Biblical "Primitive Mentality"

Perhaps the most influential statement contrasting ancient "biblical" persons and modern (British) persons was the essay by H. Wheeler Robinson concerning "corporate personality" in ancient Israel (published in 1936). Robinson's description of ancient Israelite corporate personality derived from L. Lévy-Bruhl's popularization of how contemporary primitives think. Anthropologist Lévy-Bruhl (1923; 1926) and others of his day were much taken by "primitive mentality." From his distinctive conception of this category, he deduced a distinctive primitive personality, namely, a corporate personality. The characteristic feature of this model of the primitive lies in the observation that primitives never perceived themselves as single beings but believed themselves to be irreducibly a part of a larger group. To use modern jargon, such primitives were not simply codependent, but totally dependent, in their self-awareness. They were not individualists but collectivists. Obviously early ethnologists like Lévy-Bruhl accurately intuited a number of the features of collectivist personality. Yet his articulation of the intuition proved inadequate, if only because some 70 percent of the population of the planet today (hence surely not primitive) are socialized and enculturated to become collectivist selves (Triandis 1990). Furthermore, by modern standards his data set was simply inadequate.

Robinson, in turn, gets credit for using anthropology to understand ancient Israel, even if he never defined "corporate personality" in any adequate way. This inadequacy undoubtedly had to do with the faults of Lévy-Bruhl's articulation. Be that as it may, a number of biblical scholars took up the idea of "corporate personality" to explain various phenomena in the Old Testament as well as the New Testament (e.g., the sin of Adam in Genesis and in Paul, as in De Fraine 1965). Influential works similar to Robinson's and based on presuppositions of different mentalities include those of Claude Tresmontant (1960) and Thorlief Boman (1960). In this regard, the reprint of Robinson's essay (1980) includes a valuable introduction by Gene Tucker describing the history of the influence of Robinson's work and the position taken by its critics, as well as a historically relevant bibliography. In sum, it would seem that "corporate personality" has the same standing as "primitive mentality." Today both essentially serve as historical curiosities.

Easy Ethnocentrisms:
People Like Us

Our excursion into "corporate personality" underscores the fact that biblical scholars must indeed be dependent on social scientists when it comes to learning and articulating a sophisticated, comparative model that might serve to understand persons of other cultures as well as persons of ancient cultures. Fair and responsible readers must use our contemporary experts to assist us in the task of building comparative, adequate scenarios to interpret others.

Yet many scholars tend to go the way of intuition and bypass colleagues whose disciplines focus specifically on accumulating empiric data for cross-cultural comparison of personhood. This intuitive way, more often than not, seems rooted in the willingness to yield to the temptation to project our individualist psychology upon New Testament persons. One constantly reads about the tensions, psychological struggles, or personality traits of Paul, Jesus, and others. We suggest that such statements are ethnocentric and anachronistic projections, without the slightest basis outside the imagination of the modern writer. Modern psychology is rooted in individualist culture. And there simply were no individualist cultures before the sixteenth century (although some would give honors to the seventeenth or eighteenth century; see Martin 1994, 134–35 n.5).

> The fundamental assumption of modernity, the thread that has run through Western civilization since the sixteenth century, is that the social unit of society is not the group, the guild, the tribe, or the city, but the person. (Bell 1976, 16).

Because we are concerned with persons in the first-century Mediterranean, we shall concentrate on what is meant by a collectivist or group-oriented culture. And to aid readers in this, we provide an appendix to this book that compares and contrasts individualist and collectivist cultures. We are reminded that Mediterraneans are still known for their anti-introspective and anti-psychological approaches to life. Yet in biblical scholarship, popular psychology remains quite pervasive in nearly all descriptions of ancient Mediterraneans still innocent of social-scientific

concerns. And this is true not only of the countless books offering immediate relevance of the biblical text to modern Euro-Americans but in
works presented as biblical scholarship. For example, Jerome Murphy-
O'Connor tells of "a feeling of frustration" that was inevitable in first-
century Corinth. For "what was the point of a life in which the full exploitation of one's talents was blocked by circumstances outside one's
control?" (1984, 153). He imposes modern notions of the psychology of
individualist personal fulfillment upon a culture that was fundamentally
collectivist. Something is radically askew. Wayne Meeks, in turn, attempts to explain why first-century Mediterraneans might join and adhere to a Pauline-type church in terms of loneliness, anxiety, and need for
mobility—all psychological categories used to describe modern neuroses
in overcrowded, impersonal cities in our individualist culture. Persons afflicted with loneliness and anxiety, he argues, would find a welcome
refuge in the intimacy of Christian groups, while the daring, self-confident
social climber would be allowed to break out of constraining social structure (1983, 164–92). Despite his claim to provide a social description of
"urban" Christianity, Meeks presumes to know what an ancient city was
like and imagines modern urban psychological dynamics existed in ancient urban environments. (For a welcome corrective, see Rohrbaugh
1991a, 1991b). Similarly, largely ethnocentric psychological models
shape the way Meeks presents ancient Mediterranean moral behavior, although his work is largely told in the words of the ancients (1986, 1993).
The words are the words of Esau, but the hands are those of Jacob.

Others proceed in like manner and envision the world of Paul and
Jesus as one in which "a strong individualism prevails in most segments
of Greek society alongside of a search for community" (Doohan 1989, 49).
Such retrojections of contemporary experience into the world of early
Christianity might seem to make the ancient world relevant to modern
readers of the New Testament, but they do not describe ancient Mediterraneans in any fair and responsible way. While hypothetical intuitions
about early Christian personages deriving from the discipline known as
the history of ideas are interesting (for example Stendahl's intuition about
Paul, 1963), such intuitive approaches offer little by way of testable explanation and remain in the category of pop psychology.

The Problem of Psychology

On the other hand, Gerd Theissen's psychobiology and Terrence
Callan's rather straightforward psychology overlook the difficulties involved in psychological analysis without a present subject (Theissen
1987; Callan 1987 gives an excellent overview of previous psychological
studies; and Callan also offers a full study in 1990). Even the insistence,
for example, of Helen Doohan (1984) or Albert Vanhoye (1986) that it is

necessary and legitimate to study Paul's unique personality in terms of modern psychology does not deal with the fundamental obstacles to applying modern psychology to the past.

The question is not the obstinacy of the critic but lack of a workable method to carry off the task in some intellectually responsible manner. Historians as a rule give little attention to the problem of the implicit models they inevitably use. And most New Testament scholars would describe themselves as historians of antiquity. This inattention to implicit models holds all the more so for their selection from among many analytic frameworks that do exist (Prochaska 1979). Moreover, historians often ignore the formidable impediments to an adequate psychological assessment of absent, idiosyncratic subjects. These impediments have been well articulated by David Stannard. Yet Stannard's arguments do not seem to faze psychohistorians, even when he quietly concludes:

> The time has come to face the fact that, behind all its rhetorical posturing, the psychoanalytic approach to history is—irremediably—one of logical perversity, scientific unsoundness, and cultural naivete. The time has come, in short, to move on. (1980, 156)

Yet such anachronistic studies do serve a purpose. For they tell us what someone like Paul, given the minimum of idiosyncratic data available, would have been like to a very limited extent *had he been alive today.* To say that Paul was a human being whose psychological reactions would be just like those of other persons in his day and age is simply trifling. Rather the real problem is to discover what were the typical psychological reactions of persons of that day and age. And that is our quest: the typical, but not the idiosyncratic and unique. We seek, if you will, ancient social psychology, not modern individualist psychology. Psychology in a collectivist culture will be quite different from that in an individualist one.

MODAL PERSONALITY:
THE TYPICAL PERSON

We turn to the reports of our native Mediterranean informants to provide us with their contemporary categories and evaluations of persons that are quite suited to that collectivist culture. For in order to imagine the qualities of the persons we confront as we read the New Testament, we need adequate scenarios that respect the collectivist culture of the world we are visiting. Given the various constraints involved in dealing with psychological personality in cross-cultural perspective, it seems that at present the best we can attempt is a type of social psychology built upon a Mediterranean *modal personality,* along with the idiosyncrasies of the culture and distinctiveness of social structure in that time and place. As we previously noted, the term "modal personality" refers to a model of the typical qualities expected in a society's ideal, stereotypical, successful person who embodies a culture's definition of the ideal human being. Modal personality study might also be called regional (or national) character study (see Hsu 1983, 435). Such typical personality, then, points to some ideal, personal embodiment of a group's "native theory of success":

> A native theory of success thus includes knowledge of the range of available cultural tasks or status positions, their relative importance or value, the competencies essential for attainment or performance, the strategies for attaining the positions or obtaining the cultural tasks, and the expected penalties and rewards for failures and successes. A people's theory of success develops out of past experiences with cultural tasks, social rewards and relative costs. The theory is either reinforced or altered by contemporary experiences, that is, by perceptions and interpretations of available opportunity structures. . . . Nevertheless to suggest that natives (be they white middle-class Americans, black ghetto residents or African tribesmen) usually have a good knowledge of their status system and of what it takes to make it as behavioral guides is not too far removed from reality. (Ogbu 1981, 420)

The study of modal personality is a type of regional character study patterned after the national character studies of the 1940s and 1950s (Inkeles and Levinson 1954). These studies have picked up support once again, now under the aegis of social psychology (see Seelye 1985, 35–36). In our case the goal will be a social psychology built upon a Mediterranean modal personality, along with the idiosyncrasies of the culture and distinctiveness of social structure in the given time and place. On the basis of such a configuration, we might discuss cultural groups and the types of personalities such groups might allow for. The following chapters of this book are intended to provide a general orientation for Euro-American New Testament readers as they attempt to imagine the types of persons found in the pages of their biblical reading.

OUR HYPOTHESIS:
A GENERAL ORIENTATION

Our hypothesis is that first-century Mediterranean persons were strongly group-embedded, collectivist persons. Since they were group-oriented, they were "socially" minded, as opposed to "psychologically" minded. They were attuned to the values, attitudes, and beliefs of their in-group, with which they shared a common fate due to generation and geography. Thanks to their in-group enculturation, they were used to assessing themselves and others in terms of stereotypes often explained as deriving from family "history" and the geographical location of their group. Furthermore, because these persons were strongly embedded in groups, their behavior was controlled by strong social inhibitions along with a general lack of personal inhibition. Their prevailing social institution was kinship. Familism, belief in the central role and value of the "household," was foremost in people's minds. The primary way they made sense of their local world was in terms of gender and geography, by viewing spatially situated persons as well as things as male and female (for more information, see Malina and Neyrey 1991b).

While elites shared in many of the orientations of the majority population, the prevailing elite social institution was the *polis.* The word *polis* is usually translated "city," "state," or "city-state." None of these words actually carries the freight that polis does, largely because of the radical change in social systems from antiquity to modern times. The pre-industrial, pre-Enlightenment, pre-medieval market/central place called the polis was a social institution where elites who controlled the surrounding agricultural and forest lands lived. The polis was the center of political religion (with temples), political economy (with market and storage in temples), and political life (with buildings for meeting) in general. It also had residences for the elites, buildings for their entertainment, and housing for their retainers. Elite males were *politai* (citizens); on the basis of their residence and land control, they could participate in the decision-making processes that affected those living in the polis (thus meeting as "legislature," "court," "jury," and the like). Elites described themselves in terms of the polis to which they owed their allegiance (e.g., Philo of Alexandria, Paul of Tarsus). Nonelites constituted the vast majority of the population and named themselves after their parentage, for instance, Jesus, whom Mary bore; or Jesus, son of Joseph; Simon, son of Jonah. Also note that Jesus, his disciples, and more than 90 percent of the Mediterranean world simply had no citizenship because they were not elites in any polis. Yet everyone had a place in some *oikos,* or household.

The polis was made up of individual households, or *oikoi.* The oikos consisted of the house itself, its land, and the people, animals, and objects that it housed. It was headed by a male landowner, and its continuity depended on the continuation of this man's line, but it was not simply a family of kinship. Membership involved a combination of blood relationship and physical residence, for nonkin (including slaves) who lived in the house were regarded as part of the oikos, while those who lived in other oikoi were considered to be outsiders and rivals even if they were kin, unless the kin group as a whole was faced with a threat. Consequently, when a woman went in marriage to the oikos of her husband, she became a member of that household and ceased being a member of the household of her birth (although the break was not complete). Through marriage, women connected male groups. Men lived in the dual world of polis and oikos, but women's status and role were determined entirely in terms of membership—or lack of membership—in an oikos.

The polis had an in-group and an out-group dimension, as did all of Mediterranean living. Political life consisted of group-embedded individuals interacting with a view to effective collective action toward the outside, yet with concerns for honor acquisition on the inside. The persons described in the ancient documents, the aristocrats and elites of the Greco-Roman world, had ascribed identities due to solidarity with the groups in which they were embedded, primarily the kinship group, yet with their fellow polis members as well. They were known either by their family of origin or polis of origin or both. Kin group and polis alike were units of religion and economics. And elites were much concerned about both domestic religion and domestic economics, as well as about political religion and political economics. As we shall see from their own norms for interaction, they dealt with each other in extremely stereotypical fashion. They were, in fact, anti-introspective. It was the significant groups, the kin group and the polis group, that served as conscience and guide.

We now turn to the documents of rhetoric and physiognomy to verify our hypothesis. We develop our theme with a view to assisting readers to form a more accurate scenario of the types of persons that present themselves in the pages of the New Testament. With the scenarios that develop, the modern reader will gain greater insight into the New Testament world and thus prove to be a more considerate reader of the witness our ancestors in faith have provided us in the documents we cherish as God's New Testament.

2

The Encomium:
A Native Model of Personality

We continue to read the letters of Paul today because we accept them as part of the New Testament. Yet it is interesting, to say the least, that contemporary readers of these ancient letters claim to understand what Paul said and meant. For Paul's references to himself or to Apollos, Stephanus, Timothy, Euodia, and Phoebe, or any other person should really be quite difficult for modern readers to envision. The reason for this is that whenever Euro-Americans today start talking about someone, their inevitable frame of reference is psychological and individualist. Notice how, for example, the nightly news highlights the extraordinary and its impact on the individual, how the soap operas rivet on the individual's psychological perplexities, or how talk shows focus on individualist idiosyncrasies. If our television fare is any indication, people today are totally bent on understanding the individual self, on solving individual problems in an individualist way, and on realizing individual potential. Our common stories portray the individual self pursuing its self-fulfillment in a competitive, often unfriendly society (Berman 1987, 100–102). When Euro-American Christians read Paul, they inevitably call up a set of scenarios in which persons are understood individualistically. Such scenarios envision first-century Mediterraneans as though they were twentieth-century persons. Yet Paul and his contemporaries surely did not understand themselves as individualist persons. We are certain of this from the many historical studies that underscore the emergence of individualism only in rather recent historical times (see Bell 1976; Duby and Braunstein 1988). Hence to retroject our mode of being persons onto first-century Mediterranean personages would be anachronistic.

Given this state of affairs, we propose an alternative scenario for modern Christian readers of the Bible to facilitate an empathetic and historically attuned reading of the New Testament. Our ancient Mediterranean sources serve as native informants providing us with an alternative scenario depicting how first-century persons viewed themselves and others in their society. The first type of source consists of manuals that describe how a speaker ought to proceed in convincing and persuading other people. In antiquity, such works devoted to persuasion were called manuals of "rhetoric." The second type of document we use was drawn up in ancient times to help assess the character of other persons on the basis of where they came from and how they looked. Such manuals for evaluating others were based on what our ancient informants called "physiognomy." We have chosen these two types of documents because they offer sustained reflection from well-educated persons at the start of the first millennium about what a human being was like. Although those ancients did not have the word "person" and did not share in the rich psychological overtones that the Romantic period of Euro-American history has given to that word, they did know one another, but not very well *by our standards* since they did not know one another psychologically. Consequently we offer a scenario that consists of people who think "sociologically," in terms of group-oriented principles of birth and place of origin, of status and gender-based roles, and with constant concern for public rewards of respect and honor. The core items in this "sociological" scenario, we shall see, are generation, geography, and gender. This alternative scenario suggests that (a) Paul and his audience perceived human beings quite differently from the way Euro-Americans usually do, and hence (b) first-century Mediterraneans thought quite differently about who a person might be and what might be the expected range of human behavior.

PROGYMNASMATA AND HOW TO SPEAK/WRITE ABOUT PERSONS

The Roman world of the first-century A.D. consisted of the rather broad regions bordering the Mediterranean sea, called by its Greek-speaking inhabitants the *oikoumenê,* the inhabited, civilized world. They considered this geographical expanse a political and cultural unity that was being civilized by the expansion of Roman military might and culture. This oikoumene was dotted with central, residential and administrative places called *poleis* in Greek (singular: *polis*). Around these cities dwelt countless persons clustered in hamlets and villages that were connected in various ways to the larger central places (Rohrbaugh 1991b, 129–33). For elites, the proper place to live was in a polis, and the proper way to live in a polis was as a *politês* (citizen). Living in such a polis was, of course, the ideal of nonelites and noncitizens as well. While human beings might be grouped as tribes, peoples, and tongues (e.g., 1 Sam. 9:1; 2 Sam. 3:2–5), there were no territorial countries or states or nations in our sense of the word. Translators often lead modern readers astray by translating the word *polis* as "state" or "city," or both. And modern maps are equally deceptive in that they mark off territories with boundaries that no ancient could ever conceive of. Similarly, in modern experience a "nation" invariably refers to a social entity that emerged in the early nineteenth century A.D.: The "nation" as a legal and political ego presumed to function as a concrete subject, a "nation-state," such as the United States, Germany, Russia, and the like (Anderson 1983). Yet the word *nation* is also used to translate the Native American word for a group of people, for example, "the Sioux nation," as well as Latin and Greek words that refer to rather limited ethnic groups. In fact, our common understanding of countries, states, and nations is quite recent. As Anderson has observed, a nation is an imagined community, imagined as inherently limited, ethnically identical (horizontal comradeship), and sovereign (replacing the divinely ordained, hierarchical dynastic realm). The word *nation* is about two hundred years old, rooted in the Enlightenment and revolutions of the eighteenth century. With the Enlightenment and the dusk of Christendom, nation-states come to offer the continuity that religion did. "France is eternal!" National states "always loom out of an immemorial past, and, still more important, glide into a limitless future. It is the magic of nationalism to turn chance into destiny" (Anderson 1983, 18). In sum, there were no such countries, states, and nations in antiquity at all. Hence, for the sake of avoiding anachronism and ethnocentric scenarios, we shall refer to ancient central places of a residential and administrative nature as "poleis" and not as "city" or "state." We feel confident the reader will be able to construct appropriate scenarios to empathize with our ancient Mediterranean informants.

It is as important to be aware of such terminological differences as it is to know the broad residential arrangement of the ancient oikoumene. For our task is to understand how and why elite persons learned to relate with other persons in the ancient world. These elites were *politai* (singular: *politês*), legally recognized participants in the life of some polis. And one of the life-goals of politai was to maintain the honorable status into which they were born in some specific polis. After all, the body of politai together (called the *politeuma*) made legislation; and members of the politeuma likewise served as jury for any litigation. A *politês* originally represented himself as plaintiff or defendant. Finally, at public meetings on many and varied occasions, politai were expected to celebrate the significance of the persons and groups in whose honor the occasion was held. To these ends, it was necessary to become adept at public speaking and the persuasion of others that that entailed. This skill was called rhetoric, as previously noted.

Now on the way to formal studies in persuasion, students were initially taught to organize what they would have to say in terms of generally accepted, conventional topics. These topics were considered necessary themes for a person to master in order to function as a *politês* in the polis. Thus students learned composition by following rather standardized exercises, thereby assimilating clear sets of rules of composition. Creativity consisted in developing ever more consistent ways to imitate the past and to carry out what one was taught. The rules and exercises for learning how to write came to be known as *progymnasmata* (collected in some of the first "how to" books). We possess but a fraction of ancient Hellenistic progymnastic documents from what must have been a substantial literature. (For documents consulted for this study, see Appendix 1. See also Neyrey 1994a, 177; Hock and O'Neil 1986, 10–11). Yet as one would expect, the extant examples reveal rather consistent patterns.

In the cultures of the Hellenistic world, an author's originality and creativity consisted in finding ever better ways to follow the usual, accepted practices. Conventionality ruled the day, and so predetermined kinds of composition had to be mastered, each with its fixed parts, developed in quite standardized ways. A stock list of topics or kinds of composition to be learned in the progymnasmata included specific training in writing and speaking about the following:

1. Myths (*mythoi:* narrating fables and tales from history)
2. Chreia and proverbs (*chreia:* developing a topic by iteration, enthymeme, contrast, illustration, example, and testimony of authority)
3. Refutation and confirmation (*anaskeuê, kataskeuê:* analyzing myths to show that the story was not obscure, incredible, impossible, inconsistent, unfitting, or inexpedient)
4. Commonplaces (*gnômê:* enlarging on praise of virtue and condemnation of vice)
5. Encomium and vituperation (*enkômion:* praising a person or thing and condemning another as vicious)
6. Comparison (*synkrisis:* comparing and arguing which of the two is better or worse)
7. Personalized speeches or prosopopoeia (*êthopoia:* composing an imaginary monologue that might be appropriately spoken or written by a historical, legendary, or fictitious person under given circumstances)
8. Description (*ekphrasis:* vividly presenting details of sight and sound)

9. Thesis (*thesis:* arguing for or against a general question such as "Should a man marry? Seek office?")
10. Legislation (*nomon eisphora:* speaking for or against a law, usually from ancient history)

For our first window on how persons were perceived in the ancient Mediterranean world, we focus on the fifth exercise in the progymnasmata listing, namely, the description of persons in the encomium, the speech of praise. This part of the progymnasmata offers us clear access to how elite ancient Mediterraneans perceived and presented persons in their Hellenistic world. The encomium contains concepts of what persons at that time and in that culture deemed important and essential for portraying human beings according to their cultural conventions and expectations. The elements might seem quite stereotyped, hackneyed, and foreign to what modern biographers deem important. But for all that, the encomium is a valuable and accessible ancient native model of personhood, rooted in an implicit theory of person, and composed by the ancients for the ancients and reflecting their ancient social system(s). In order to be considerate readers of the New Testament, we will have to trust our ancient informants to provide us an adequate native scenario for understanding persons on their terms.

AN ENCOMIUM

An encomium is a speech of praise. One might praise another person or some object that would be personified, such as a place or a polis. The counterpart to this speech of praise was the speech of blame. Praise and blame form natural counterpoints, as Paul, for example, indicates in 1 Cor. 11:2 (" I commend you . . .") and 17 ("I do not commend you"). Although we present a compressed version of an encomium here, a sampling of the actual documents is available in Appendix 1.

The ancients not only had a specific cultural meaning for praise, but they perceived and expressed such praise in terms of stereotyped categories. When composing an encomium, the classical writer was advised to cover the following fixed categories: the subject's origin and birth, nurture and training, accomplishments, and outstanding qualities. Of course, each of these aspects was further subdivided to present a well-rounded portrait:

1. Origin and birth (*eugeneia*) entailed consideration of a range of aspects: origin (*genos*) included ethnic affiliation (*ethos*), home locale (*patris*), ancestors (*progonoi*), and parents (*pateres*); birth (*genesis*) dealt with phenomena at birth (stars, visions, and so forth) and family.

2. Nurture and training (*anastrophê*) presented personality and character formation, as well as general education (*paideia*); this involved one's teachers, arts and skills (*technê*), and grasp of laws (*nomoi*).

3. Accomplishments (*epitêdeumata*) and deeds (*praxeis*) looked to body, soul, and the happenstances of life. Considerations of the body (*kata sôma*) included beauty, strength, agility, might, and health; those of the soul (*kata psychên*) looked to justice (*dikaiosynê*), wisdom (*phronêsis*), moderation rooted in a sense of shame (*sôphrosynê*), manly courage (*andreia*), and respect for those who control one's existence (*pistis, eusebeia*). Happenstances of life, that is, fate or fortune (*kata tychên*), treated power (*dynasteria*), wealth (*ploutos*), friends (*philoi*), children, their number and beauty, as well as fame and fortune, length of life, happy death.

4. Comparison (*synkrisis*) is the final feature. By comparing the subject with others, the speaker or writer highlights the outstanding quality of the person in question.

In sum, a speech of praise involved four features: a subject's origin, formation, accomplishments, and comparison with others. To appreciate these categories and to assess the way they contribute to an understanding of what it means to be a person, we will have to elaborate further on their native meanings. To this end we offer the following description from Greek and Roman authors. Our task here remains to learn how natives thought about persons and the values they believed persons might embody.

Origin and Birth (*Eugeneia*)

Honorable people derive from and are rooted in honorable locales, regions and poleis; they are made honorable by connection with equally praiseworthy clans and families. Hence, a person's role and status in society should be considered a function of such noble regional and blood connections. To know someone means to know their roots, ancestry, and genealogy. Noble families, moreover, stem from noble soil and live in noble poleis. The converse is equally true. Ignoble persons bespeak ignoble families, low-quality regions, and contemptible poleis. Nathanael's question, "Can anything good come out of Nazareth?" (John 1:46), illustrates the first step in determining honorable or dishonorable origins. On the other hand, when Paul presents himself as "a Judean, born at Tarsus in Cilicia, but brought up in this city [Jerusalem]" (Acts 22:3), he pulls out all the honorable stops; for Tarsus was "no low-status city"

(Acts 21:39), and Jerusalem was the major city of Judea and site of Israel's temple.

Origin

We begin by considering what someone such as Aristotle said about "noble birth." First, however, a note of caution. We cite available translations as they are, even though such social categories as "race," "nation," "state," "city," or "citizen" are always misleading for the modern reader because they never mean what we normally mean by the words. "Race" and at times "nation" both refer to a person's ethnic identity, based on people and place of origin, customs and behavior of people in that place of origin, regional characteristic of that place of origin, and the like. On the other hand "state," "city," and often "nation" refer to central administrative and residential clusters, the polis, while "citizen" is an elite resident of a polis. "Country" always refers to "countryside," "region," "locale." "Land," finally, refers either to acreage or to the place where an ethnic group can be found; for example, Persia is where the Persians can be found. The "Promised Land" is the place where the people "of the promise" would eventually be found. In antiquity, space and time ("the days of King Herod") were not so much abstract entities as designations primarily marking the presence of people.

To return to Aristotle, the philosopher notes the following:

> Noble birth, in the case of a nation or State, means that its members or inhabitants are sprung from the soil, or of long standing; that its first members were famous as leaders, and that many of their descendants have been famous for qualities that are highly esteemed. In the case of private individuals, noble birth is derived from either the father's or the mother's side, and on both sides there must be legitimacy; and, as in the case of a State, it means that its founders were distinguished for virtue, or wealth, or any other of the things that men honour, and that a number of famous persons, both men and women, young and old, belong to the family. (*Rhet.* 1.5.5, 1360b, Loeb)

Aristotle reflects the common cultural expectation that children will be chips off the old block (see Deut. 23:2; 2 Kings 9:22; Isa. 57:3; Hos. 1:2; Sir. 23:25–26; 30:7); specifically: like father, like son (e.g., Matt. 11:27), and like mother, like daughter (e.g., Ezek. 16:44). If the parents or ancestors were "landed," or politai of a free polis, then the ancients deemed the root stock of the family noble. If the ancestors were distinguished in virtue, they should be expected to breed virtue. Plato stated it clearly: "They were good because they sprang from good fathers" (*Menex.* 237, Loeb). Quintilian carried on this tradition: " 'Birth,' for persons are generally regarded as having some resemblance to their parents and ancestors, a resemblance which leads to their living disgracefully or honorably, as the case may be" (*Inst. Orat.* 5.10.24, Loeb).

In Menander Rhetor's progymnasmata, his instructions on writing this part of an encomium read as follows:

> If the city has no distinction, you must inquire whether his nation as a whole is considered brave and valiant, or is devoted to literature or the possession of virtues, like the Greek race, or again is distinguished for law, like the Italian, or is courageous, like the Gauls or Paeonians. You must take a few features from the nation . . . arguing that it is inevitable that a man from such a [city or] nation should have such characteristics, and that he stands out among all his praiseworthy compatriots . . . If neither his city nor his nation is conspicuously famous, you should omit this topic and consider whether his family has prestige or not. If it has, work this up. If it is humble and without prestige, omit this likewise. (2.369.26–370.12)

This late writer (end of the third century A.D.) confirms the cultural expectation that noble ancestors and a noble source of origin (whether ethnic group, that is, "nation," or polis or segment of the ethnic group, that is, the "tribe") determine the sort of person one is. As he said, "it is *inevitable* that a man from *such parentage* . . . should have *such characteristics*" (emphasis added). We note that these characteristics are deemed to be inherited, acquired, innate, and not learned, achieved, or absorbed. They derive from group affiliation. They are not individual characteristics, developed individualistically, but rather are group features.

Birth

The birth of an honorable person might be accompanied by visions, celestial phenomena (stars, comets, lightning, and so forth), and signs and wonders, which testify to the exceptional qualities of the person whose birth they herald. This material is already known to readers of the New Testament from form-critical comparisons of biblical and classical materials (Dungan and Cartlidge 1974, 7–32), but we locate it in its proper rhetorical context, the encomium. Menander Rhetor instructs the composer of an encomium to note such phenomena:

> If any divine sign occurred at the time of his birth, either on land or in the heavens or on the sea, compare the circumstances with those of Romulus, Cyrus, and similar stories, since in these cases also there were miraculous happenings connected with their birth—the dream of Cyrus' mother, the suckling of Romulus by the she-wolf. (2.371.5–14)

The ancients treasured accounts of such phenomena as indicators of status. Whatever happened in the macrocosm of the sky mirrored and foretold what was soon to occur in the microcosm of the earth. But in essence, such phenomena constituted status markers (see Malina 1993a, 1995a, 30–44).

Nurture and Training (*Anastrophê*)

In the contemporary world, education is almost always about instruction, the mastering of some information, or the development of some skill. In contrast, ancient education focused on the moral, mental, and "personality" formation of a human being. The education process aimed to produce a well-rounded person of character and integrity, someone worthy of the label "human being." Once again, modern scholars already know this material under the rubric of form-criticism (Dungan and Cartlidge 1974, 33–35), but we situate it in its proper historical and cultural matrix, the progymnastic encomium. Aphthonius of Antioch (third century A.D.) provides rules for an encomium that instruct us tersely to note three things about the education of a person: "inclination to study, talent and rules." Again Menander Rhetor indicates what seems worthwhile to note about the education and training of a person:

> Next comes "nurture." Was he reared in the palace? Were his swaddling-clothes robes of purple? Was he from his first growth brought up in the lap of royalty? Or, instead, was he raised up to be emperor as a young man by some felicitous chance? If he does not have any distinguished nurture (as Achilles had with Chiron), discuss his education, observing here: "In addition to what has been said, I wish to describe the quality of his mind." Then you must speak of his love of learning, his quickness, his enthusiasm for study, his easy grasp of what is taught him. If he excels in literature, philosophy, and knowledge of letters, you must praise this. If it was in the practice of war and arms, you must admire him for having been born luckily, with Fortune to woo the future for him. Again: "In his education, he stood out among his contemporaries, like Achilles, like Heracles, like the Dioscuri." (2.371.17–372.2)

We highlight several things here. Individuals were thought to be shaped, molded, and formed by their mentors and teachers, whose stamp they henceforth bore. Given the reverence for the past and the importance of living up to ancestral tradition (the *mos maiorum*) in antiquity, young men were only as good as their teachers and those who formed in them the social values enshrined in their past culture. Jesus is reported to have alluded to this truism: "A disciple is not above his teacher, but every one when he is fully taught will be like his teacher" (Luke 6:40; Matt. 10:24). This correlates with the preceding notion of family stock. If the parents were noble, so must the children be; if the teachers were excellent, so must the disciple be. An unspecified assumption operates here about the expectation of constancy of character, which is quite unlike modern developmental notions of personality. An honorable man *must* have been an honorable youth; a dutiful or courageous or wise adult *must* have already borne those traits in childhood. Thus, if the ancients perceive an adult to be noble in some way, it is presumed that he *always* was thus. Consequently they found it quite easy to describe the childhood and youth of a distinguished adult because those periods *must* have mirrored his adult accomplishments. No further facts are needed other than adult acccomplishments. Thus a person's biography was expected to reflect lifelong constancy, with childhood and youth a retrojection of adult attainments.

Accomplishments and Deeds
(*Epitêdeumata kai Praxeis*)

Before specific deeds are to be mentioned, the authors of the progymnasmata instruct us to attend to "accomplishments" (*epitêdeumata*), that is, the choices a person makes that reveal character. Menander Rhetor, our Mediterranean informant, states:

> "Accomplishments" also will give scope for discussion ("accomplishments" are qualities of character not involved with real competitive actions) because they display character. For example: "He was just (or temperate) in his youth." Isocrates used this idea in Evagoras, in the passage where he shortly goes on to say: "And when he became a man, all this was increased, and many other qualities were added." Similarly, Aristides in the Panathenaicus shows that Athens was humane (he treats this quality as an "accomplishment") in harboring the refugees. (2.372.2–13)

Cicero, an earlier Mediterranean informant (died 43 B.C.), offers considerable help in understanding this aspect. By "accomplishments," he means learned or acquired good habits:

> By habit [*habitus*] we mean a stable and absolute constitution of mind or body in some particular, as, for example, the acquisition of some capacity or of an art, or again some special knowledge, or some bodily dexterity not given by nature but won by careful training and practice. (*Inv.* 1.24.36)

Once more, we highlight how important it is to note that information concerning arts, skills, and "accomplishments" developed in a person's later life serves as proof and warrant enough for an author to indicate that such were present in that person's youth. As we noted, the perspective is one of constancy of character; such a person *always* was thus-and-such.

After listing "accomplishments," writers then turn to "actions" (*praxeis*): "Next to 'accomplishments' now comes the topic of 'actions'" (Menander 2.372.14). As noted above, a person's deeds are classified according to three categories: those of the body, the soul, and fortune.

Deeds of the Body

Aristotle briefly mentions the accomplishments of the body: "bodily excellences, such as stature, beauty, strength, athletic powers" (*Rhet.* 1.5.6,

1361a). While this is quite a short description, the progymnasmata did not contain much more instruction either. Hermogenes (second century A.D.) mentions "beauty, stature, agility, might"; Aphthonius notes "beauty, swiftness, strength"; and Theon (first century A.D.) specifies "health, strength, beauty, quick sensibility." Since Aristotle is an early witness to this topic (see *Rhet.* 1.5.10–14, 1361b), consider what he means by these features:

> *Health* [is] bodily excellence . . . , and of such a kind that when exercising the body we are free from sickness; for many are healthy in the way Herodicus is said to have been, whom no one would consider happy in the matter of health, because they are obliged to abstain from all or nearly all human enjoyments.

> *Beauty* varies with each age. In a young man, it consists in possessing a body capable of enduring all efforts, either of the racecourse or of bodily strength while he himself is pleasant to look upon and a sheer delight. This is why the athletes in the pentathlum are most beautiful, because they are naturally adapted for bodily exertion and for swiftness of foot. In a man who has reached his prime, beauty consists in being naturally adapted for the toils of war, in being pleasant to look upon and at the same time awe-inspiring. In an old man, beauty consists in being naturally adapted to contend with unavoidable labours and in not causing annoyance to others, thanks to the absence of the disagreeable accompaniments of old age.

> *Strength* consists in the power of moving another as one wills, for which purpose it is necessary to pull or push, to lift, to squeeze or crush, so that the strong man is strong by virtue of being able to do all or some of these things.

> *Excellence in size* (stature) consists in being superior to most men in height, depth, and breadth, but in such proportion as not to render the movements of the body slower as the result of excess.

> *Athletic excellence* consists in size, strength, and swiftness of foot; for to be swift is to be strong. For one who is able to throw his legs about in a certain way, to move them rapidly and with long strides, makes a good runner; one who can hug and grapple, a good wrestler; one who can thrust away by a blow of the fist, a good boxer; one who excels in boxing and wrestling is fit for the pancratium, he who excels in all for the pentathlum.

Aristotle seems to have a male warrior or an athlete in mind. For the philosopher, the young *politês* ought to be fit to fight for the polis. In either case, such a person embodies what is needed to be a public figure in the culture of the time, hence to gain public honor. "Health" is the ability to use one's body; "beauty" pertains to endurance and exertion in contests. Thus these qualities have to do with imposing one's will, acting assertively, performing heroic deeds, and thus gaining honor and respect.

Deeds of the Soul

Deeds of the soul are divided according to the commonplace of the four classical virtues; wisdom (*phronêsis*), temperance or sense of shame (*sôphrosynê*), justice (*dikaiosynê*), and courage (*andreia*). Menander Rhetor, when he instructs an author to organize his material according to all four, is himself reflecting an old, established tradition:

> Always divide the actions of those you are going to praise into the virtues (there are four virtues: courage, justice, temperance, and wisdom) and see to what virtues the actions belong and whether some of them, whether in war or in peace, are common to a single virtue: e.g., wisdom, for it belongs to wisdom both to command armies well in war and to legislate well and dispose and arrange the affairs of subjects to advantage. (2.373.5–14).

Duane Stuart's observations about the prevailing cultural expectations of excellence in the ancient world indicate the antiquity and pervasiveness of Menander's remarks. Stuart has observed that an encomiast began his writing with the knowledge that "there were foreordained excellencies without which lofty character could not be imagined as existing" (1928, 65). Such "foreordained excellencies" point to stereotypical require-ments. These consisted of the four cardinal virtues—courage, wisdom, temperance, and justice—which, "evolving naturally in the moral con-sciousness of Greece, were systematized into criteria of ethical valuation, furnished measuring rods." By demonstrating these in the life of the per-son being described, the encomiast sought to show that "his hero lived up to this standard of all that did become a man." Thus, writers and their audiences already possessed a clear idea of what characterizes a noble person, namely, the four cardinal virtues. Moreover, they also shared a common understanding of what constituted each of those four virtues.

This part of the encomium would seem to be of considerable impor-tance to Menander Rhetor, for he both repeats and develops it at consid-erable length. When speaking of the accomplishments of a politeuma (population of a polis), he notes that residents would be "assessed in terms of the virtues and their parts" (1.361.11–13). After naming the four virtues, he then discusses the parts of each virtue, a topic that is impor-tant for our grasp of how ancient Mediterranean natives understood these features. By surveying this material briefly, we can be quite sure we un-derstand what Menander and other progymnastic writers meant by these four virtues.

The parts of justice are piety, fair dealing and reverence. . . . There are two tests of temperance, in public life and in private domesticity. . . . Similarly with prudence. In public affairs. . . . On the private side. . . . Courage is assessed in peace and war. (1.361.17–365.4)

It should be noted that other encomia in the extant progymnasmata have longer lists of virtues as illustrations of the deeds of the soul. Besides the four cardinal virtues, "piety, nobility and sense of greatness" and being "pious, free and magnanimous" are noted.

Deeds of Fortune

In the ancient world, one's role and status were tied to what we consider circumstances essentially external to the person. Although elites knew they had little if any control over their fortune, they were deemed responsible for how they dealt with events that cropped up in life. Thus items such as land, wealth, social connections, and the like are always seen as an integral part of a person's existence over which one has no control. After all, some have more and some have less. But why? These aspects are considered under the rubric of "fortune." They indicate divine favor showered on the individual. For we must not lose sight of the goddess Tychê (Fortune), a deity who showed patronage and benefaction unequally. Consequently a divinely favored person would necessarily assume a higher and more distinctive status in ancient society, precisely because of this divine connection.

The encomium of Hermogenes affords a brief summary of what ancients meant by the deeds of fortune:

Then external resources, such as kin, friends, possessions, household, fortune, etc. Then from the (topic) time, how long he lived, much or little; for either gives rise to encomia. Then, too, from the manner of his end, as that he died fighting for his fatherland, and, if there were anything extraordinary under that head, as in the case of Callimachus that even in death he stood. You will draw praise also from the one who slew him, as that Achilles died at the hands of the god Apollo. You will describe also what was done after his end, whether funeral games were ordained in his honor, as in the case of Patroclus, whether there was an oracle concerning his bones, as in the case of Orestes, whether his children were famous, as Neoptolemus. (Baldwin 1928, 32)

Again, we turn to the ancients for their native appreciation of the meaning of these "deeds of fortune." Aristotle's description of "happiness" serves as a convenient compendium of the deeds of fortune. He lists its component parts: "plenty of friends, good friends, wealth, good children, plenty of children, a happy old age . . . fame, honor, good luck" (*Rhet.* 1.5.3, 1360b). Then he describes the component parts of each:

The blessing of good children and numerous children needs little explanation. For the commonwealth it consists in a large number of good
young men, good in bodily excellences, such as stature, beauty, strength,
fitness for athletic contests; the moral excellences of a young man are self-
control and courage. For the individual it consists in a number of good
children of his own, both male and female, and such as we have described.
(*Rhet.* 1.5.6, 1360b–1361a)

Wealth consists in abundance of money, ownership of land and proper-
ties, and further of movables, cattle, and slaves, remarkable for number,
size, and beauty. . . . In a word, being wealthy consists rather in use than in
possession; for the actualization and use of such things is wealth. (*Rhet.*
1.5.7, 1361)

A good reputation consists in being considered a man of worth by all. . . .
Honour is a token of a reputation for doing good; and those who have already done good are justly and above all honoured. . . . The components of
honour are sacrifices, memorials in verse and prose, privileges, grants of
land, front seats, public burial, State maintenance, and among the barbarians, prostration and giving place, and all gifts which are highly prized in
each country. For a gift is at once a giving of a possession and a token of honour; wherefore gifts are desired by the ambitious and by those who are
fond of money, since they are an acquisition for the latter and an honour for
the former; so that they furnish both with what they want. (*Rhet.* 1.5.8–9,
1361a–1361b).

The meaning of numerous and worthy friends is easy to understand
from the definition of a friend. A friend is one who exerts himself to do for
the sake of another what he thinks is advantageous to him. A man to whom
many persons are so disposed, has many friends; if they are virtuous, he
has worthy friends. (*Rhet.* 1.5.16, 1361b)

Good fortune consists in the acquisition or possession of either all, or
the most, or the most important of those goods of which fortune is the
cause. . . . Speaking generally, the goods which come from fortune are such
as excite envy. (*Rhet.* 1.5.17, 1361b–1362a)

"Deeds of fortune" describe the archetypal honorable man in the public
world of the polis. He can command respect for his family in public, and
because of the number of its members, the head of the family can readily defend the family's honor. His bequeathed wealth serves as an index
of status and honor as well as of his "reputation" (fame and glory). He
enjoys excellent connections (i.e., friends), either high-ranking patrons
or loyal clients. And he enjoys success in the eyes of all and thus pro-
vokes envy.

Envy readily produces enmity. Yet for a man to have incurred the enmity of others who will eventually seek out some form of vengeance
against him usually redounds to his credit, because such a man of honor
must have successfully overcome opposition some time in the past. Aris-

totle presents a detailed discussion of envy in his rhetorical treatise as a *pathos* used in all species of rhetoric, including that of praise (*Rhet.* 2.10.1–11, 1387b–1388a).

Comparison (*Synkrisis*)

Finally, we come to comparison. Although comparison is one of the ten exercises to be learned in the progymnasmata and has its own special rules, it also appears as a recommended part of an encomium. Menander Rhetor describes it adequately:

> You should then proceed to the most complete comparison, examining his reign in comparison with preceding reigns, not disparaging them (that is bad craftsmanship) but admiring them while granting perfection to the present. You must not forget our previous proposition, namely that comparisons should be made under each head; these comparisons, however, will be partial (e.g., education with education, temperance with temperance), whereas the complete one will concern the whole subject, as when we compare a reign as a whole and in sum with another reign, e.g., the reign of Alexander with the present one. (2.377.1–9; see 2.421.1–10)

Thus authors may compare two people using one or more of the standard categories of the encomium.

The encomium, then, constitutes a native's view of what was deemed important to know about a person in antiquity. It provides us with exact historical and ethnographic descriptions of persons who differ from us not only temporally but culturally. The encomium contains information about a person from birth to death. While seemingly chronological in outline, it is structured around the native concept of *aretê* (virtue), ultimately rooted in generation, geography, and gender. Everything in the encomium, moreover, is cast in fixed categories or stereotyped terms. Such stereotypes both presume a common, shared culture and socialize new writers and speakers in that culture. The encomium, quite obviously, provides an invaluable native perspective on what constituted a person in antiquity.

PAUL'S SELF-DESCRIPTION IN HIS LETTERS: GALATIANS, PHILIPPIANS, AND 2 CORINTHIANS

As an opening gambit into our subject, the rules for an encomium provide the modern student of the Greco-Roman world with the ancient native's way of perceiving and valuing other persons. Concern with "proper" generation, geography, and gender, with positively valued origins, formation, and accomplishments—all in comparative presentation—duly describe the praiseworthy person. Personified places or things might also be described. In the case of Paul the apostle, we believe that the encomium's conventional categories can serve as a template to surface and organize what Paul says about himself in his letters. We are not arguing that Paul formally wrote apologetic encomia for himself, although George Lyons has pointed out how Galatians 1—2 reflects the content and formal terminology of an encomium (Lyons 1985, 130–35). But for purposes of developing a model of person that derives from and fits the ancient Mediterranean, a comparative sampling from the traditional genres such as the encomium and Paul's letters suffices to bring out fundamental cultural concerns. We hope to show that Paul does, in fact, present himself in these conventional ways. After describing the data available from Paul's writings, we shall inquire into the sort of person who might consider such a characterization sufficient to sum up the distinctive features of a person.

Encomiastic Elements in Gal. 1:12–2:14

Any reading of Paul's remarks in Gal. 1:12–2:21 will necessarily have to be sensitive to the rhetorical analysis of the letter by Hans-Dieter Betz (1979, 14–25). Arguing that Galatians should be read in light of ancient rhetoric, Betz outlined the structure of the document in terms of the typical sequence of elements found in both actual speeches and rhetorical handbooks:

I.   Exordium (1:6–11)
II. Narratio (1:12–2:14)
III. Propositio (2:15–21)
IV. Probatio (3:1–4:31)
V.   Exhortatio (5:1–6:10)

Betz's analysis prompted an important discussion of questions such as the structure of the argument and its rhetorical aims and strategy. For example, in the "narratio" section (1:12–2:14) he underscored the importance of "denial" of certain charges and the presentation of certain facts favorable to the correct viewing of Paul's claims. In his exposition, however, he gave scarce attention to the content of the so-called autobiographical remarks in Galatians 1—2, except to mention a tradition of apologetic autobiography (Betz 1979, 14–15). Other scholars were quick to pick up Betz's discussion and offered slight (Hester 1984, 223–33) and major (Hall 1987, 277–87) modifications of his analysis. Yet rhetorical analysis alone does not satisfactorily inform us of the conventional content of the "statement of facts" in Gal. 1:12–2:14.

In a doctoral thesis, George Lyons has attempted to fill in this lacuna by developing Betz's own suggestion about "autobiography" vis-à-vis Galatians 1—2. With recourse to different areas of rhetoric, Lyons offered a more detailed form-critical view of Paul's autobiographical remarks in the light of the conventions of biography. Like Betz, he situates his analysis within a formal discussion of ceremonial or demonstrative (*epideiktikos*) rhetoric, noting that one of the key proofs in any speech "is the argument of the speaker's ethos, his distinguishing or customary moral character" (1985, 27). In this regard he indicates that rhetorical amplification of this part of a speech might entail customary topics similar to those noted earlier in this chapter. Thus, Lyons (1985, 135) suggested a fresh template of categories for perceiving the autobiography in Galatians 1—2.

I.   Opening (*prooimion*) 1:10–12 — Paul's divine gospel
II. Lifestyle (*anastrophê*) 1:13–17 — Paul's ethos
    A.   1:13–14 — As persecutor of the church
    B.   1:15–17 — As preacher of the gospel
III. Deeds (*praxeis*) 1:18–2:10 — Paul's conduct
    A.   1:18–20 — In Jerusalem
    B.   1:21–24 — In Syria and Cilicia
    C.   2:1–10 — In Jerusalem
IV. Comparison (*synkrisis*) 2:11–21 — Cephas and Paul
    A.   2:11–14 — Incidental: In Antioch
    B.   2:15–21 — General: Paul and Judean Messianists
V.   Conclusion (*epilogos*) 2:21 — Paul and divine favor

This is how the passage looks when outfitted with the appropriate encomiastic titles.

I.   *Prooimion* 1:10–12 — Paul's divine gospel

> Am I now seeking the favor of men, or of God? Or am I trying to please men? If I were still pleasing men, I should not be a servant of Christ. For I would have you know, brethren, that the gospel which was preached by me is not man's gospel. For I did not receive it from man, nor was I taught it, but it came through a revelation of Jesus Christ.

II.   *Anastrophê* 1:13–17 — Paul's ethos

    A.   1:13–14 — As persecutor of the church

> For you have heard of my former life following Judean political religion, how I persecuted the church of God violently and tried to destroy it; and I advanced in Judean political religion beyond many of my own age among my people, so extremely zealous was I for the traditions of my fathers.

    B.   1:15–17 — As preacher of the gospel

> But when he who had set me apart before I was born, and had called me through his grace, was pleased to reveal his Son to me, in order that I might preach him among the Gentiles, I did not confer with flesh and blood, nor did I go up to Jerusalem to those who were apostles before me, but I went away into Arabia; and again I returned to Damascus.

III.   *Praxeis* 1:18–2:10 — Paul's conduct

    A.   1:18–20 — In Jerusalem

> Then after three years I went up to Jerusalem to visit Cephas, and remained with him fifteen days. But I saw none of the other apostles except James the Lord's brother. (In what I am writing to you, before God, I do not lie!)

    B.   1:21–24 — In Syria and Cilicia

> Then I went into the regions of Syria and Cilicia. And I was still not known by sight to the churches of Christ in Judea; they only heard it said, "He who once persecuted us is now preaching the faith he once tried to destroy." And they glorified God because of me.

    C.   2:1–10 — In Jerusalem

> Then after fourteen years I went up again to Jerusalem with Barnabas, taking Titus along with me. I went up by revelation; and I laid before them (but privately before those who were of repute) the gospel which I preach among the Gentiles, lest somehow I should be running or had run in vain. But even Titus, who was with me, was not compelled to be circumcised, though he was a Greek. But because of false brethren secretly brought in, who slipped in to spy out our freedom which we have

in Christ Jesus, that they might bring us into bondage—
to them we did not yield submission even for a moment,
that the truth of the gospel might be preserved for you.
And from those who were reputed to be something
(what they were makes no difference to me; God shows
no partiality)—those, I say, who were of repute added
nothing to me; but on the contrary, when they saw that
I had been entrusted with the gospel to the uncircumcised, just as Peter had been entrusted with the gospel
to the circumcised (for he who worked through Peter
for the mission to the circumcised worked through me
also for the Gentiles), and when they perceived the
grace that was given to me, James and Cephas and John,
who were reputed to be pillars, gave to me and Barnabas
the right hand of fellowship, that we should go to the
Gentiles and they to the circumcised; only they would
have us remember the poor, which very thing I was ea-
ger to do.

IV.   *Synkrisis* 2:11–21 — Cephas and Paul

   A.   2:11–14 — Incidental: In Antioch

But when Cephas came to Antioch I opposed him to his
face, because he stood condemned. For before certain
men came from James, he ate with the Gentiles; but
when they came he drew back and separated himself,
fearing the circumcision party. And with him the rest
of the Judeans acted insincerely, so that even Barnabas
was carried away by their insincerity. But when I saw
that they were not straightforward about the truth of
the gospel, I said to Cephas before them all, "If you,
though a Judean, live like a Gentile and not like a
Judean, how can you compel the Gentiles to live like
Judeans?"

   B.   2:15–21 — General: Paul and Judean Messianists

We ourselves, who are Judeans by birth and not Gentile
sinners, yet who know that a man is not justified by
works of the law but through faith in Jesus Christ, even
we have believed in Christ Jesus, in order to be justified
by faith in Christ, and not by works of the law, because
by works of the law shall no one be justified. But if, in our
endeavor to be justified in Christ, we ourselves were
found to be sinners, is Christ then an agent of sin? Certainly not! But if I build up again those things which I

> tore down, then I prove myself a transgressor. For I
> through the law died to the law, that I might live to God.
> I have been crucified with Christ; it is no longer I who
> live, but Christ who lives in me; and the life I now live in
> the flesh I live by faith in the Son of God, who loved me
> and gave himself for me.

V.   *Epilogos* 2:21 — Paul and divine favor

> I do not nullify the grace of God; for if justification were
> through the law, then Christ died to no purpose.

Subjects or items of information set out in rather conventional form are
called *topoi* (our word *topic* is related). Here Paul sets out biographical
topoi, as Lyons has indicated. His observations offer a valuable and valid
complement to Betz's rhetorical analysis. Given our concern with ancient
Mediterranean person, we shall now work out Lyons's suggestions in
some detail. We can readily do so because biographical topoi contain far
more comparative cultural data than most people realize. Consider the following features.

> 1:13   *For you have heard of my former life following Judean politi-
> cal religion, how I persecuted the church of God violently and tried to
> destroy it;* [14]*and I advanced in Judean political religion beyond many
> of my own age among my people, so extremely zealous was I for the tra-
> ditions of my fathers.*

Paul talks first about "my former (way of) life" (*tên emôn anastrophên*).
The Greek for "way of life" here is *anastrophê*, the technical term we have
observed in the list of elements in an encomium for "manner of life."
When he tells us that "I advanced in Judean political religion beyond
many among my people of the same age" (v. 14), he indicates his ethnic
group (*ethnos,* "among my own people"), Israel. The Israelite worldview
and customary behavior based on that worldview were called "Judaism,"
after the Roman-controlled "kingdom" of Judea. Non-Israelites, as a rule,
believed all Israelites came from Judea, hence called them "Judeans" and
their customs "Judaism." (Paul's Judean political religion, situated in
Judea and focused on Jerusalem and the Temple there, ought not to be
confused with later Jewish domestic religion deriving from Mishnah and
Talmud.)

Be that as it may, wherever Paul was, he was trained in the behavior
and customs typical of people from Judea (*en tôi Ioudaismôi*). He boasts
that he was preeminent in his manner of life, which was rooted in respect
for ancestors: "for I was far more zealous for the traditions of my ancestors" (v. 15). This zeal showed itself in his uncompromising devotedness

to the Israelite status quo, which accounted for his authorized persecution and destruction of "the churches of God" (see Malina 1994a, 51–78; Seland 1995, 6–16). Thus three terms with emphatic placement quickly tell us of the unsurpassing excellence of Paul's manner of life: (a) "violently" (*kata hyperbolên*), (b) "advanced" (*proekopton*), and (c) "extremely zealous" (*perissoterôs zêlôtês*).

Yet the further description of his "manner of life" would create problems for ancient readers. For the mention of change in his manner of life would normally be viewed with suspicion. The culture valued stability and constancy of character. Hence, "change" of character was neither expected nor praiseworthy. Normally adult persons were portrayed as living out the manner of life that had always characterized them. All that is in the mighty oak was already in the acorn. In a recent dissertation, Jon Bailey (1993, 85–88) has shown how in certain philosophical circles, such as the Stoics, change or repentance was negatively viewed. He cites Cicero, quoting the Stoic view: "The philosopher surmises nothing, repents of nothing, is never wrong, and never changes his opinion" (*Pro Murena* 61, Loeb; see Aesop, *Fable* 48). Paul would need some clever explanation to indicate why it would not be shameful for him to change his manner of living from "the customary behavior of Judeans" to that of the "churches of God." Of course, the explanation is forthcoming, and it duly exonerates Paul, for God is responsible for the change!

> 1:15 *But when he who had set me apart before I was born, and had called me through his grace, was pleased* [16]*to reveal his Son to me, in order that I might preach him among the Gentiles, I did not confer with flesh and blood,* [17]*nor did I go up to Jerusalem to those who were apostles before me.*

Paul now goes on to tell something about his birth (*genesis*) that might explain the change in his manner of life. As is well known, the birth of Jesus was accompanied by customary marks of the birth of a noble person (signs in the sky: Matt. 2:2, 7–10; visions and dreams: Matt. 1:20–23; 2:12, 13, 19; and other strange events: Matt. 2:16–18). Paul, on the other hand, notes his birth more simply, yet in a way not without significance for this inquiry. For he explains his unusual qualities by indicating the special role God played in that event: "From my mother's womb," he says, God both "set me apart" and "called me through his favor." He was, then, beloved of God ("called through his grace"), favored by God ("it pleased God"), and ascribed distinction by God ("he set me apart"). These features constitute a powerful claim to honor. In fact, they account for the change in Paul's behavior in a positive way.

To begin with, these features identify Paul as a person to whom God ascribed the specific role of prophet (Betz 1979, 69–70).

Paul's Version	Prophet's Version
1. ... who had set me apart	*Jer. 1:5* Before I formed you in your mother's womb, I knew you; before you were born, I consecrated you.
	Isa. 49:1b ... from the body of my mother he named my name.
2. and had called me	*Isa. 49:1c* The Lord called me though his grace from the womb
3. to reveal his son to me	*Isaiah 6; Ezekiel 1*
4. in order that I might preach to the nations	*Jer. 1:6* I appoint you a prophet to the nations
	Isa. 49:6 I will give you as a light to the nations

Paul describes his birth, then, in terms of the conventions of a prophetic calling, thus claiming a unique role and status in the household of God.

But Paul did not initially act as God's prophet. The first part of his life was marked by unswerving devotedness to God's will as expressed in Israel's traditions. This is undoubtedly what he learned through his ethnic enculturation. The result was his dedication to authorized violence on behalf of the status quo, to Judean customary behavior, and to the tradition of his ancestors. With the hindsight accompanying his new point of view, he could clearly see that his previous way of life was itself in marked contrast to what God had originally intended for him. Hence his present role was not so much a change as simply a return to where he originally should have been. Because his former "manner of life" set him against God's revealed purposes, it was incumbent upon him finally to take up what God wanted for him. Thus he was not an opportunist, a fickle person, or a flatterer! By invoking God as the agent of change, Paul claims that his new manner of life was ordained by God and thus should be regarded as highly honorable. God's "revealing" to him again marks Paul as a person of high standing, even as it confirms him in the role of a prophet. He always was a prophet, even from his mother's womb, although previous circumstances thwarted the emergence of this dimension of his way of life. His prophetic calling was ascribed to him by the

very God "who raised Jesus from the dead" (Gal. 1:1; Rom. 8:11). All of
his subsequent actions, then, are to be viewed as the legitimate fulfillment
of his divinely ascribed role, not as an alteration or deviation indicative of
inconstancy.

This reference to Paul's prophetic status seems to be rooted in a conflict over roles, which is intimated in this letter. There are evidently apostles in the church, at least in the Jerusalem church (Gal. 1:17–19). But in
the church of the Galatians, a controversy rages over whether Paul qualifies as an apostle (1:1). His claim to be a prophet might well position Paul
in a role higher than that of apostle. Prophets had immediate experience
of God, whereas apostles were commissioned by the man Jesus. Further,
Paul uses immediacy of revelation later to rank Abraham's covenant over
that of Moses, which was "ordained by angels through an intermediary"
(3:19). Revelations from God, moreover, must count as more honorable
than the experience of merely seeing and hearing Jesus. Thus in 1:15–16,
Paul shows how change in his "manner of life" (*anastrophê*) is no deviation but something quite expected, given his "birth" (*genesis*). His compliance with God's will for him is eminently honorable because it is ordained by God. And so his divinely ascribed role as prophet must likewise
be respected.

> 1:17b   *But I went away into Arabia; and again I returned to Da-
> mascus.*
> *18Then after three years I went up to Jerusalem to visit Cephas, and
> remained with him fifteen days. 19But I saw none of the other apostles ex-
> cept James the Lord's brother. 20 (In what I am writing to you, before God,
> I do not lie!) 21Then I went into the regions of Syria and Cilicia. 22And
> I was still not known by sight to the churches of Christ in Judea; 23they
> only heard it said, "He who once persecuted us is now preaching the faith
> he once tried to destroy." 24And they glorified God because of me.*

If we take our cue from the encomium conventions for describing a
"life" (*bios*), these verses have to do with typical observations about a person's education (*paideia*), an important element in describing a manner
of life. The Acts of the Apostles relate that Paul studied his Pharisaic lore
under Gamaliel (22:3). Yet regarding his "knowledge" of Christ and God's
ways, Paul claims here that he did not have a human teacher. In effect, he
was taught by God, who "revealed his Son to me" (1:16a). While the truism indicated that a disciple cannot exceed his teacher, there was no such
saying about the relative standing of teachers. Yet because Paul has God
as teacher, surely he can exceed any other human teacher!

He thus begins his account of his life by disclaiming having any human
teachers in his formation. He insists that "the gospel proclaimed by me is
not of human origin (*kata anthrôpon*), for I did not receive it from a

human source (*para anthrôpou*), nor was I taught it" (1:12). No human
teachers were involved because he received it "through a revelation" (*di'
apokalypseôs*), that is, he was instructed, informed, and formed exclusively by God. This would likewise seem to be the force of the disclaimer
in 1:16–17 that after the "revelation of his Son in me," Paul did not confer
with flesh and blood, nor did he even go up to Jerusalem to those who
were already apostles before him. There simply was no need, because he
had no human teachers. He knew what he knew because of God's "revelation" (vv. 12, 15).

In John's Gospel (6:45), being "taught by God" serves as a mark of divine selection or special status; there the expression is rooted in Isa.
54:11. In 1 Cor. 2:13, Paul boasts that he imparts knowledge "not taught
by human wisdom but taught by the Spirit." Paul himself seems to have
coined a term for "taught by God" (*theodidaktos*), which he used in 1
Thess. 4:9. Considerable attention has been given to this term in recent
Pauline scholarship, with specific reference to Philo's discussion of persons who are taught by others or self-taught. We are thus apprised of the
cultural importance attached to education by a teacher compared to education by another and higher source. We suggest that when Paul claims
that "I did not confer with flesh and blood" (1:16b), he is informing his
readers of the source of his education. He has been formed in his Christian way of life, not by human teachers such as "the apostles before me,"
but by a higher teacher, namely, God. Hence, he stands above others,
given the standing of his teacher!

Next Paul claims that after three years he went up to Jerusalem to
"visit" Cephas (v. 18). It has been argued that this term "visit" (*historêsai*)
means much more than just "talk about the weather" for two weeks. Dictionaries translate this word as "to visit a person for the purpose of inquiry" (Lidell, Scott, and Jones 1968, 842; Dunn 1985, 138–39). In this
sense, Paul would have come to Jerusalem to make inquiries, to get informed, to find out things from Cephas. This meaning has been challenged by Hofius (1984, 73–85) and Ulrichs (1990, 262–69), who argue
from linguistic grounds for a more neutral meaning such as "to get to
know a person." From the perspective of the encomium's directives on
"education," we would have to opt for the more neutral meaning of the
term. Paul was already the type of person God intended him to be, with
knowledge of everything he needed to know. In that light Paul insists that
he was *not* taught by any earthly teachers (Acts 22:3), for he was formed,
informed, and taught by God.

If he really had nothing to learn from them, why would a Mediterranean
such as Paul want to visit Cephas and James? We can be sure of one thing:
His purpose did not derive from a social system like that of modern Westerners and their experience of ready mobility and keeping family ties alive

over long distances. Paul's mention of the timing of the encounter may offer a clue to his motivation. For having previously been taught by God, and away from Israel's central place, Jerusalem, Paul already knows about God's plan for humankind, which is rooted in Jesus the Messiah. Hence Paul's decision to go to Jerusalem is not based on seeking information; he has nothing to "inquire" of Cephas. Yet by Mediterranean cultural standards, his claim that he was "taught by God" needs to be acknowledged by others if it is to be a valid claim to honor and status. What seems important in Gal. 1:18–19 is Paul's positioning himself on par with Cephas and James, the Lord's brother. Paul meets only with the leaders of the group, both as their peer and as a person acknowledged to have been taught by God—at least these seem to be Paul's own rhetorical claims. Thus, his studied insistence that he did not go to Judea or Jerusalem is indication of his independence and acknowledged divine "education" in matters pertaining to his gospel and Christ Jesus.

> 2:1 *Then after fourteen years I went up again to Jerusalem with Barnabas, taking Titus along with me. ²I went up by revelation; and I laid before them (but privately before those who were of repute) the gospel which I preach among the Gentiles, lest somehow I should be running or had run in vain. ³But even Titus, who was with me, was not compelled to be circumcised, though he was a Greek. ⁴But because of false brethren secretly brought in, who slipped in to spy out our freedom which we have in Christ Jesus, that they might bring us into bondage— ⁵to them we did not yield submission even for a moment, that the truth of the gospel might be preserved for you. ⁶And from those who were reputed to be something (what they were makes no difference to me; God shows no partiality)—those, I say, who were of repute added nothing to me; ⁷but on the contrary, when they saw that I had been entrusted with the gospel to the uncircumcised, just as Peter had been entrusted with the gospel to the circumcised ⁸(for he who worked through Peter for the mission to the circumcised worked through me also for the Gentiles), ⁹and when they perceived the grace that was given to me, James and Cephas and John, who were reputed to be pillars, gave to me and Barnabas the right hand of fellowship, that we should go to the Gentiles and they to the circumcised; ¹⁰only they would have us remember the poor, which very thing I was eager to do.*

At this point in an encomium, an author would begin to discourse on a person's "accomplishments" (*epitêdeumata*) and "deeds" (*praxeis*). Many rhetorical authors indicate that when praising a person's deeds and accomplishments, we may present them either chronologically or thematically. Quintilian (died ca. A.D. 96) states:

> It has sometimes proved the more effective course to trace a man's life and deeds in due chonological order, praising his natural gifts as a child, then

his progress at school, and finally the whole course of his life, including words as well as deeds. At times on the other hand it is well to divide our praises, dealing separately with the various virtues, fortitude, justice, self-control and the rest of them and to assign to each virtue the deeds performed under its influence. (*Inst. Orat.* 3.7.15)

These modes of presentation were not mutually exclusive, for even a chronological sequence is to contain indication that the person's accomplishments illustrate the four conventional virtues. Evidently, Paul presents a chronology of his labors ("immediately," 1:16b; "then after three years," v. 18; "then," v. 20). The chronology, however, ought to illustrate the more important issue of virtue. For Paul must demonstrate that his life is lived in accord with one or another of the conventional virtues, such as justice, wisdom, temperance, courage, and the like. Such are the requirements of the formal conventions of an encomium.

Modern readers need to pause and reflect on how the ancients defined the four cardinal virtues and viewed each as a broad category or genus with a variety of species. As we noted earlier, it had become commonplace in antiquity to identify four cardinal virtues: prudence, justice, temperance, and fortitude. Occasionally a fifth or sixth virtue, such as piety, might be listed. But in time, the famous four held pride of place. Depending on the rhetorical situation of a given author, one or another of the four cardinal virtues might be said to be the chief or primary virtue. Josephus, for example, makes "religion" or "piety" (*eusebeia*) the virtue that includes the rest (*The Life* 14; also Philo, *Spec. Leg.* 4.147). Philo, reading Gen. 15:6, cited faithfulness as the queen of the virtues (*Abr.* 270) and the most perfect of them (*Quis rerum divinarum Heres* 91). In 4 Maccabees 1:18, the primary virtue is wisdom.

Of particular interest to our examination of Galatians are Hellenistic discussions of justice (*dikaiosynê*). Aristotle described "justice" or "righteousness" (*dikaiosynê*) as follows:

> To righteousness it belongs to be ready to distribute according to desert, and to preserve ancestral customs and institutions and the established laws, and to tell the truth when interest is at stake, and to keep agreements. First among the claims of righteousness are our duties to the gods, then our duties to the spirits, then those to country and parents, then those to the departed; among these claims is piety [*eusebeia*], which is either a part of righteousness or a concomitant of it. Righteousness is also accompanied by holiness and truth and loyalty (*pistis*) and hatred of wickedness. (*Virtues and Vices* 5.2–3, 1250b, Loeb)

Thus, Aristotle defined "justice" (*dikaiosynê*) and treated it as a genus with species of piety and loyalty. Moreover, he likewise believed that when one thinks of justice, one should think of one's duties and the obligation of piety to perform them.

Justice or righteousness (*dikaiosynê*), then, is about proper interpersonal relations and the obligations entailed in these relations. It refers to keeping agreements and performing duties. Piety or religion describes the practical respect for those who control one's existence. Thus as part of justice, piety means loyalty and faithfulness to the gods. Aristotle's broad definition can be clarified by the comments of one of the authors of the progymnasmata whom we cited earlier, our native informant Menander Rhetor.

> The parts of justice are piety, fair dealing, and reverence: piety towards the gods, fair dealings towards men, reverence towards the departed. Piety to the gods consists of two elements: being god-loved (*theophilotês*) and god-loving (*philotheotês*). The former means being loved by the gods and receiving many blessings from them, the latter consists of loving the gods and having a relationship of friendship with them. (1.361.17–25)

Not only does Menander confirm piety as a part of justice, he speaks of a reciprocity between gods and mortals, benefaction from the gods to mortals, and respect and honor from mortals to the gods. As with patrons in general, the patronage of the gods establishes a duty of loyalty and faithfulness in the one receiving patronage. Thus piety means that one shows respect, obedience, and loyalty to one's patron (see Elliott 1987; Malina 1988b).

This attempt to understand the native meaning of justice and its relationship to piety and loyalty should have a bearing on how we might understand Paul's remarks in Gal. 1:20–24. Paul states that he spent fourteen years "preaching the faith he once tried to destroy" (v. 23). We would classify this consistent and habitual behavior as an illustration of piety (*eusebeia*), which is a part of justice (*dikaiosynê*). When Paul twice notes that God "revealed" mysteries to him (vv. 12, 15), this should surely be taken to mean that he is god-loved or *theophilotês*. To a sinner who persecuted God's designated Messiah and his followers, God showed incomparable benefaction: Paul was given a revelation of God's exclusive plan, knowledge of his "Son." Moreover, this revelation did not simply alter Paul's awareness, from being ignorant of some bit of information to one who was now informed about it. Rather the revelation proved to be a formative event—it served as a sort of ritual of status transformation whereby the persecutor of the gospel became its herald: ". . . so that I might proclaim him among the Gentiles" (v. 16). Paul thus demonstrates that he was blessed indeed, one "loved by God." For his part, Paul now had a duty to be God-loving. He had received both a benefaction and a commission. He owed God loyalty to fulfill the gracious commission entrusted to him.

When Paul went first to Arabia and Damascus and then to the regions of Syria and Cilicia, he tells us that he spent three and then fourteen years fulfilling God's commission (vv. 17, 20). His later visit to Jerusalem indicates continued loyalty to God, as does his situation as the defender of the faith of the Galatians. He has, then, demonstrated remarkable piety and loyalty toward God. Note also his concern that he not "run in vain" (2:2), that is, that he not fail in his commission.

In the foregoing quote from Aristotle on the parts of justice, the philosopher mentioned not only piety (*eusebeia*) but also loyalty or faithfulness (*pistis*): "Righteousness is also accompanied by holiness and truth and loyalty (*pistis*)." Significantly, Paul likewise shows concern to note his loyalty in his obedience to God's commission. Inasmuch as he was ascribed the authority and role of being an official herald "that I might preach him among the Gentiles" (1:16), he faithfully fulfilled that commission by his labors in "Syria and Cilicia" (v. 21). His second trip to Jerusalem (2:1–10) further illustrates several of Paul's conventional virtues. He again acts obediently to God's "revelation" (v. 1), demonstrating his piety both as one God-loved and as one loving God, to whom he proved loyal.

What sort of virtue might be signaled by his desire to avoid error and misrepresentation of God's gospel: "lest somehow I should be running or had run in vain" (v. 2)? His behavior in Jerusalem demonstrates his pious loyalty to his patron, God. He staunchly defends certain principles that he learned from having been "taught by God." Titus was not required to be circumcised (v. 3), although it is not clear that this was upon Paul's insistence. But it does show that others in Jerusalem acknowledged that Paul did not require circumcision of non-Israelites. It is clear that Paul's decision to go to the uncircumcised constitutes part of his commissioning by God (1:16). On the other hand, it may properly be implied that the decision not to circumcise the uncircumcised is likewise part of that "revelation." It is to be expected that Paul has enemies in Jerusalem, but he shows "courage" (*andreia*) by "not yielding submission even for a moment" (2:5). Thus Paul presents himself as a man of virtue, in particular as someone who possesses dikaiosyne in all its forms. He is both "beloved by God" and "God loving" in return; he excels in faithfulness and loyalty, and so in piety (*eusebeia*). He claims to be nothing less than a regular holy man.

Besides deeds of the soul, the encomiast is instructed to discourse also on deeds of fortune. Under deeds of fortune, the rhetoricians regularly listed all those important features that befall a person: power, wealth, friends, children, fame, fortune, and the like. In one sense, Paul was always a well-known personage, a man with fame of sorts. For his new Messianist in-group, that fame initially had to do with something negative, his persecution of the disciples of Jesus. But his reputation changed and his fame grew as a result of God's favor shown to him. The churches of Christ in Judea "heard about it," that is, about his preaching of the gospel (1:23); and they "glorified God because of me" (v. 24). His reputation, moreover, could only be enhanced by his first meeting with Cephas and James (vv. 18–19). It grew to the point that he was privileged with a face-to-face meeting with the Jerusalem leaders (2:2). They truly enjoyed fame and a good reputation, for they were known as "the pillars" and "those of repute" (*hoi dokountes*), even if this term is taken ironically. By appearing in the company of famous people and by being treated as an equal to Cephas in terms of mission (2:7–9), Paul can be said ultimately to have fame and to enjoy a very good reputation. In regard to friends, Paul claims that Cephas and the other pillars of the Jerusalem church extended the right hand of fellowship to him (*dexias . . . koinônias,* v. 9). This gesture intimated "a legally binding, reciprocal partnership or association between one person and one or more second people with regard to a particular action, thing or person" (Sampley 1977, 159). Roman law called it *societas, koinônia* in Greek. This sort of agreement depended fully on the mutual trust and faithfulness of the partners, and it had its focus on some shared goal toward which the partners (*socii*) were to contribute their property or work, or both, in the fulfillment of the shared aim. The gesture thus confirmed that just as Peter had been entrusted with the gospel to the circumcised, so Paul was entrusted with the gospel to the uncircumcised. Each would offer support to the other. Cephas had already received Paul (1:18), as had James the brother of the Lord. Paul, then, had high-ranking partners in the inner circles of the reconstituted Jesus movement group.

Regarding fortune, we have already noted how Paul proclaims that he is blessed by God. He received not only mercy for persecuting God's church but also benefactions of "revelation" and commissioning. Regarding honor, Paul's role and status were publicly acknowledged by the elite in-group of Jerusalem. In an honor/shame society such as the one in which Paul lived, claims to honor and precedence always required public acknowledgment, lest they be vain claims, ridiculed and leading to shame. Paul is acknowledged by the most important figures in his orbit, "those of repute," whose judgment carried great weight. Even Paul's sarcastic labeling of these figures in no way diminished the importance of their acknowledgment of him: "They saw that I was entrusted with the gospel to the uncircumcised" (2:7). And he proudly parades his legitimation by them: "They gave me and Barnabas the right hand of fellowship" (v. 9). Thus his claim to honor is confirmed by the most important people in the circle of Jesus' disciples. His commission is considered on par with that of Cephas.

As the foregoing indicates, Paul described this part of his career in terms that would readily be appreciated in a culture in which an encomium provided commonplace categories for organizing information about a person. He has high-ranking associates; he enjoys considerable good fortune through God's benefactions; he possesses an excellent reputation, which has been publicly acknowledged by the elite of the group. Thus, he is an eminently honorable person.

> 2:11 *But when Cephas came to Antioch I opposed him to his face, because he stood condemned. 12For before certain men came from James, he ate with the Gentiles; but when they came he drew back and separated himself, fearing the circumcision party. 13And with him the rest of the Judeans acted insincerely, so that even Barnabas was carried away by their insincerity. 14But when I saw that they were not straightforward about the truth of the gospel, I said to Cephas before them all, "If you, though a Judean, live like a Gentile and not like a Judean, how can you compel the Gentiles to live like Judeans?"*

After the exposition of the accomplishments of a person, the encomia indicate that it is appropriate to include a synkrisis or "comparison." We might examine Gal. 2:11–14 in this light. Hermogenes offers us a succinct definition of a "comparison":

> Now sometimes we draw out comparisons by equality, showing the things which we compare as equal either in all respects or in several; sometimes we put the one ahead, praising also the other to which we prefer it; sometimes we blame the one utterly and praise the other, as in a comparison of justice and wealth. (Baldwin 1928, 34)

The comparison, then, may elevate the status of a less honorable person to the level of a recognized and honorable person. Or it may praise the one and blame the other. In this regard, we might reconsider the meeting of Paul with "those of repute" in 2:1–10. He earlier maintained that he did not "confer [about his gospel] with flesh and blood" (1:16), but now he does so: "I laid [*anethemên*] the gospel before them" (2:2). The two events may be "compared" in that the second one is directed by God ("I went up by a revelation," v. 2a), whereas previously Paul was under no such constraint. The latter, then, is not an indication of inconsistency and instability. Once more Paul indicates superior and praiseworthy behavior, because it was at God's direction that he behaved as he did. At that meeting, moreover, Paul met privately with the elite of the Jerusalem group, "those of repute" (vv. 3, 6) and "those reputed to be pillars" (v. 9). On that occasion, the higher-ranking persons, James, Cephas, and John, perceived that Paul was equal to Peter in that, "just as Peter was entrusted with the gospel to the circumcised," so too they acknowledged that Paul was comparably "entrusted with the gospel to the uncircumcised" (vv.

6–7). Mention of the meeting, then, served the rhetorical function of comparing Paul with Peter and putting Paul on a par with the person commonly acknowledged to have the top management role. The world was ethnocentrically divided into two equal parts (Judeans and foreigners), and Paul was credited with being in charge of the foreign half of the world. His honor claim is not simply acknowledged, but he is also elevated in status through this comparison: he is ranked on par with Peter.

The comparison seems most evident, however, in the narration of the encounter at Antioch in 2:11–14. It is not our purpose to examine the exact nature of the controversy in all its historical particularity (see Dunn 1983; Esler 1987, 87–89). We focus only on the rhetoric of comparison and what comparison underscores about the character of Paul. Here it will be helpful to cite the rules of Theon on comparison:

> A comparison is a speech which shows what is better or what is worse. There are comparisons of characters and subjects: of characters: for example, Ajax, Odysseus; of subjects: for example, wisdom and courage. But since we prefer one of the characters over another in view of their actions, as well as whatever else about them is good, there can be one method for both. First, let it be established that comparisons are made not with matters that differ greatly from one another . . . but with matters that are similar and concerning which we disagree about which of the two we must prefer because we see no superiority of one over the other. So then, when we compare characters, we will first set side by side their noble birth, their education, their children, their public offices, their reputation, their bodily health. . . . After these items, we will compare their actions by choosing those which are more noble and the reasons for the numerous and greater blessings, those actions that are more reliable, those that are more enduring, those that were done at the proper time, those from which great harm resulted when they have not been done, those that were done with a motive rather than those done because of compulsion or chance, those which few have done rather than those that many have done (for the common and hackneyed are not at all praiseworthy), those we have done with effort rather than easily, and those we have performed that were beyond our age and ability, rather than those which we performed when it was possible. (10.1–26 in Butts 1986, 494–97)

The context of comparison, Theon says, is praise and blame: "what is better and what is worse." Two similar characters are compared: two warriors or two proclaimers of the gospel. Then their actions are compared, whether they are reliable and enduring, beneficial or harmful, free or under compulsion, requiring courage or not, or rare or commonplace. This more extended view of comparison greatly aids our reading of 2:11–14. At the very least, we can say that in this passage, one person is blamed and another praised, just as Hermogenes and Theon indicate should be the

case. Paul blames Peter: "I opposed him to his face . . . he stood condemned" (v. 11). If Peter is blamed, then Paul is to be praised. Second,
Peter is blamed for inconsistency and unreliability, hence "insincerity,"
which infected others in the group (*synypekrithêsan,* v. 13a; *hypokrisei,*
v. 13b).

In contrast, when Paul claims that Peter and others were "not acting
consistently with the truth of the gospel" (*ouk orthopodousin,* v. 14), he positions himself as one who is "sincere" and who acts straightforwardly.
Peter, moreover, acted out of "fear" of the circumcision party (v. 12). Fear
is one of the cardinal vices, a term sure to draw blame upon Peter. In contrast, Paul demonstrated "courage" by boldly challenging Peter in public
and by steadfastly defending the truth. In this, Paul can be seen to engage
in comparison that first puts him on par with Peter (vv. 1–10) and then ex-
alts him over Peter (vv. 11–14). His gospel and his manner of living are
"straightforward," "approved by the church," and "consistent." If Peter
might be charged with "pleasing men" by returning to his kosher obligations and once more not eating with Gentiles, Paul can claim consistency
in his approach and boast that he was not "pleasing men." Otherwise, he
would never have publicly challenged Peter.

From the foregoing considerations, it seems that the encomium looms
large as the model for Paul's remarks about himself in this passage from
Galatians. Most of the prescribed elements of an encomium are present:
(a) birth and attendant divine ascription of honor (1:15–16); (b) manner
of life as an advanced and observant Pharisee (1:13–14); (c) education,
not by mortals, but "taught by God" (1:16–19); (d) accomplishments and
deeds: deeds of the soul, for example, righteousness demonstrated by
piety, faithfulness (1:21–24; 2:1–10), and courage (2:11–14); and deeds of
fortune, for example, friends, fame, fortune, and honor; and (e) comparison between Paul's consistency and correctness and Peter's inconsistency (2:11–14). Further, the function of 1:12–2:14 is fully in accord with
the aims of an encomium, to praise and to blame. "Praise" is analogous to
apology, just as "blame" corresponds to polemic. These observations on
the encomiastic shape of Galatians 1—2 are not at all in conflict with other
arguments about the larger rhetorical shape of the letter. But it is essential to note the presence and function of encomium features in this part of
Paul's argument.

The Type of Person Described
in Galatians 1—2

The forms that language takes in a given society inevitably derive from
the social system of the speakers and writers of the language. For example, food or movie advertisements derive from the way people in a society
deal with preparing and selling food, or the way people produce and pre-

sent movies. It should be quite apparent, then, that the progymnasmata derive from the way people in the ancient Mediterranean world thought of and perceived persons. Since Paul followed the prescriptions of the progymnasmata in his self-description and self-presentation, he obviously followed the behavioral patterns of his society in thinking about himself and others. By adhering to the requirements of an encomium, Paul reveals what he himself thought important to know about a person, as well as what he thought his audience would want to know.

In the first place, the encomium gives both Paul and his audience a shared set of expectations and values that both constrain and liberate. They constrain because they force persons to see themselves and others only in limited, stereotyped terms. But they liberate because they set forth quite clearly and unequivocally what is required of a person to be a decent human being in that society.

Second, Paul obviously set out only information of social relevance: birth, manner of life, education, and the like. "Relevance" here refers to the code of honor into which all males were socialized in Paul's world (see Malina and Neyrey 1991a; Malina 1993b, 28–62).

Third, it is hardly a minor matter that Paul presented himself as the quintessential group-oriented person, controlled by forces greater than he: (a) God ascribes his role, status, and honor at birth; (b) Paul presents himself in terms of group affiliation, a Pharisee, a member of a specific group; (c) he claims to have learned nothing on his own but to have been taught by another, a truly noble teacher, namely, God; (d) he demonstrated the group virtues of loyalty, faithfulness, and obedience; he sought only the honoring of his patron, not his individual benefit; and (e) most important, he is ever sensitive to the opinion others have of him: either his detractors, his Galatian audience, or the Jerusalem "pillars." Acknowledgment by the Jerusalem church becomes a matter of the highest importance to this group-oriented person.

In sum, for all of the "independence" claimed for Paul by modern Western readers, he presents himself as utterly dependent on group expectations and the controlling hand of forces greater than he: ancestors, groups, God. He was a typically group-oriented person. In fact, "independence" of any group authorization would have been a major liability to him.

Encomiastic Elements
in Philippians 3:2–11

Of course, the traits Paul discloses in Galatians can also be found in his other writings. We consider here his letter to the Philippians. A cursory reading of Philippians quickly reveals that Paul knows of rival preachers of Christ Jesus who make Paul the target of their opposition (1:15–18). He sets out to persuade the Philippians not to engage in honor claims and challenges (2:1–4). To this end, he portrays Jesus the Messiah as one who pursued honor by forgoing privilege and status in obedience to God:

> 2:5   *Have this mind among yourselves, which is yours in Christ Jesus, ⁶who, though he was in the form of God, did not count equality with God a thing to be grasped, ⁷but emptied himself, taking the form of a servant, being born in the likeness of men. ⁸And being found in human form he humbled himself and became obedient unto death, even death on a cross. ⁹Therefore God has highly exalted him and bestowed on him the name which is above every name, ¹⁰that at the name of Jesus every knee should bow, in heaven and on earth and under the earth, ¹¹and every tongue confess that Jesus Christ is Lord, to the glory of God the Father.*

Now when Paul begins his polemic against "the dogs" in 3:1, he has sufficiently programmed his readers and hearers to beware of a situation of boasting and competition. He proceeds as follows:

> 3:2   *Look out for the dogs, look out for the evil-workers, look out for those who mutilate the flesh. ³For we are the true circumcision, who worship God in spirit, and glory in Christ Jesus, and put no confidence in the flesh. ⁴Though I myself have reason for confidence in the flesh also. If any other man thinks he has reason for confidence in the flesh, I have more: ⁵circumcised on the eighth day, of the people of Israel, of the tribe of Benjamin, a Hebrew born of Hebrews; as to the law a Pharisee, ⁶as to zeal a persecutor of the church, as to righteousness under the law blameless. ⁷But whatever gain I had, I counted as loss for the sake of Christ. ⁸Indeed I count everything as loss because of the surpassing worth of knowing Christ Jesus my Lord. For his sake I have suffered the loss of all things, and count them as refuse, in order that I may gain Christ ⁹and be found in him, not having a righteousness of my own, based on law, but that which is through faith in Christ, the righteousness from God that depends on faith; ¹⁰that I may know him and the power of his resurrection, and may share his sufferings, becoming like him in his death, ¹¹that if possible I may attain the resurrection from the dead.*

The autobiographical materials in 3:4–11 are prefaced in such a way as to signal the audience that Paul is about to engage in an encomiastic comparison (*synkrisis*). First, he tells the group to beware of certain people (*blepete*, three times) whom he disparagingly labels as "dogs," "workers of evil," and "mutilators." In contrast, he ironically claims to be "the circumcision"; that is the true circumcision (*peritomê*), which he contrasts with the false circumcision of those who "mutilate" (*katatomê*) the flesh.

He worships in the spirit (*en pneumati*) and does not trust in the flesh (*en sarki*), as do his rivals. Thus spirit is compared to flesh, as the true circumcision is contrasted with mutilation. The former is praised and the latter blamed.

Within this encomiastic form of a comparison, Paul compares his "confidence in the flesh" with theirs: "If anyone else has reason to be confident in the flesh, I have more" (3:4). Following the conventions of a comparison, moreover, he compares his ethnic credentials ("in the flesh") with theirs.

First he tells us of his generation or genesis, marked by mention of his ethnic group, clan, and ancestry.

> 3:5   *Circumcised on the eighth day, a member of the people of Israel, of the tribe of Benjamin, a Hebrew born of Hebrews.*

His ethnos or group of origin: the Israelite people; family or clan: Benjaminite; ancestry: a full-blooded Hebrew. His parents: If he was circumcised on the eighth day, then his parents were observant members of the house of Israel, hence honorable people, who socialized him to the customs of his family, clan, and ethnos.

Next he tells us of his manner of life (*anastrophê*): "As to the law, a Pharisee" (v. 5d). Thus we know of his formation in the strict and honorable tradition of Pharisaic study of the law. Then he announces his achievements and deeds: "As to zeal, a persecutor of the church, as to righteousness under the law, blameless" (v. 6). He tells us of his life, not in terms of chronology, but in terms of the traditional virtues or "deeds of the soul." By his own account, he epitomizes righteousness (*dikaiosynê*) to the highest degree: he is "blameless." He is truly loyal to God ("zeal" = "piety"), even to the point of persecuting the Jesus movement group, and he is "blameless" in regard to his legal duties to God.

In terms of the rhetorical strategy of a comparison, then, Paul has positioned himself not simply as the equal of those who urge circumcision and other Judean practices ("confidence in the flesh") but as their superior ("I have more . . ."). If praise derives from "the flesh," that is, from a noble birth into an honorable tribe, from a rigorous education, and from a virtuous life, then truly Paul has "more confidence" than they do.

This brief autobiographical excerpt obviously gives us a considerable amount of information about Paul. But more significantly, it provides indicators of what Paul and his audience deemed important to know about a person. Paul presumes that his readers share a common index of honor, that is, an understanding of what is socially agreed upon as bestowing worth, respect, and prestige. Hence, what he selects to tell about himself becomes culturally relevant, important information, perhaps the only information worth noting in a group-oriented culture where honor and shame are pivotal values. The features set out by Paul offer rather clear indication that group-oriented persons are basically socialized into a value system that puts a premium on nonindividualist traits.

First, Paul assures his addressees of his honorable pedigree in terms of ascribed characteristics of birth: the right ethnic origin ("Israelites"), the correct ancestry ("a Hebrew of Hebrews"), and the appropriate tribe ("Benjamin"). Paul, then, is a blue blood of the ethnic stock required to situate him socially to make the claims he does. Second, the manner of life into which he was socialized and formed stands second to none, for he was trained as a Pharisee to know and observe "the law." Those who controlled his formation set him on the most desirable course conceivable. Finally, regarding his deeds of the soul, areas for which he might be judged responsible by others, he was "blameless" in the virtue of righteousness.

From the viewpoint of modern biography, we must admit that we know nothing of his character, personality, idiosyncrasies, likes and dislikes, and other vast sections of his life. The most we can say is that he was a group-oriented person, not at all an individualist. But in terms of ancient Mediterranean concerns, we do not need to know any more than we do; for, from what he tells us, we can fill in all that is necessary to know the man in his society. We can expect that as he was raised in an observant family ("circumcised on the eighth day"), and trained as a youth as a zealous observer of the law, so he was always faithful to the Torah, both oral and written. His later behavior was in total continuity with his birth and training. All these features allow their possessor full "confidence in the flesh."

Yet interestingly enough, in Paul's case "confidence in the flesh" is not a subject for boasting and honor. And his own life, although once supremely "confident in the flesh," was changed. Once again, in a social system that downgraded personal "change" as ancient Mediterranean society did, this change too required explanation, for Paul no longer boasts of his past life and shames those who do. He offers the example of Jesus Messiah who underwent radical personal change by giving up status, privilege, and honor. But he did so in order to carry out God's bidding and so to please God. Paul intimates that his situation directly resembles that of Jesus. He now regards all former "gains" as "loss" because of Christ (3:7). He contrasts himself with those who boast of "confidence in the flesh" by claiming that only the pattern established by Jesus Messiah, according to 2:6–11, is what is truly honorable. Jesus had "former" glory but gave it up for the greater glory that obedience to God entails. Paul, too, had glory in living as an upstanding Israelite, blameless and zealous for the law, but he gave it all up for the greater glory that comes from conformity to Christ's resurrection (3:10–14). Thus Jesus' "obedience" (2:8) is superior to Paul's old "righteousness" (3:9). And so he allows the old righteousness to fall by the way in favor of God's inbreaking righteousness, a process that actually entails "loyalty" (*pistis*) to God.

We might note that while Paul contrasts himself and Judaizers, he likewise compares himself with Christ according to the pattern of the hymn. In the hymn, we know of Jesus' genesis ("in the form of God") and his manner of life ("he did not exploit it"). We learn of his deeds of the soul ("obedient"), his noble death (death on a cross), and his subsequent fame and fortune ("God highly exalted him . . . a name above every other name"). Thus the features highlighted in the encomium form also account for the features listed as significant for the "life" of Jesus Messiah. Paul in turn shows how his "life" conforms to the pattern of honorable change characteristic of Jesus Messiah. Although he has a noble birth and an honorable manner of life, like Jesus he forswore it and gave it up at God's behest. He seeks new deeds of the soul, not blameless righteousness (*dikaiosynê*) under the law, but the imitation of Christ and especially imitation of his loyalty or "faith." He desires to share in Christ's noble death (3:10), and so to qualify to share in Christ's fame and fortune (vv. 11, 14, 20–21). In contrast, his opponents cling to past birth, education, and deeds of life, which Paul labels as "loss" (vv. 7–8) and "rubbish" (v. 8b). Theirs will not be a noble death with subsequent fame and fortune, for "their end is destruction" (v. 19a). For them there is no true "glory" but only "shame" (v. 19b). They will not become politai of the "celestial body of citizens" (v. 20), that is, the polis in the sky, because their thoughts are on things of earth. Thus Paul, using the traditional categories of the encomium to portray the "life" of Jesus Messiah, argues that Jesus' mode of life alone is honorable. All who imitate Jesus' life, by undergoing change in obedience to God, then, deserve praise and honor. Not so the Judaizers, who argue for constancy and the status quo of Judean political religion, hence a life different from that of Jesus Messiah, a life that Paul says will bring only shame and dishonor.

Encomiastic Elements
in 2 Corinthians 11:21–12:10

Fitzgerald (1988) has published a work on the "catalogues of hardship" in Paul's Corinthian correspondence. He presents a persuasive case that Paul was following well-known conventions when enumerating "autobiographical" details, such as the list of hardships (2 Cor.

4:7–12; 6:3–10). Paul's remarks are conventional both in terms of literary form and content of the *peristasis* catalogues. Fitzgerald is most concerned about the form and literary function of such lists in the ancient Mediterranean world, yet he does make due reference to rhetorical comparison. However, he offers only brief comments concerning 2 Cor. 11:21–12:10, largely because of his focus on the lists of hardships in the earlier part of the document. Yet we can also make good use of his study as a valuable source of information for the proper interpretation of 11:21–12:10.

Consider what Paul has to say in the following passage:

> 11:21 *To my shame, I must say, we were too weak for that! But whatever any one dares to boast of—I am speaking as a fool—I also dare to boast of that. 22Are they Hebrews? So am I. Are they Israelites? So am I. Are they descendants of Abraham? So am I. 23Are they servants of Christ? I am a better one—I am talking like a madman—with far greater labors, far more imprisonments, with countless beatings, and often near death. 24Five times I have received at the hands of the Judeans the forty lashes less one. 25Three times I have been beaten with rods; once I was stoned. Three times I have been shipwrecked; a night and a day I have been adrift at sea; 26on frequent journeys, in danger from rivers, danger from robbers, danger from my own people, danger from Gentiles, danger in the city, danger in the wilderness, danger at sea, danger from false brethren; 27in toil and hardship, through many a sleepless night, in hunger and thirst, often without food, in cold and exposure. 28And, apart from other things, there is the daily pressure upon me of my anxiety for all the churches. 29Who is weak, and I am not weak? Who is made to fall, and I am not indignant? 30If I must boast, I will boast of the things that show my weakness. 31The God and Father of the Lord Jesus, he who is blessed for ever, knows that I do not lie. 32At Damascus, the governor under King Aretas guarded the city of Damascus in order to seize me, 33but I was let down in a basket through a window in the wall, and escaped his hands.*
>
> 12:1 *I must boast; there is nothing to be gained by it, but I will go on to visions and revelations of the Lord. 2I know a man in Christ who fourteen years ago was caught up to the third heaven—whether in the body or out of the body I do not know, God knows. 3And I know that this man was caught up into Paradise—whether in the body or out of the body I do not know, God knows— 4and he heard things that cannot be told, which man may not utter. 5On behalf of this man I will boast, but on my own behalf I will not boast, except of my weaknesses. 6Though if I wish to boast, I shall not be a fool, for I shall be speaking the truth. But I refrain from it, so that no one may think more of me than he sees in me or hears from me. 7And to keep me from being too elated by the abundance of revelations, a thorn was given me in the flesh, a messenger of Satan, to harass me, to keep me from being too elated. 8Three times I*

besought the Lord about this, that it should leave me; ⁹but he said to me,
"My grace is sufficient for you, for my power is made perfect in weak-
ness." I will all the more gladly boast of my weaknesses, that the power
of Christ may rest upon me. ¹⁰For the sake of Christ, then, I am content
with weaknesses, insults, hardships, persecutions, and calamities; for
when I am weak, then I am strong.

Paul is clearly engaging in a comparison (*synkrisis*), a regular item in
the progymnasmata, as we have seen. The comparison is normally made
about the very items that comprise the encomium (origin and birth; nurture and training; and accomplishments and deeds: deeds of the body, of
the soul, and of fortune). Any or all of the elements in an encomium are
suitable topics for a comparison, because these are the features worth
comparing to make socially relevant points. Given the information provided by 2 Cor. 11:21–12:10, the comparison here employs most of the elements of a typical encomium.

Paul opens the passage by noting: "Whatever any one dares to boast
of, I also dare to boast of that" (11:21). He seems outraged to find himself
the object of anyone else's comparison. He disclaims practicing such a
ploy: "We do not venture to class or compare ourselves with some of
those who commend themselves" (10:12a). And he shames those who
seek honor by doing so: "When they measure themselves by one another,
and compare themselves (*synkrinontes*) with one another, they are fools"
(v. 12b). But he himself later conducts his own comparison, even admit-
ting that by doing this he, too, is a "fool" (12:11). He begins his comparison with the typical initial encomiastic element of origins:

> 11:22　*Are they Hebrews? So am I! Are they Israelites? So am I! Are*
> *they seed of Abraham? So am I!*

If honor and status derive from one's generation, that is, from one's ancestry and ethnicity, then Paul enjoys as much honor as his opponents
because he too shares in their noble origins. Unlike Phil. 3:5–6, Paul here
omits all mention of his nurture and formation. Because the accomplishments of "superapostles" constitute in large measure the basis for
their denigration of Paul (11:5–6, 7–9), he too dwells on his own accomplishments and deeds. Now he claims superiority to his rivals: "Are they
servants of Christ? I am a better one" (v. 23). "Servant" (*diakonos*) need
not be interpreted as a humble slave. In one study, John N. Collins has
argued that in the Greco-Roman world, "servant" (*diakonos*) normally
means someone functioning as an agent of a high-ranking person, either
as an intermediary in commercial transactions or as a messenger or a
diplomat (Collins 1990, 77–95, 169–76). As agent of God, Paul boasts that
he has been proven a loyal and steadfast agent, in fact, more loyal and

more honorable because of his faithful service through "far greater labors, far more imprisonments, with countless beatings, and often near death" (v. 23). What follows is a list or catalogue of hardships, such as those Fitzgerald has examined. But unlike those other lists of hardships, 2 Cor. 11:23–33 is no mere free-floating catalogue that might stand as a literary form in its own right. Rather, this list is a sequence of items constituting the topics of an encomium. Hence, we should examine Paul's list here in comparison with its co-text, that is, the encomiastic category of deeds, either of the body, of the soul, or of fortune. Consider Paul's list first in terms of the encomiastic category "deeds of the body." Among these deeds, the progymnasmata include beauty, strength, agility, might, and health. Now in one passage (1 Cor. 9:24–27; see 2 Tim. 4:7–8), Paul does compare himself to an athlete who might be presumed to have strength, agility, might, health, as well as beauty. But here in 2 Cor. 11:23–33, Paul boasts of his ability to endure hardships, thus boasting of his strength and might.

He begins his account of his deeds of the body in 11:23 with a list of the generic hardships he has endured: labors (*kopois*), imprisonments (*phylakais*), beatings (*plêgais*), and dangers of death (*thanatois*). This list seems to function as a topical statement that is subsequently developed point by point. First, he catalogues his beatings (vv. 24–25a), then his near death experiences (v. 25b). But he spends most of his time enumerating his labors (vv. 26–28). Finally he mentions an imprisonment by the king of Damascus (vv. 31–33).

While admittedly equal to his rivals in terms of ancestral and ethnic origin, Paul claims superiority to them in terms of his deeds of the body ("far greater . . . far more . . . countless . . . often"). He actually numbers his beatings ("five times . . . three times"), his stonings ("once"), his shipwrecks ("three times") to emphasize strength and endurance. He makes "frequent" journeys, during which he faces "dangers" from rivers, seas, deserts, and cities; from robbers and false brethren; and from Judeans and foreigners, as well. The people, locale, and terrain to which he refers bespeak his broad experience in the wide world, as well as the challenges from the whole world that he has been forced to face in obedience to God's mandate. Whatever and wherever the crisis, Paul has successfully endured. And it is precisely on this point that he contrasts his own experiences with those of his rivals.

The latter's credentials consist in their strength and in the absence of events with shameful outcomes. Not so Paul. For when he boasts, he boasts "of the things that show his weakness" (v. 30). But how may "weaknesses" be considered praiseworthy deeds of the body? Insofar as such deeds demonstrate his endurance and strength of resolve, they may serve as the basis for praise, but they would be deeds of the soul rather than of the body. Fitzgerald believes bearing "things that show weakness" demonstrates the virtue of "courage" (*andreia;* 1988; 87–90). He points out that in the estimation of some, courage was "the quintessential virtue" deemed worthy of honor. It is also the "mother" of related virtues, such as patient endurance, derring-do, stoutheartedness, and perseverance. Paul's list of hardships, then, can be seen as illustrating his courageous character, in particular his obedient endurance and perseverance.

Moreover, Paul's list contains deeds of fortune. In the rules for the encomium in the progymnasmata, we learn that deeds of fortune might include power, wealth, friends, children, fame, fortune, length of life, and happy death. Obviously many of these did not befall Paul: Paul lists neither children nor wealth (v. 27) nor power (vv. 24–25). And up to this point, he has not experienced a noble death, although he might be said to boast of "length of life" because of his constant escape from imminent death (vv. 23–33). Yet he has "friends" who aided his escape from King Aretas in Damascus (vv. 31–33).

Another significant deed of fortune is fame or good reputation. As Aristotle noted, "Fame means being respected by everybody, or having some quality that is desired by all men" (*Rhet.* 1.5.8, 1361a). Yet Paul cannot claim fame, respect, or a good reputation here. As a matter of fact, he begins this part of the document by noting his bad reputation among the Corinthians: "His letters are weighty and strong, but his bodily presence is weak and his speech is of no account" (2 Cor. 10:10; see Neyrey 1986c). In the estimation of the Corinthians, Paul lacks honorable accomplishments, and if he is perceived as a flatterer, he also lacks praiseworthy deeds of the soul. He chafes at being considered "unskilled in speaking," even as he claims a reputation for skill in "knowledge" (11:6). His bad reputation is further bolstered by failure to accept financial support from the Corinthians, a serious breach of fellowship and reciprocity (see Marshall 1987, 1–34). Yet he does seek good repute by offering the typical honor-riposte to all of the challenges to his reputation. He insists that he is equal to his rivals in origins; he is superior to them in labors and dangers endured; he surpasses them in revelations and in all forms of God-given favor and fortune. His bad reputation and lack of fame, then, are utterly undeserved. Indeed he "boasts" constantly of his various deeds. In a just world, then, Paul claims that he merits a good reputation, fame, and renown. Regarding "power," one of the deeds of fortune, Paul makes ironic claims. For him it is honorable to "boast of things that show my weakness" (v. 30). At the moment, he does not explain how shame (weakness) is transformed into honor (power). Later, when speaking of the weakness of "the thorn in the flesh," he quotes God's verdict on weakness: "My power [*dynamis*] is made perfect in weakness" (12:9). Hence Paul will gladly boast of his weakness that "the power [*dynamis*] of Christ" will be at work in him (v. 9b).

Paul, then, can claim strength and power in his weakness (12:10), that is, the good fortune of having God's very power at work in him. In terms of the deeds of fortune, Paul most enjoys God's favor, or simply "fortune." Divine providence and heavenly favor have constantly befallen Paul in his rescue from shipwrecks (11:25), "deaths" (v. 23), and dangers (v. 26). Divine favor, however, has been most dramatically manifested in Paul's "visions and revelations." He was taken to Paradise and heard things that "cannot be told, which mortals may not utter" (12:3–4). He had such "an abundance of revelations" that God also favored him with a "thorn in the flesh" to keep him from excess (v. 7).

At the end of the comparison Paul remarks how shameful it was to catalogue these deeds, either deeds of the body, the soul, or fortune. He offered the list only to prove that "I was not at all inferior to these superlative apostles" (v. 11). He states that the marks of an apostle are "signs and wonders and mighty works" (v. 12). Yet the comparison in 2 Cor. 11:21–12:13 contains various elements of an encomium that allow for a person to be praised. These include not just "signs and wonders and mighty works," but also origins, honors, and deeds. The deeds, moreover, may pertain to the body (strength, endurance), the soul (virtues, such as piety, faithfulness, justice, and courage), as well as fortune (gifts of heavenly power, favor, revelation, protection). Where honorable and praiseworthy aspects of his person may be cited, Paul follows conventional rhetoric of praise. But there are many things that connote shame and weakness that he must transform into honor and strength. In the comparison, Paul devotes most attention to ways in which he is equal, if not superior to, the "superapostles." These include his endurance of labors, hardships, and dangers, his virtuous courage in face of adversity, and his acknowledgment of how God's power compensates for his weakness and how ill repute deriving from the service of God is in fact a mark of virtue.

SUMMARY AND OVERVIEW

The encomium is an ancient Mediterranean form of writing and speaking rooted in the social system of the Hellenistic cultural world. This literary and speech pattern covers a person's origins, formation, accomplishments, comparisons (with the origins, formation, and accomplishments of others). It ideally begins with the presentation of some person's origins (birth, ancestry, clan, family, parentage). It then considers a person's formation and training ("teachers"), moving on next to deal with a person's accomplishments (deeds of body, soul, fortune). In conclusion, comparisons are made between any of the foregoing features and the same features as found in others, invariably of lesser distinction.

The encomium thus essentially underscores everything a person has received from others or that has befallen a person, features that lay beyond the control of the individual. The fact is, the person described in encomia, whether in the manuals or by Paul, was simply not in control of life at all. The deeds of body and of soul further underscore inherited qualities that a person might develop should the person seize the responsibility. And a person is praised for taking responsibility—yet in a situation totally controlled by other persons, human or divine.

Moreover, if the persons thus described have had appropriate nurture and training, they would have been instructed and socialized into a group's notions of morality. Thus, they can be said to have learned not just the social expectations for their gender and status, but the moral and ethical expectations of their culture as well. Praise and blame, which are the group's verdict on individual persons, would be allotted precisely according to an individual's conformity to the norms of the group. And because it is the group's verdict that ultimately counts, to follow one's conscience means to follow the expected verdict.

Both as written and spoken form, all of the features of the encomia highlight how persons are known exclusively in terms of their embeddedness in others, that is, their group heritage and consequent social relationships. Most important are the vertical relationships that include ancestors, clan, parents, teachers, and patrons, including God or gods, as well as one's general group affiliation, such as the polis. In this regard, the term "friends" does not necessarily refer to peer relationships but more often to the endless patron-client relationships that constituted the social network of individuals in antiquity.

And so persons are known to themselves and to others in terms of their group embeddedness and resultant social connections, their standing in the network of relationships, and their prestige deriving from these connections. Relations rooted in birth and ancestral family connections are replicated in status-based polis connections. Those with whom one has social connections form one's in-group. Such persons share a common fate: of generation and status, of heritage and geography, and of gender. Social norms and obligations are defined by the in-group to please significant others in the in-group; they are not determined in order to get personal satisfaction by realizing individual interests. Persons harbor beliefs shared with the rest of the in-group members, rather than beliefs that distinguish them from the in-group. And group members put great stock on readiness to cooperate with other in-group members.

Paul reveals himself to be a typical member of his society. His altered state-of-consciousness experiences (Pilch 1993b, 1995) convinced him of his dependence on the God who revealed himself as the one who raised Jesus from the dead (Gal. 1:1; Rom. 8:11). This God is now Paul's patron, in whose service Paul has become a "group organizer," ever sensitive to those grants of honor given him by the various Messianist groups with which he interacts.

The encomia reveal Paul as the typical collectivist, group-oriented person. He labors for the group's well-being, integrity, solidarity, and health. His list of accomplishments puts the emphasis on the views, needs, and goals of his in-group, rather than on single group members, whom he seldom mentions. The virtues Paul notes are essentially social virtues, as one would expect of a collectivist personality. Justice, temperance, fortitude, and prudence all have as their outcome the benefit of the group and its significant members (God, parents, patrons, fellow members); Paul does not identify individualist virtues resulting in individual success for the individual's own sake. In sum, the values and virtues deemed praiseworthy are those in which the individual manifests loyalty to the group. "Justice" has to do with paying one's dues to those to whom they are owed. When this is spelled out as an aspect of "piety," honorable persons know and pay their debt to the gods, parents, or ancestors. Josephus praises the person who prays not for his own welfare but for that of the group (*Against Apion* 2.195–96). In his rules for speeches of praise, Quintilian insisted that authors "emphasize what was done for the sake of others rather than what he performed on his own behalf" (*Inst. Orat.* 3.7.16). Thus a person might be praised for benefaction to the polis, obedience to law or to God, or loyalty to the family. Any quality Paul possesses that cements and supports interpersonal relationships is noted, with the expectation that others will value it as well.

Paul's goal in life is the security, survival, and honor of the limited range of in-groups in which he finds himself embedded. The outcome of his successes in founding various Messianic groups is an increase in his own reputation, which contributes to the in-group's goals. Rather than seeking personal satisfaction, Paul shows that he will do what he must as dictated by his group commitments and by those in authority over the group: God, various patron figures, and the like.

We conclude, therefore, that the person described in an encomium reflects accurately what social psychologists call a group-oriented person typical of collectivist cultures (see Triandis 1990). As a set of formal rules followed by hosts of writers in the ancient Mediterranean world, the encomium reflects the social system of those who composed progymnasmata and embodies certain general cultural expectations about persons. Those cultural expectations, we noted, pertain to a group-oriented person. By means of such cultural cues, the group-oriented person derives identity, status, and honor by stable embeddedness in others and by living up to the expectations of others. At times the rhetorical form of comparison dominates, but the contents of Paul's comparison with super-apostles are rooted in the encomium (how to praise a person). He both defends and underscores his honor. Yet in the end he tells us nothing about his individualist psyche, about his psychological frame of mind, about his idiosyncratic and unique personhood or personality. Did Paul think his "personal" descriptions were complete pictures of himself? By the standards of the encomium, he really omits nothing. There was nothing more to say.

3

The Public Defense Speech: Describing Persons

Rhetoricians trained polis elites in other forms of speaking along with the encomium. Elites, of course, were expected to take part in public affairs with distinction. To this end, rhetoricians provided these elites with public speaking guidelines and instructions for describing persons in those conflict situations called litigation. We would call these "courtroom" interactions. One type of speech that had to be delivered "in court" before a jury of all assembled citizens was the speech of public defense. The name for this sort of speech is the "forensic defense speech." The forensic defense speech belongs to the genus or general category of judicial rhetoric, one of the three kinds discussed in ancient rhetorical literature.

In this chapter, we shall first study the form of the public defense speech as it was described and explained by our ancient Mediterranean informants. In this case we possess the rhetorical handbooks of Cicero and Quintilian, who set out this genre in its most abstract form. Then we shall inquire into whether this sort of public, legal defense speech might serve as a pattern for understanding Luke's portrayal of Paul in his various court speeches in Acts 22—26. Given the way in which the elite politai of the day were instructed in public legal defense, what did Luke consider important or necessary in an adequate portrait of Paul for presentation to his Hellenistic audience? The descriptions of persons customarily presented in this rhetorical genre provide us with another ancient native's point of view of person. We shall compare this description with that offered in the encomium with the purpose of ferreting out common perceptions and categories. Finally, the salient features of persons presented in the forensic defense speech will be marshaled with features described in the previous chapter to develop a fuller anthropological model of person in the ancient Mediterranean.

THE FORENSIC DEFENSE SPEECH

According to Quintilian, a forensic defense speech consists of five parts: "the exordium [*prooemium*], the statement of facts [*narratio*], the proof [*probatio*], the refutation [*refutatio*], and the peroration [*peroratio*]" (*Inst. Orat.* 3.9.1). Because we are investigating how persons were perceived and described in the ancient world, we focus on the parts of the defense speech that depict a person's character (*êthos*), whether the person in question be the speaker, plaintiff, or witness. Yet to appreciate this feature, in all fairness to the genre we must view character features in the context of the other parts of the defense speech as well.

The Exordium

The opening part of a forensic speech is called the *exordium* or *prooemium* (*Rh. Her.* 1.4.6; Cicero, *Inv.* 1.15.20; Quintilian, *Inst. Orat.* 4.1.1–4). It functions to prepare the members of the audience so that they will be positively inclined to lend a ready ear to the rest of the speech. In short, this formal opening is to render the audience "well disposed, attentive, and receptive" (*Inv.* 1.15.20). Cases differ, and each case requires distinctive tact and skill. Cicero listed five types of cases, each with its own difficulty:

> *Honorable:* This case wins favor in the auditor's mind at once, without any speech of ours.
>
> *Difficult (admirabile):* This case alienates the sympathies of those listening.
>
> *Mean (humile)*: Auditors make light of this case and think it unworthy of their attention.
>
> *Ambiguous:* The "point of decision" is doubtful in this case or engenders both goodwill and ill will.
>
> *Obscure:* In this case, the auditors are either slow of wit or it involves matters hard to grasp.

In honorable cases, the speaker can presume on the favor of the audience. But in difficult cases, where sympathies are ostensibly alienated, the speaker must practice "insinuation" to win goodwill and hence to gain a receptive hearing (*Rh. Her.* 1.6.9; *Inv.* 1.15.20–16.21; *Inst. Orat.* 4.1.45–50).

According to Cicero, goodwill derives from four quarters: from the person of the speaker, from the person of the opponent, from the person of the judge, and from the case itself. Because goodwill is rooted in how people present themselves or depict others, this feature deserves a closer look.

1. We will win goodwill *from our own person* if we refer to our own acts and services without arrogance; if we weaken the effect of charges that have been preferred, or of some suspicion of less honorable dealing which has been cast upon us; if we dilate on the misfortunes which have befallen us or the difficulties which still beset us; if we use prayers and entreaties with a humble and submissive spirit.

2. Goodwill is acquired *from the person of the opponents* if we can bring them into hatred, unpopularity, or contempt. They will be hated if some act of theirs is presented which is base, haughty, cruel, or malicious; they will become unpopular if we present their power, political influence, wealth, family connections, and their arrogant and intolerable use of these advantages, so that they seem to rely on these rather than on the justice of their case. They will be brought into contempt if we reveal their laziness, carelessness, sloth, indolent pursuits, or luxurious idleness.

3. Goodwill will be sought *from the persons of the auditors* if an account is given of acts which they have performed with courage, wisdom, and mercy, but so as not to show excessive flattery; and if it is shown in what honorable esteem they are held and how eagerly their judgment and opinion are awaited. (See *Inv.* 1.16.22, emphasis added)

Sentiments of honor and shame lie at the roots of the varied contents and overall aims of these goodwill strategies (see Malina 1993b, 28–62). Cicero advised the speaker not to focus so much on claims of great honor but to give a riposte to the diverse challenges put by opponents. As Quintilian said, "If he is believed to be a good man, this consideration will exercise the strongest influence at every point in the case" and lead the hearers to accept him as an absolutely reliable witness (*Inst. Orat.* 4.1.7). Hence, orators were instructed to develop in the opening of their speech their own positive qualities, as well as those of the person they represent, "to paint their characters in words as being upright, stainless, conscientious, modest, and the like" (Cicero, *Orat.* 2.43.184, Loeb). This is to be done by telling of their "merits, achievements or reputable life" (2.43.182 and 2.79.321).

Quintilian, moreover, urges the speaker to indicate that his motives for taking part are devoid of any trace of personal gain or advancement:

It is pre-eminently desirable that he should be believed to have undertaken the case out of a sense of duty to a friend or relative, or even better, if the point can be made, by a sense of patriotism or at any rate some serious moral consideration . . . it is necessary for the parties themselves to create the impression that they have been forced to take legal action by some weighty and honorable reason or even by necessity . . . the authority of the speaker carries greatest weight, if his undertaking of the case is free from all suspicion of meanness, personal spite or ambition. (*Inst. Orat.* 4.1.7–8)

Loyalty to family, kin, or fellow ethnic group members would not be understood as an aggressive claim to honor but as a legitimate and expected riposte to an honor challenge. A speaker would thereby present himself as a group-oriented person, rightly embedded in his social fabric and loyal to it. In this way the speaker will avoid every appearance of individualist behavior, such as self-centered ambition or claim to self-centered honor.

Aristotle was well aware of the cultural value attached to group-oriented behavior. When listing the signs of virtue, he highlighted the honorable quality of deeds done with an eye toward others, rather than for the promotion of oneself:

> and things absolutely good and whatever someone has done for his country, overlooking his own interest; and things good by nature and that are not benefits to him, for such things are done for their own sake; and whatever can belong to a person when dead more than when alive . . . and whatever works are done for the sake of others (for they have less of the self); and successes gained for others, but not for the self and for those who have conferred benefits (for that is just); and acts of kindness (for they are not directed to oneself). (*Rhet.* 1.9.17–19, 1366b–1367a)

Thus Aristotle both identifies a group-oriented person and highlights what makes such a person virtuous in that culture.

Yet when it comes to opponents, the speaker must vigorously challenge their honor by bringing them into "hatred, unpopularity or contempt." This is done by pointing out their dishonorable behavior: arrogance, misuse of power, and indulgence. In short, they are perceived as rank individualists who are selfish and self-serving and who totally lack the virtues of justice and temperance. Finally, in regard to the person of the audience, the speaker should honor them but without flattery.

The exordium, then, stands out as a place where the ethos or character of a person will be most carefully and attentively presented. For example, in the book of Acts, especially because Paul always appears in trial scenes as one accused of being a traitor to Israel's traditions, Luke must take great pains to make a positive impression on the audience with what the Roman's called *captatio benevolentiae* ("grabbing goodwill"). He must attend here to Paul's ethos as a pious and devout follower of Israel's God.

Statement of Facts (*Narratio*)

The second structural part of a forensic speech contains the statement of facts or *narratio*. It is that part of a forensic speech in which the court is addressed "as to the nature of the case under dispute" (Quintilian, *Inst.*

Orat. 4.2.31). It formally intends "to prepare the mind of the judge" (*Inst. Orat.* 4.2.4–5). Four aspects of the statement of facts are traditionally listed: (1) the main question at issue, (2) the line of defense, (3) the point for the judge's decision, and (4) the foundation or basic argument for the defense (*Inst. Orat.* 3.11.6–7).

The main question at issue (*quaestio/zêtêma*) is the chief subject of the debate: "whether a thing has been done, what it is that was done, whether it was rightly done" (Cicero, *Inv.* 1.13.18; Quintilian, *Inst. Orat.* 3.11.2). The speaker must address the issue of what was supposed to have been done and whether it actually was done. Given that it actually was done, what reasons might explain what was done. This last feature leads into the strategy the speaker ought to adopt. For the next element, the line of defense (*ratio/aition*), sets out the defendant's motive or justification for the act in question (*Inv.* 1.13.18; *Inst. Orat.* 3.11.4). The judge is to base his decision (*iudicatio/krinomenon*) on what was actually done and the motive behind the action (*Inv.* 1.13.18; *Inst. Orat.* 3.11.5–6). The judge must ultimately rule on what the defendant states about his actions and motives. Finally, the strongest argument the defense can make forms the foundation (*firmamentum/synechon*) of the case; it is to address the point on which the judge's decision pivots (*Inv.* 1.14.19; *Inst. Orat.* 3.11.9).

To illustrate the four points, Cicero cites the classical case of Orestes, who murdered his mother, Clytemnestra: (1) The main question in this case does not involve a question of fact; Orestes admittedly killed Clytemnestra. The point at issue is whether he was justified or not. He is charged with matricide, but he claims to be avenging a patricide. The proper definition of the act under judgment emerges as the paramount question. (2) His line of defense consists of his motive, namely, vengeance for Clytemnestra's murder of his father. (3) The point for the judge's decision, then, is whether it was right that even a guilty mother be slain by her son. (4) The central argument or foundation for the defense, according to Cicero, becomes Orestes's avowal that "the disposition of his mother toward his father, himself and his sisters, the kingdom, the reputation of the race and the family was such that it was the peculiar duty of her children to punish her" (*Inv.* 1.13.18–14.19; see *Rh. Her.* 1.10.17; *Inst. Orat.* 3.11.4–13).

Once more, values such as honor and shame offer insights into the matter. In the culture, fathers always come first. Fathers are the locus of the family's honor, just like the king is the locus of the kingdom's honor. The justification mentioned above has to do with Orestes's response to his mother's challenge to his father's honor. Moreover, by dishonoring her husband, she equally dishonors the family and all of its members. The reputation of the royal family was dishonored; the son was duty bound to avenge that dishonor. At stake, then, are typical Mediterranean notions of royalty, family, and kinship, which are themselves illustrative of the values of honor and shame. Not to have acted in defense of his father's honor would have meant to shame the central personages of the political institution (Agamemnon, Orestes, and Greek nobility), as well as of the familial institution.

The *statement of facts,* then, can easily provide an important window into the ethos of a person, for in it a speaker attempts to show how an individual embraced group norms and ideals, and acted, not individualistically, but in order to live up to group expectations.

Proof (*Probatio*)

The third structural part of a forensic defense speech is called the proof (*probatio/pistis*). At this point witnesses, arguments, and evidence are marshaled forth. Rhetorical handbooks are rather inconsistent about the order of presenting proof. "First among the proofs" according to the rhetoricians, "must be placed the evidence of witnesses and confessions that are obtained by torture" (Aristotle, *Rh. Al.* 36, 1442b; 37). For example, Isocrates (*Trapeziticus* 17.54) claims that such testimony has the highest value in a court of law: "I see that in private and public causes you judge that nothing is more deserving of belief or true than testimony given under torture." Then note that in Paul's case, Luke tells us that the arresting officer intended "to examine him by scourging" to obtain Paul's testimony, "to find out why they shouted thus against him" (Acts 22:24). Yet, if such testimony is not convincing, say the handbook authors, it needs confirmation from "probability, examples, tokens, signs and maxims" (*Rh. Al.* 36, 1442b; 39–1443a, 6). The best evidence is testimony confirmed by tokens (*tekmêria*) and signs (*semeia*).

Cicero, however, begins his explanation of the proof section of the speech by noting that all statements in litigation are supported by attributes of persons or actions. He cites nine qualities to be treated when presenting a description of a person's character: name, nature, manner of life, fortune, habit, feeling, interests, purposes, achievements (including incidents that befell a person and the speeches he made about them). Because this is one of the clearest items in which the forensic defense speech indicates how to perceive and describe persons, we examine these nine categories in detail and present Cicero's and Quintilian's views rather extensively. These two Roman rhetoricians label their lists differently, but upon closer analysis, we note that they are basically talking about the same items. Table 1 attempts to give a synoptic view of the comparable lists of important information about ancient persons from classical rhetorical literature.

TABLE 1.

Comparative List of Cicero's and Quintilian's Views on a Person's Character

Cicero	Quintilian

Name (*nomen*). Name is that which is given to each person, whereby he is addressed by his own proper and definite appellation.

Nature (*natura*). In regard to humans, their nature is considered first as to sex (*in sexu*) whether male or female, and as to ethnicity, place of birth, family, and age.

Sex (*sexus*). A man is more likely to commit a robbery, a woman to poison.

As to ethnicity (*natio*), whether one is a Greek or a foreigner; as to place of birth (*patria*), whether an Athenian or a Lacedaemonian; as to family (*cognatio*), what are one's ancestors and kin; as to age (*aetas*), whether one is a boy, or youth, of middle age, or an old man.

Ethnicity (*natio*). Ethnic groups have their own character, and the same action is not probable in the case of a barbarian, a Roman and a Greek.

Country (*patria*). There is a like diversity in the laws, institutions and opinions of different states.

Birth (*genus*). Persons are regularly regarded as having some resemblance to their parents and ancestors, a resemblance which sometimes leads to their living disgracefully or honorably, as the case may be.

Age (*aetas*). Different actions suit different ages.

Besides, we take into consideration such advantages and disadvantages as are given to mind and body by nature, as for example: whether one is strong or weak, tall or short, handsome or ugly, swift or slow; whether bright or dull, retentive or forgetful, affable or unmannerly, modest, long-suffering, or the contrary.

Bodily Constitution (*habitus corporis*). Beauty is often induced as an argument for lust, strength as an argument for insolence, and their opposites for opposite conduct.

Manner of life (*victus*). Under this should be considered with whom he was reared, in what tradition and under whose direction, what teachers he had in the liberal arts, what instructors in the art of living, with whom he associates on terms of friendship, in what occupation, trade or profession he is engaged, how he manages his private fortune, and what is the character of his home life.

Formation and Training (*educatio et disciplina*). It makes a great difference who were the instructors and what the method of instruction in each individual case.

(TABLE CONTINUES)

TABLE 1 (CONTINUED)

Fortune (*fortuna*). Under fortune one inquires whether the person is a slave or free, rich or poor, a private citizen or an official with authority, and if he is an official, whether he acquired his position justly or unjustly, whether he is successful, famous, or the opposite; what sort of children he has. And if the inquiry is about one no longer alive . . . about the nature of his death.

Fortune (*fortuna*). The same acts are not expected from rich and poor, or from one who is surrounded by troops of relations, friends or clients and one who lacks all these advantages.

Circumstances (*conditio*). It makes a great difference whether a man be famous or obscure, a magistrate or a private individual, a father or a son, a citizen or a foreigner, a free man or a slave, married or unmarried, a father or childless.

Habit (*habitus*). By habit we mean a stable and absolute constitution of mind or body in some particular, as, for example, the acquisition of some capacity or of an art, or again some special knowledge, or some bodily dexterity not given by nature but won by careful training and practice.

Natural Disposition (*animi natura*). Avarice, anger, pity, cruelty, severity and the like may often be adduced to prove the credibility or the reverse of a given act; it is for instance often asked whether a man's way of living be luxurious, frugal or parsimonious. Then there is occupation, since a rustic, a lawyer, a man of business, a soldier, a sailor, a doctor all perform very different actions. We must also consider the personal ambitions of individuals, for instance whether they wish to be thought rich or eloquent, just or powerful.

Feeling (*affectio*). This is a temporary change of mind or body due to some cause: for example, joy, desire, fear, vexation, illness, weakness and other things which are found in the same category.

Passion (*commotio*). By this we mean some temporary emotion such as anger or fear.

Interest (*studium*). Interest is unremitting mental activity ardently devoted to some subject and accompanied by intense pleasure, for example interest in philosophy, poetry, geometry, literature.

Disposition of Mind (*habitus animi*). We inquire whether one man is the friend or enemy of another.

Purpose (*consilium*). This is a deliberate plan for doing or not doing something.

Purpose (*consilia*). They also add design, which may refer to past, present or future.

Achievements, accidents, speeches (*factus, casus, orationes*). What he did, what happened to him, what he said; what he is doing, what is happening to him, what he is saying; or what he is going to do, what is going to happen to him, what language he is going to use.

Past Life and Previous Utterances (*acta dictaque*). These are also subject for investigation, since we are in the habit of inferring the present from the past.

DATA FROM *INV.* 1.24.35—25.36 AND *INST. ORAT.* 5.10.24–29.

Regarding Cicero's understanding of *name* and *nature,* we note first of all that one's name in antiquity generally contained indication of one's place of origin, or of one's father and clan (Malina and Neyrey 1991b, 74–75). Examples of persons named in terms of a significant polis include Paul of Tarsus and Philo of Alexandria. Jesus called "Jesus of Nazareth" (Mark 1:24) is ambiguous because Nazareth was not a polis. On the other hand, Peter is "Simon, son of Jonah" (Matt. 16:17). Alternately, nature highlights gender, geography, and generation.

Gender is significant because in antiquity the self is always a gendered self. The primary personal identification factor in antiquity was gender (male or female). This aspect was replicated in the totally gender-divided worldview of the ancients. Moreover, gender in antiquity came with elaborate stereotypes of what was appropriate male or female behavior (Neyrey 1994b, 79–83). Quintilian observes that males are more likely to commit robbery, but females poisoning.

Persons are known from *geography,* the region of their birth (e.g., Uriah the Hittite [2 Sam. 11:3, 6] and Ittai the Gittite [2 Sam. 15:19, 22]) or the central place of their birth ("This one was born in Jerusalem!" Ps. 87:4–5). Both Jesus and the disciples, moreover, are "Galileans" (Matt. 26:69; Acts 1:11). Commenting on the geographical factor, Quintilian expresses the latent stereotype that "ethnic groups have their own character" and that barbarians do not act as Greeks or Romans do.

Persons were also known in terms of their parents and tribe, their *generation.* The infamous Achan of Joshua 7:1 is presented as "Achan the son of Carmi, son of Zabdi, son of Zerah, of the tribe of Judah." Sheba is not only "son of Bichri" but he is also "a Benjaminite" (2 Sam. 20:1). Interrelated geography and generation come together in the question put to Jonah by his fellow travelers: "What is your occupation? And whence do you come? What is your country? And of what people are you?" (Jon. 1:8). On the other hand, Quintilian surfaces the stereotypical expectation that "persons are regularly regarded as having some resemblance to their parents and ancestors." He is not referring to inherited genetic traits but to "a resemblance which leads to their living disgracefully or honorably."

Manner of life allows a speaker to expand on a person's education, namely the teachers, mentors, and other formative figures who socialized the person. Students could not hope to surpass their teachers but only to imitate them. Knowledge of mentors and teachers conveys vital information about proper socialization and upbringing. In this chapter, we often speak of "embeddedness" as a quality of group-oriented persons. Embeddedness is a social-psychological quality describing that dimension of group-oriented persons by which all members of the group share a certain perspective, a virtual identity with the group as a whole and with its individual members. There is no opposition between the individual and the group in which she or he is embedded. No one really has his or her "own" opinion, nor is anyone expected to. A group-embedded person carries values and voices that echo many years, even after the person is transplanted to some new location. The formation and thorough enclosure of the person in the social reality of the group might be likened to the formation and enclosure of an embryo in the womb, but in this instance, life in the "womb" is a mode of social-psychological being in the group.

Group-oriented persons assimilate the expectations of those who have a superior role or status in their lives. In this light, teachers and mentors are far more than purveyors of information. Rather they are figures to whom a person might grow attached because they convey the group's values and norms. Plutarch remarked that all life, even for elite males, entails interaction with members of the group into which the individual grows embedded: "The nurse rules the infant, the teacher the boy, the gymnasiarch the youth, his admirer the young man who, when he comes of age, is ruled by law and his commanding general. No one is his own master, no one is unrestricted" (*Dialogue on Love* 754D, Loeb).

Manner of life also underscores a person's occupation, profession, or trade, which is normally closely linked to generation since these derive from one's parent. Note the cultural disdain for those who work for wages and admiration for leisured elites in the following passage:

> Now in regard to trades and other means of livelihood, which ones are to be considered becoming to a gentleman and which ones are vulgar, we have been taught, in general, as follows. First, those means of livelihood are rejected as undesirable which incur people's ill-will, as those of tax gatherers and usurers. Unbecoming to a gentleman, too, and vulgar are the means of livelihood of all hired workmen whom we pay for mere manual labor, not for artistic skill; for in their case the very wages they receive is a pledge of their slavery. Vulgar we must consider those also who buy from wholesale merchants to retail immediately; for they would get no profits without a great deal of downright lying; and verily, there is no action that is meaner than misrepresentation. And all mechanics are engaged in vulgar trades; for no workshop can have anything liberal about it. Least respectable of all are those trades which cater to sensual pleasures: "Fishmongers, butchers, cooks, and poulterers, and fishermen," as Terence says. Add to these, if you please, the perfumers, dancers and the whole corps of public entertainers. But the professions in which either a higher degree of intelligence is required or from which no small benefit to society is derived—medicine and architecture, for example, and teaching—these are proper for those whose social position they become. Trade, if it is on a small scale, is to be considered vulgar; but if wholesale and on a large scale, importing large quantities from all parts of the world and distributing to many without misrepresentation, it is not to be greatly disparaged. Nay, it even seems to deserve the highest respect, if those who are engaged in it, satiated, or rather, I

should say, satisfied with the fortune they have made, make their way from the port to a country estate, as they have often made it from the sea into port. But of all the occupations by which gain is secured, none is better than agriculture, none more profitable, none more delightful, none more becoming to a freeman. (Cicero, *De Officiis* 1.42.150–151, Loeb)

Also encoded here is mention of one's social relations, namely, one's "friends," that is, one's patrons or clients.

Fortune refers to one's inherited social status: slave or free, rich or poor, sojourner or citizen. As we shall see in the next chapter, these groupings are not simply indications of status. Rather, they intimate social categories of qualitatively different kinds of persons: slaves are thus-and-such and politai are thus-and-such. Moreover, one's specific place in the social hierarchy is appropriately noted, as well as one's reputation. Persons who enjoy good fortune are characterized as "beloved of god," which adds to their reputation and stature. Like nature, fortune describes the passive lot of an individual, not one's personal achievements. The modern Western notion of a "self-made" person was literally unthinkable in antiquity.

Habit tells us about the disciplines and philosophies into which a person has been schooled. The ancients always praised "excellence" (*aretê*), not so much as an individual achievement but as the product of living according to the group's notions of virtue and as the outcome of conformity to the group's traditions of athletics and soldiering. Constancy, not change, is valued.

Feeling, although celebrated in our modern individualist culture, was by no means a valued or important thing in antiquity. If constancy counts and passions are suspect, then "temporary change of mind or body" is noteworthy but hardly praiseworthy. Here an orator could indicate that persons are either subject to change and passion or masters of them. Ideally persons are to be self-controlled and disciplined in their bodies, not subject to dissolution or crippled by misfortune.

Interest points to the culturally valued pursuits with which leisured elites would pass their time. Following convention, Cicero celebrates mind over body and so praises "philosophy, poetry, geometry and literature," all subjects taught in the trivium and quadrivium. This sort of *paideia,* moreover, reinforces the information conveyed in manner of life, and suggests a particular social status of persons wealthy enough for such an education.

In short, the list of items for describing the ethos of a person in the forensic defense speech portrays a person according to a fixed set of group expectations. Speakers are decidedly less interested in portraying individual characteristics than in presenting the degree to which a person conformed to social expectations, values, and roles. The portrayal of a person's ethos aims to emphasize conformity, not novelty and embeddedness, not distinctiveness.

The features noted by both Cicero and Quintilian relative to this type of speech readily overlap with the features mentioned in the encomium pattern. Both authors are concerned about a person's origins and birth: country, ethnicity, locale, as well as clan, ancestors, and parents. Because of the ancient Mediterranean appreciation of stereotypes about generation, gender, and geography, it was believed that general knowledge about any population always yields accurate and specific knowledge about individuals belonging to that population. As Vergil said of the devious Greek, Sinon, "Learn about them all from this one instance" (*ab uno disce omnes, Aen.* 2.65). Both authors likewise consider it important to know how a person was formed by others; hence, they required information about the way persons were educated and trained, their teachers, mentors, and course of studies. Furthermore, they both concern themselves with the deeds of the body (bodily constitution, strength, weakness, and so forth), the deeds of the soul (passions, virtues, habits), as well as the deeds of fortune (wealth, power, patronage, status, and the like). Although Cicero does not use the word "achievement" (*epitêdeumata*), he is concerned with the life choices made in youth that persist throughout adult life. Special consideration is given to past achievements, deeds, and speeches, for an argument is often made about the consistency of a person's life, how "history repeats itself" for good or ill.

Refutation and Peroration

The final segments of the forensic speech are the refutation and the peroration. Cicero explains the refutation as follows:

> The refutation is that part of an oration in which arguments are used to impair, disprove, or weaken the confirmation or proof in our opponents' speech. It utilizes the same sources of invention that confirmation does, because any proposition can be attacked by the same methods of reasoning by which it can be supported. For nothing need be considered in all these quests for arguments except the attributes of persons and of actions. (*Inv.* 1.42.78; see Quintilian, *Inst. Orat.* 5.13.1)

Notice that the focus of the refutation is the person and the person's actions. Now what dimension of the person or person's action are worth attention? Cicero's own practice amply indicates that emphasis here ought be on dishonoring or shaming the opposition by demonstrating the opponent's lack of honor, lack of dignity, lack of sense of shame (see Swarney 1993, 137–55). The point is that the merits of the argument or the case are of little consequence. What counts is the honor/dishonor rating of the person involved and the honorable or dishonorable quality of his actions.

But such is not the approach to be followed in the final segment of the speech, the peroration or summing up. Again Cicero:

> The peroration is the end and conclusion of the whole speech; it has three parts, the summing-up, the indignatio or exciting of indignation or ill-will against the opponent, and the conquestio or the arousing of pity and sympathy. (*Inv.* 1.52.98; see Quintilian, *Inst. Orat.* 6.1.1–12)

Quintilian, in turn, notes this: "The peroration is the most important part of forensic pleading, and in the main consists of appeals to the emotions ..." (*Inst. Orat.* 6.2.1).

We stress that at the close of the speech, as speakers sum up their arguments, they formally attempt to arouse specific emotions in the audience. If the exordium might stress the ethos of the speaker, the *peroratio* becomes the place to develop *pathos* or emotional responses. Two questions emerge: (a) Why the appeal to pathos? and (b) What emotions? Aristotle codified the prevailing wisdom that emotion or pathos plays a significant role in presenting a person to an audience. When he begins his discussion of the role of character and emotion in persuasion, Aristotle comments:

> it is not only necessary to consider how to make the speech itself demonstrative and convincing, but also that the speaker should show himself to be of a certain character and should know how to put the judge into a certain frame of mind. For it makes a great difference with regard to producing conviction—especially in demonstrative, and, next to this, in forensic oratory—that the speaker should show himself to be possessed of certain qualities and that his hearers should think that he is disposed in a certain way toward them. (*Rhet.* 2.1.2–3, 1377b)

Evoking the appropriate, culturally expected emotions will ensure sympathy. But what emotions? Discussion of the cultural aspects of emotions remains in its infancy, but anthropologists are pointing the way toward a fruitful consideration of "the cultural and social construction of emotion" (Lutz 1986, 417–27), a direction which has been picked up by New Testament writers (Pilch and Malina 1993). In essence, certain emotions might be considered typical of a group, while a given range of emotions might also be endowed with special meaning in the group. Aristotle selectively comments only on anger, calmness, friendly feeling or enmity, fear or confidence, shame or shamelessness, kindliness or unkindliness, being indignant, envy, and emulation (*Rhet.* 2.2–11). It seems apparent that most of these emotions are rooted in the ancient Mediterranean understanding of honor, for what is involved is some dimension of anger, envy, enmity, shame, or being indignant or zealous concerning one's own or another's honor and status. Other emotions relate to notions of reciprocity that arise out of patron-client relations. In short, pathos or emotion seems itself to be a window on what persons value and hold in common. Specific emotions encode group values and expectations, either fulfilled or neglected.

In summary, the typical forensic defense speech can provide valuable information from ancient Mediterranean informants about how to describe and perceive another human being in that time and space. We focus in particular on the exordium and the peroratio. In the former, the ethos of a person is carefully presented according to group-acceptable categories; in the latter, pathos is invoked, which likewise reflects stereotypical, group-oriented values. But it is especially the ethos of the person that we will examine further for native comments on how persons were perceived and presented in the ancient Mediterranean world.

APPLICATION TO PAUL
IN ACTS 22—26

Scholars have shown interest in forensic features of the Acts of the Apostles for some time now. Various legal issues surrounding Paul's trials in Acts 22—26 have been studied by H. J. Cadbury (1937: 5.297–338) and more recently by A. N. Sherwin-White (1963, 48–70) and J. Dupont (1967, 527–52). The apologetic character of Paul's defense speeches was the subject of a dissertation and subsequent essay by F. Veltman (1975, 1978), and the forensic aspect of the term "to give testimony" (*martyrein*) and its compounds has been treated in many recent studies (Strathmann 1967, 4.474–514; Beutler 1972; Trites 1977). A general survey of the forensic terminology in Acts was presented by Trites (1974, 278–84). There has, therefore, been no lack of interest in the forensic aspect of Acts (see Gilchrist 1967, 264–66; Black 1981, 209–18).

We believe such interest is on target. Our approach here will be to adopt the profile of forensic defense speeches as these are described in the rhetorical handbooks and to read the trial speeches of Paul in Acts 22—26 in light of these formal structures. Our specific interest is to note how Paul is perceived and described according to the ancient native categories set forth in the forensic defense speech.

Exordium and Ethos of the Person

The first of Paul's forensic speeches in the book of Acts is found in Acts 22:1–21:

[1]"Brethren and fathers, hear the defense which I now make before you." [2]And when they heard that he addressed them in the Hebrew language, they were the more quiet. And he said: [3]"I am a Judean, born at Tarsus in Cilicia, but brought up in this city at the feet of Gamaliel, educated according to the strict manner of the law of our fathers, being zealous for God as you all are this day. [4]I persecuted this Way to the death, binding and delivering to prison both men and women, [5]as the high priest and the whole council of elders bear me witness. From them I received letters to the brethren, and I journeyed to Damascus to take those also who were there and bring them in bonds to Jerusalem to be punished.

[6]"As I made my journey and drew near to Damascus, about noon a great light from heaven suddenly shone about me. [7]And I fell to the ground and heard a voice saying to me, 'Saul, Saul, why do you persecute me?' [8]And I answered, 'Who are you, Lord?' And he said to me, 'I am Jesus of Nazareth whom you are persecuting.' [9]Now those who were with me saw the light but did not hear the voice of the one who was speaking to me. [10]And I said, 'What shall I do, Lord?' And the Lord said to me, 'Rise, and go into Damascus, and there you will be told all that is appointed for you to do.' [11]And when I could not see because of the brightness of that light, I was led by the hand by those who were with me, and came into Damascus.

[12]"And one Ananias, a devout man according to the law, well spoken of by all the Judeans who lived there, [13]came to me, and standing by me said to me, 'Brother Saul, receive your sight.' And in that very hour I received my sight and saw him. [14]And he said, 'The God of our fathers appointed you to know his will, to see the Just One and to hear a voice from his mouth; [15]for you will be a witness for him to all men of what you have seen and heard. [16]And now why do you wait? Rise and be baptized, and wash away your sins, calling on his name.'

[17]"When I had returned to Jerusalem and was praying in the temple, I fell into a trance [18]and saw him saying to me, 'Make haste and get quickly out of Jerusalem, because they will not accept your testimony about me.' [19]And I said, 'Lord, they themselves know that in every synagogue I imprisoned and beat those who believed in thee. [20]And when the blood of Stephen thy witness was shed, I also was standing by and approving, and keeping the garments of those who killed him.' [21]And he said to me, 'Depart; for I will send you far away to the Gentiles.'"

Luke goes on to describe the raucous reaction to Paul and the outcome of the speech (vv. 22–30):

[22]Up to this word they listened to him; then they lifted up their voices and said, "Away with such a fellow from the earth! For he ought not to live." [23]And as they cried out and waved their garments and threw dust

into the air, ²⁴the tribune commanded him to be brought into the barracks, and ordered him to be examined by scourging, to find out why they shouted thus against him. ²⁵But when they had tied him up with the thongs, Paul said to the centurion who was standing by, "Is it lawful for you to scourge a man who is a Roman citizen, and uncondemned?" ²⁶When the centurion heard that, he went to the tribune and said to him, "What are you about to do? For this man is a Roman citizen." ²⁷So the tribune came and said to him, "Tell me, are you a Roman citizen?" And he said, "Yes." ²⁸The tribune answered, "I bought this citizenship for a large sum." Paul said, "But I was born a citizen." ²⁹So those who were about to examine him withdrew from him instantly; and the tribune also was afraid, for he realized that Paul was a Roman citizen and that he had bound him. ³⁰But on the morrow, desiring to know the real reason why the Judeans accused him, he unbound him, and commanded the chief priests and all the council to meet, and he brought Paul down and set him before them.

The second speech is in Acts 26:1–23:

¹Agrippa said to Paul, "You have permission to speak for yourself." Then Paul stretched out his hand and made his defense: ²"I think myself fortunate that it is before you, King Agrippa, I am to make my defense today against all the accusations of the Judeans, ³because you are especially familiar with all customs and controversies of the Judeans; therefore I beg you to listen to me patiently. ⁴"My manner of life from my youth, spent from the beginning among my own nation and at Jerusalem, is known by all the Judeans. ⁵They have known for a long time, if they are willing to testify, that according to the strictest party of our religion I have lived as a Pharisee. ⁶And now I stand here on trial for hope in the promise made by God to our fathers, ⁷to which our twelve tribes hope to attain, as they earnestly worship night and day. And for this hope I am accused by Judeans, O king! ⁸Why is it thought incredible by any of you that God raises the dead? ⁹I myself was convinced that I ought to do many things in opposing the name of Jesus of Nazareth. ¹⁰And I did so in Jerusalem; I not only shut up many of the saints in prison, by authority from the chief priests, but when they were put to death I cast my vote against them. ¹¹And I punished them often in all the synagogues and tried to make them blaspheme; and in raging fury against them, I persecuted them even to foreign cities. ¹²Thus I journeyed to Damascus with the authority and commission of the chief priests. ¹³At midday, O king, I saw on the way a light from heaven, brighter than the sun, shining round me and those who journeyed with me. ¹⁴And when we had all fallen to the ground, I heard a voice saying to me in the Hebrew language, 'Saul, Saul, why do you persecute me? It hurts you to kick against the goads.' ¹⁵And I said, 'Who are you, Lord?' And the Lord said, 'I am Jesus whom you are persecuting. ¹⁶But rise and stand upon your feet; for I have appeared to you for this purpose, to appoint you to serve and bear witness to the things in which you have seen me and to those in which I will appear to you, [17]delivering you from the people and from the Gentiles—to whom I send you [18]to open their eyes, that they may turn from darkness to light and from the power of Satan to God, that they may receive forgiveness of sins and a place among those who are sanctified by faith in me.' [19]Wherefore, O King Agrippa, I was not disobedient to the heavenly vision, [20]but declared first to those at Damascus, then at Jerusalem and throughout all the country of Judea, and also to the Gentiles, that they should repent and turn to God and perform deeds worthy of their repentance. [21]For this reason the Judeans seized me in the temple and tried to kill me. [22]To this day I have had the help that comes from God, and so I stand here testifying both to small and great, saying nothing but what the prophets and Moses said would come to pass: [23]that the Christ must suffer, and that, by being the first to rise from the dead, he would proclaim light both to the people and to the Gentiles."

Again, Luke describes the outcome of the speech, this time as follows (vv. 24–32):

[24]And as he thus made his defense, Festus said with a loud voice, "Paul, you are mad; your great learning is turning you mad." [25]But Paul said, "I am not mad, most excellent Festus, but I am speaking the sober truth. [26]For the king knows about these things, and to him I speak freely; for I am persuaded that none of these things has escaped his notice, for this was not done in a corner. [27]King Agrippa, do you believe the prophets? I know that you believe." [28]And Agrippa said to Paul, "In a short time you think to make me a. Christian!" [29]And Paul said, "Whether short or long, I would to God that not only you but also all who hear me this day might become such as I am—except for these chains." [30]Then the king rose, and the governor and Bernice and those who were sitting with them; [31]and when they had withdrawn, they said to one another, "This man is doing nothing to deserve death or imprisonment." [32]And Agrippa said to Festus, "This man could have been set free if he had not appealed to Caesar."

It has long been noticed that these two of Paul's forensic speeches in Acts begin with an exordium. This is usually discussed only in terms of the *captatio benevolentiae,* or appeal to the audience (Lösch 1931). Yet the handbooks indicate that it is precisely in the exordium that the ethos of the defendant may be presented. And this seems to be the case in Luke's adaptation of the form of the defense speech (see Sattler 1957; Kennedy 1972).

While rhetorical handbooks present the general, abstract rules for composing a speech, the extant examples from Isocrates, Cicero, and others do not evidence any wooden, slavish adherence to those rules in the creative arrangement of materials. Luke himself adapted the form of the forensic defense speech, focusing on certain parts and omitting others. In particular, Luke's exordium contains an elaborate presentation of Paul's ethos at the very beginning of the two speeches. To an exceptional degree, the exordia in both contain the nine attributes that rhetorical tradition indicated ought to be developed as relevant to the ethos of the speaker. Recall these include name, nature, manner of life, fortune, habit, feeling, interest, purpose, achievements.

Name: In the contexts of these speeches, Luke previously reports Paul as asserting that he was not the Egyptian revolutionary but Paul of Tarsus (21:38–39).

Nature: By ethnic origin Paul is a Hebrew; his place of birth was Tarsus in Cilicia (22:3).

Manner of Life: He was reared in Jerusalem (22:3; 26:4), educated by the eminent teacher Gamaliel (22:3), instructed in the tradition of the Pharisees (26:5). His way of living followed the strict manner of the law. With regard to piety, he was zealous for God (22:3; 26:5). His associates comprised the leading religious figures of Jerusalem (22:5). With regard to occupation, he spent his time persecuting the politically heterodox Way, deputized by the Jerusalem Temple elite (22:4; 26:9–11).

Fortune: Paul claimed to be an authorized official, deputized in Judea and Damascus by Jerusalem's "high priests and the whole council of elders" (22:5; 26:9–12).

Habit: During his entire early life he was steadily "zealous for the law according to the strict manner of the Pharisees" (22:3).

Feeling: He experienced a strong and unusual change in mind and body in the theophany on route to Damascus, from confident hostility to the Way to acceptance of it (22:7–8; 26:14–15), from sight to blindness to sight again (22:11).

Interest: Both when persecuting the Way and later when preaching it, Paul displayed unremitting and ardent devotion to the core values and ideals of Israel: he was "zealous for God" (22:3), "was not disobedient to the vision" (26:19), persecuted deviants to the utmost (22:4; 26:10–11), and proclaimed the gospel to all (26:20).

Purpose: When persecuting the Way, he acted according to a deliberate plan that was duly authorized (22:15; 26:16–18).

Achievements, accidents, speech: Paul tells us in detail what happened on route to Damascus, what he said, what Jesus said, and what he, Paul, subsequently did (22:6–11; 26:12–18).

The exordia of Paul's two speeches, then, contain all of the vital information that pertains to a favorable portrayal of the ethos of a defendant or witness in a difficult case. On the basis of Paul's education, piety, and authorization, he is shown to be a witness of reputable social standing, an upright, stable, and pious man, whose testimony deserves a fair hearing in court. The formal understanding of the exordium helps us to appreciate the function of Paul's autobiographical statements in the first part of his defense speeches. One can grasp the importance of this item in a forensic defense speech by contrasting the way Paul is presented as an educated and socially respectable person with the way Peter and John are treated in their trial in Acts 4. For those judging Peter and John "perceived that they were uneducated, common men" (4:13) and so dismissed them as the sort of characters who were not worthy of a hearing.

What makes a good witness? Or who may give testimony? In general Greek and Roman courts excluded as witnesses women, slaves, and children; only adult males in full possession of civic rights were acceptable as witnesses in court (Greenidge 1901, 482–83; Bonner 1905, 27–28, 32; 1927, 185–88). According to Josephus, slaves may not give testimony "because of the baseness of their souls since they will not attest the truth whether from cupidity or fear" (*Ant.* 4.219, Loeb). Women, he continues, are unacceptable because of the "levity and temerity of their sex" (ibid.). Israelite traditional laws proscribed as witnesses "usurers, dice-players, pigeon-flyers, and so forth"—in short, anyone considered wicked or lawless.

The social status of the witness, however, was of considerable importance in Israelite as well as in Greco-Roman courts. Harvey states the issue most succinctly: "Whose word can we trust? If a citizen who enjoyed the respect of society solemnly affirmed that something was the case, this was all one could ask for . . . the all-important question was the character of the witnesses" (1976, 21). Josephus's remarks further illustrate this point: ". . . had my case against John been tried and had I produced some two or three excellent men as witnesses to my behavior, it is evident that you would have been compelled, after inquiries into their character, to acquit me of the charges brought against me" (*The Life* 49, Loeb). Character, however, does not simply mean moral probity. Rather, only a person of birth-based, respectable social status and of the male gender can possibly have the requisite "character" required for the acceptance of a witness's testimony. Character or ethos is rooted in the cultural perception of what constitutes an honorable person.

Conversely, low social standing radically depreciated a witness's testimony. Paul claimed respectable social standing in the presentation of his ethos, but the testimony of Peter and John was dismissed in their trial largely on the basis of their low social standing (Acts 4:13). Such common, uneducated persons were labeled *'am ha'aretz* in Hebrew. The term means literally "people of the land," a phrase with double meaning, referring both to rustics as well as to the original inhabitants or "natives" of the land, namely, Canaanites (Moore 1927, 1.435–45; Schlier 1965, 215–16). The Babylonian Talmud records a statement about the legal status of these "natives": "Our rabbis taught: six things were said of an *'am ha'aretz;* we do not commit testimony to them; we do not accept testimony from them" (*b. Pesaḥ* 49b). The presentation of Paul's status and character in the opening of his speeches, then, was calculated to prevent his dismissal as a "common, uneducated" person, as had been done with Peter and John. In Luke's eyes, it was necessary to secure a good hearing for Paul's testimony by favorably presenting his character, especially his pedigree, education, and piety. For our purposes, it is important to note here how the estimate of a person's character derives essentially from social standing, and social standing in turn derives from gender and kinship. Thus a person's worth, as a rule, is all a matter of birth, not of moral probity.

Statement of Facts

The next part of the forensic defense speech is the statement of facts. An appreciation of this structural part has bearing on our understanding of certain parts of Paul's defense speeches. We might recall that the statement of the facts of a case (*narratio*) consists of four items: (1) the main question, (2) the justifying motive, (3) the point of judgment, and (4) the foundation of the defense. Because these have much to do with the way Paul's collectivist, group-oriented identity and motives are presented, we should examine each element in detail. Paul evidences continued concern for group integrity.

The *main question* of Paul's trial, the accusation against him, is a point of considerable elaboration. In Acts 21:38 he is charged with "teaching men everywhere against the people and the law and this place." Paul is accused of being a political deviant: anti-Israel, anti-Torah, and anti-Temple (including its personnel and practices). To advocate opposition to one's ethnic group, its "constitution," and its most sacred shrine is nothing less than treason, and this of the most heinous sort. Were the accusations against Paul true, he would in effect be accused of renouncing and rejecting his embeddedness in family, clan, and ethnic group. He would, in short, be accused of being an individualist, a degenerate who deviates from the cultural ideal of the group-oriented person. In the face of such serious charges, Paul attempts to show that he is not a traitor to Israel, its "constitution," or its God (24:12–13). He argues, on the contrary, that "according to the Way, which they call a [political] party, I worship the God of our fathers, believing everything laid down by the law or written in the prophets" (24:14). The case concerns political religion, religion embedded in politics or public religion (see Malina 1986c, 1994c). The question for Paul is not one of treason but of the true understanding of the law, which entails faith in the resurrection. Thus Paul is presented as maintaining basic loyalty to his Patron and Sovereign, as well as keeping fidelity to the core values of Israel. He insists that he is no individualist rebel but a group-oriented person who remains faithfully embedded in his society.

In the course of Paul's trials, it becomes clear that the main issue is not the charges alleged against him in 21:38 or 24:5–8. ("For we have found this man a pestilent fellow, an agitator among all the Judeans throughout the world, and a ringleader of the [political] party of the Nazarenes. He even tried to profane the temple, but we seized him. By examining him yourself you will be able to learn from him about everything of which we accuse him.") Rather, the main issue is an entirely different question (see O'Toole 1978, 33). The tribune Claudius Lysias remarked: "I found that he was accused about questions (*zêtêmaton*) of their law, but charged with nothing deserving death or imprisonment" (23:29). Festus tells Agrippa that the main issue is not the alleged charges but a question of the meaning of events (Jesus' resurrection) in light of Israel's "constitution," the Torah: "When his accusers stood up, they brought no charge in his case of such evils as I supposed; but they had certain points of dispute (*zêtêmata*) with him about their own superstition and about one Jesus, who was dead, but whom Paul asserted to be alive" (25:18–19).

In his own defense speeches, on the other hand, Paul repeatedly insists that the main question is in fact the resurrection of Jesus—as a fact, as God's doing, and as the point of Israel's scriptures. In the trial before the Judean court in Acts 23, he insists that the main matter is the resurrection: "With respect to the resurrection I am on trial" (v. 6). In the trial before Felix in Acts 24, even as Paul dismisses the charges that Tertullus brought against him (vv. 10–13, 17–20), he admits that the issue is the rightness of his interpretation of Israelite political religion and its requirement of orthodox belief in God: "I admit that according to the Way I believe everything laid down by the law or written in the prophets, having a hope in God which they themselves accept that there will be a resurrection of both the just and the unjust" (vv. 14–15). The main question, he tells the court, is "with respect to the resurrection" (v. 21). Finally, in the trial before Festus, Paul once more defines the main question of the forensic proceedings: "I stand here on trial for hope in the promise made by God to our fathers, to which the twelve tribes hope to attain. And for this hope I am accused by the Judeans" (26:6–7). The main question according to the defense, then, is the *issue of God's power and sovereignty as manifested in Jesus' resurrection* (the same main question in the case of Peter in Acts 4:2). Paul claims, moreover, that this belief does not betray Israel's political religion rooted in a covenant with its ancestral God but rather is the point of the Israelite scriptures (see 26:22–23). God's honor, then, is on trial.

Concerning the second part of the statement of facts, the *justifying motive,* Tertullus imputes a dishonorable motive to Paul's actions in the charges made against him in 24:5–6. The prosecution portrays his preaching of the resurrection as an act of political agitation or sedition, a point fully in accord with instructions in rhetorical handbooks (*Rh. Her.* 2.2.3–3.4; Cicero *Inv.* 2.5.16–8.28). But in his own defense, Paul puts forward the true and justifying motive (called *aition* in Acts 19:40) for his proclaiming the resurrection (*Rh. Her.* 1.16.26). He tells the court of a divine command to preach (26:16–18), a solemn authorization to speak, quite similar to the commissioning of Israel's prophets (see Lohfink 1976, 70–71). His motive for taking up this task is identical to that of Peter in 5:29 ("We must obey God rather than men"), namely, obedience to divine directives: "Wherefore I was not disobedient to the divine vision, but declared first to those at Damascus, then at Jerusalem, and throughout all the country of Judea" (26:19–20). Divine help, moreover, sustained Paul throughout his commission to preach: "to this day I have had the help that comes from God" (26:22). Just as the motive for his preaching is obedience to a divine command, so its substance is not sedition or treason but the truth of God's scriptures, "saying nothing but what the prophets and Moses said would come to pass" (26:22; see 24:14). The main question is God's power to raise the dead, and the justifying motive for preaching this power was a command from this God. The motives, then, are honorable as well as laudable. Paul claims to be faithful to the basic cultural values of Israel, obedience to Israel's supreme Lord and Patron, the ancestral God.

The point for the judge's decision is clearly brought out in Paul's defense speeches. What must be judged by Israelite and Roman judges alike is the legitimacy of Paul's main question, God's having raised Jesus from the dead. The defense speeches call attention to this point when they note that what must be judged (*krinetai, krinomenon*) is the issue of the resurrection:

23:6 "With respect to the hope of the resurrection of the dead I am on trial [*krinomai*]"

24:21 "With respect to the resurrection of the dead I am on trial [*krinomai*]"

26:6–7 "I stand on trial [*krinomenos*] for hope in the promise made by God to our fathers"

26:8 "Why is it judged [*krinetai*] incredible by any of you that God raises the dead?"

Paul presents himself as a person loyal to Israel's tradition. Far from being a deviant, he claims to defend God's honor by heralding the great deeds of God, namely, God's raising of Jesus. In this, he casts himself in the role of defender of God's honor against the challenges of the Temple elite. His motives, then, are honorable; he is not seeking his own honor but God's. Paul remains embedded in the basic values and traditions of Israel; he steps forward as chief spokesman for and defender of these values and traditions.

Proof

Next the speaker presents proof. In the proof sections of Paul's defense speeches, the prime evidence in support of the main question (that is, the resurrection) is the testimony of the witness, Paul. Paul indicates that he can serve as a valid legal witness to the resurrection because he has been duly authorized to attest to it. On trial he emphasizes that his authorization came through the divine vision, in which he was informed: "I have appeared to you for this purpose: to appoint you to serve and bear witness to the things in which you have seen me" (26:16; see 22:15).

The authors of rhetorical manuals note that although the authorized testimony of an honorable witness constitutes the foremost proof, it may need confirmation from "probability, examples, tokens, signs and maxims" (Aristotle, *Rh. Al.* 36, 1442b–1443a). Confirmation of Paul's testimony about the resurrection derives from the appearances of Jesus that Paul saw. Paul was an eyewitness, and it was eyewitness testimony that ancient courts required (e.g., Demosthenes, *Against Eubulides* 4; Philo, *Spec. leg.* 4.59; *Conf.* 141). Luke's own terminology in regard to the appearances of Jesus highlight this phenomenon precisely as forensic evidence.

Necessary Proof

As far back as Aristotle, two types of proof were distinguished: (1) necessary proof, from which a definite conclusion could be drawn; and (2) credible proof, from which no necessary conclusion can be drawn. The rhetoricians called the former irrefutable proof (*tekmêrion*) and the latter probable proof (*eikota/semeia/signa*) (Aristotle, *Rhet.* 1.2.16–17, 1357b). Necessary proof (*tekmêrion*) is one that cannot be refuted; from it a cogent and logical syllogism can be constructed. Credible or probable proof (*eikota*), however, is of great value when taken in conjunction with other proofs, for together they enable one to infer that something did indeed happen (Quintilian, *Inst. Orat.* 5.9.3–9).

Luke designates the appearances of Jesus raised by God as irrefutable and necessary proof: "To them he presented himself alive after his suffering by many proofs [*tekmêriois*], appearing to them forty days" (Acts 1:3). In another place Luke underscores the role of those who can offer special evidence or proof of the resurrection of Jesus: "God raised him up and made him manifest; not to all the people but to us who were chosen by God as witnesses, who ate and drank with him after being raised from the dead" (Acts 10:41). This recalls the proof of the resurrection offered to the eleven when Jesus appeared and ate with the witnesses, thus demonstrating he was no ghost (Luke 24:37–43; Cadbury 1937, 99–108). This irrefutable evidence serves as the basis for a more formal argument, which concludes that Jesus is "Lord and Christ" (2:36), the author of life (3:15), and the savior of the world (4:10–12). The witnessed appearances are proof that God raised him from the dead and enthroned him as Lord and Messiah (Kurz 1980, 171–95).

In the course of his forensic defense in Acts 22 and 26, Paul attests to the resurrection of Jesus. As we saw earlier, he focused the main question of the trial on the resurrection. Yet his testimony is not entirely convincing to this court, so he must confirm it. To this end, Paul recounts in considerable detail in 22:6–12 and 26:12–16 the irrefutable proof (*tekmêrion*) of his testimony concerning Jesus' appearance to him as he traveled to Damascus. According to Acts, then, the narrative of the appearance of Jesus functions as the necessary proof of Paul's defense concerning the resurrection.

Just to finish the rhetorical argument, we note that in other places Luke uses a second term for forensic proof, *pistis*. The resurrection of Jesus functioned as formal proof of God's plan to judge the world. When arguing with the Athenians, Paul affirmed God's cosmic, providential role, how he will "judge the world in righteousness by a man whom he has appointed" (17:31a). The proof of this lies in the fact that this same God raised Jesus from the dead: "Of this God has given proof [*pistin*] to all by raising him from the dead" (17:31b). *Pistis* is a technical rhetorical term for forensic proof (noted in Aristotle, *Rh. Al.* 7, 1428a, and Quintilian, *Inst. Orat.* 5.10.8).

Probable Proof

Besides the necessary and irrefutable proof of Paul's testimony, we ought to take note of the other type of evidence mentioned by Aristotle, the *eikota* or probable, credible signs. These types of signs set out confirmatory evidence; they allow us to infer that something did in fact happen. As the handbooks say, "One thing is a sign of another—not any casual thing of any other casual thing, nor everything whatever of everything whatever, but only a third that normally precedes or accompanies or follows a thing" (*Rh. Al.* 12, 1430b).

With regard to the signs that confirm Paul's testimony, the incidents accompanying the divine revealing of the raised Jesus on the way to Damascus may be treated as *eikota,* signs with supportive probative value. First, the appearance of Jesus was accompanied by a great light in the sky (22:6, 9; 26:13). The light was admittedly an extraordinary phenomenon, "brighter than the sun"; it was seen by Paul "and by those journeying with me" (26:13). On the basis of similar depictions in other ancient writings, literary scholars have labeled the pattern or literary form of the Damascus account as an epiphany of a divine being. Some typical motifs of such epiphanies are lights from the sky, mighty voices, and animate beings falling to the ground (Lohfink 1976, 61–68). The light from sky, then, is perceived as a typical sign that regularly accompanies an appearance from the realm of the divine. In Paul's defense speeches, this sign functions forensically as evidence that Paul was receiving some sort of divine revelation. From it we infer that something has indeed happened. According to rhetorical handbooks, this sort of sign normally accompanies something else, with which it has to be coupled to provide stronger evidence.

Second, Paul's blindness and subsequent healing are still another sign (22:11, 13; see 9:7–9, 17). The renewal of Paul's sight serves as a symbolic act of Paul's enlightenment about Jesus. Yet of themselves the light from the sky and renewed sight do not involve Jesus' resurrection in any sort of "necessary" way. Revelatory lights flashed around Daniel (Dan. 10:5–9) and Aseneth (Joseph and Aseneth 14:1–2); Tobit was blinded and subsequently healed (Tob. 11:11–13). In the categories of Aristotle, these signs, however, enable us to infer that something else has happened, something other than the occurrence of light from the sky and renewed sight. That something else was Paul's experience of a divinely caused appearance of the raised Jesus, an experience that provided irrefutable proof for his testimony about the resurrection. God revealed the resurrected Jesus to Paul!

A speaker's testimony can be corroborated by witnesses who can confirm all the relevant aspects of his testimony. In Paul's case, witnesses can confirm every point set out in the exordia: his loyal Israelite upbringing and education "is known by all Judeans" (26:4); his zeal as a Pharisee can be verified by local witnesses, "if they are willing to testify" (v. 5). His initial hatred of the Way can be corroborated by excellent witnesses: "The high priest and the whole council of the elders bear me witness" (22:5). And his authorization for persecuting the followers of the Way in Damascus can be supported by written documents: "From them I received letters to the brethren" (v. 5).

Paul's experience on route to Damascus can also be confirmed by corroborating witnesses. His traveling companions likewise saw the light (22:9; 26:13); they too fell to the ground (26:14). They can verify the extraordinary light, as well as Paul's blindness and healing (22:11), credible signs (*eikota*) from which one can infer Paul's experiencing the divine. These events have still another witness who can confirm them, Ananias. He is a trustworthy witness whose standing in the court is unimpeachable: "A devout man according to the law and well spoken of by all the Judeans who lived there" (v. 12). He too received a divine revelation in a dream about the events on the way to Damascus; he can verify that Paul experienced the raised Jesus: "the God of our fathers has appointed you . . . to see the Just One and hear a voice from his mouth" (v. 14). After healing Paul of his blindness, Ananias confirmed Paul's authorization to attest to the resurrection: "For you will be a witness for him to all men of what you have seen and heard" (v. 15). Thus Ananias can corroborate Paul on every point of his testimony about the raised Jesus and the events on route to Damascus. According to correct forensic procedure, then, there are two witnesses providing necessary proofs.

In an excellent study of this material, Wikenhauser called attention to the motif in Acts of "double dreams," a motif common in Greco-Roman and Israelite literature (1948, 100–111). This motif consists of a heavenly revelation to a principal figure and a simultaneous parallel revelation to a friend or relative who can corroborate the main revelation. Such a motif, which occurred in the case of Peter and Cornelius in Acts 10, is found also in the appearances of Jesus to Paul and Ananias in 9:3–6, 10–16 and 22:6–10, 12–16. And so the appearance to Ananias functions as confirmation of the appearance to Paul.

Proofs Verifiable from General Experience

Further confirmatory evidence in support of Paul's testimony comes from proofs that the handbooks call "probabilities." The term has the connotation that something is readily provable, testable, and verifiable from general experience. When setting forth a statement to judge and jury, an orator should "pay attention to the question of whether he will find his hearers possessed of a personal knowledge of the things of which he is speaking, as that is the sort of statement they are most likely to believe" (Aristotle, *Rh. Al.* 7, 1428a; see Quintilian, *Inst. Orat.* 5.10.16–19). Is there a common experience to which the orator can appeal (*Rh. Al.* 7, 1428a)? Will the audience understand? This type of proof, "probability," seems to have been taken into consideration in the composition of the proof section of Paul's forensic speeches narrating Jesus' appearance to Paul. In the first place, the revelation of the raised Jesus is recounted according to the typical form that Lohfink has described as an epiphany account. Comparing the appearance accounts in Acts 9, 22, and 26 with Old Testament examples such as Gen. 31:11–13; 46:2–3; and Exod. 3:2–10, Lohfink suggested the following formal elements (1976, 62–66):

A1	introductory formula	. . . saying to him
A2	address: double vocative	Saul! Saul!
B1	introductory formula	but he answered
B2	question	who are you, Lord?
C1	introductory formula	But he . . .
C2	self-presentation of appearing figure	I am Jesus, whom you
C3	commission	But rise and go . . .

A court familiar with Old Testament stories would presumably understand the traditional form of Paul's account of Jesus' appearance and Paul's "probable" claim to have received a divine revelation (see Hubbard 1978, 187–98). Similarly, Lohfink has shown that the account of Paul's commissioning to preach the resurrection in 26:16–18 is modeled on a mosaic of citations from the prophets about their vocation commissionings, as the following synopsis indicates (1976, 70–71):

(a)	Acts 26:16	"Stand on your feet"
	Ezek. 2:1	"Stand on your feet"
(b)	Acts 26:17	"delivering you from the people and the nations"
	Jer. 1:8	"be not afraid of them, for I am with you to deliver you"
(c)	Acts 26:17b	"from the nations to whom I send you"
	Jer. 1:7	"to whomever I send you, you shall go"
(d)	Acts 26:18	"to open their eyes that they may turn from darkness to light"
	Isa. 42:6–7	"a light to the nations, to open the eyes that are blind"

Again the form and content of Paul's testimony about his commission to preach the resurrection are phrased in such a way as to appear verifiable from experience to a court familiar with the Old Testament, suggesting a prophetic commissioning.

Paul is appealing to what is common or "probable" in the experience of his audience when he repeatedly maintains that the resurrection is not a novel or disloyal concept. He insists that it is a "probability," a statement fully in accord with the views of his hearers. For example, he confesses in his defense in 24:14–15 that he "believes everything laid down in the law or written in the prophets," which includes "the hope in God which they themselves accept that there will be a resurrection of both just and unjust." In 26:6–7, he insists again that his hope in the resurrection is the same thing "to which our twelve tribes hope to attain." He remarks that by testifying to the resurrection, he is "saying nothing but what the prophets and Moses said would come to pass" (26:22). The resurrection, then, is a "probable" phenomenon to Paul, indeed, a longstanding Israelite tradition.

In summary, what we hope to have shown in this section is that Luke's Pauline trial speeches in Acts deserve to be described formally as forensic defense speeches according to the models presented in the rhetorical handbooks. The forensic defense speech is an appropriate scenario for appreciating the structure of Paul's speeches and for grasping the function of the individual items in those speeches. Knowledge of forensic speeches and forensic procedure is indispensable for understanding the book of Acts. Table 2 conveniently summarizes the data in this section:

TABLE 2.

Structure of Paul's Speeches in Acts 22—26

Exordium				
appeal to judge	—	—	—	26:2–3
ethos of speaker	22:4–5	23:1	—	26:4–5
Statement of Facts				
main questions	—	23:6	24:10–20	26:6–7
justifying motive	22:10, 14–15	—	—	26:16–20
point for judge's decision	—	23:6	24:14–15, 21	26:6–8
Proof				
martyria	22:15	—	—	26:16
tekmerion	22:6–10	—	—	26:12–18
semeion	22:6, 11, 13 (blindness)	23:9 (light)	—	26:13 (light)
corroborating witnesses	22:5, 9, 12–15	—	—	26:5, 12–13
probabilities	22:7–10 (epiphany)	—	—	26:14–16 (epiphany); 26:16–18 (prophetic commissioning)

ENCOMIA AND
FORENSIC DEFENSE SPEECHES
FROM A SOCIAL SCIENCE PERSPECTIVE

When studying encomia and forensic defense speeches, we have examined two different ancient Mediterranean models for describing persons. We have also studied the way these native models have been applied to the figure of Paul according to the cultural norms of antiquity. Because we are interested in discerning the general conventions by which the ancients perceived and described persons, we must now compare the encomium and forensic defense speech in this regard. We do not find it at all surprising that these two types both are concerned with the same aspects of human description and address those features in roughly the same order. After all, part of our broader hypothesis remains that the conventional perception of reality is quite selective, rooted in the common enculturation and socialization of members of a group.

Generation

Generation refers to birth and its attending meanings and values. Both the encomium and the forensic defense speech would have speakers relate as much as possible about their generation—provided this information is positive. A person's worth is determined, by and large, by generation. In the encomium, writers and speakers begin by telling of a person's family of origin (*eugeneia*), so as to inform others of their honor rating. Social pedigree is based on embeddedness in a social group. The encomium specifically speaks of a person's origins (*genos:* ethnic group, region, general ancestry) and attending circumstances (*genesis:* family, phenomena at birth). Because honor is symbolized by blood, one's blood lines (specific ancestors, family) indicate a person's ascribed precedence. And because stereotypes ("Cretans are always liars!") convey information about ethnic groups, native regions, social status rooted in profession or occupation, and the like, it is important to have information about a person who presumably embodies the traditions and traits of ethnic group, native region, profession, and so forth. The encomium, therefore, focuses on group embeddedness and group-shared attributes, not on unique, individual traits.

The manuals that deal with forensic defense speeches likewise instruct speakers to comment on a person's "nature" (Cicero) or "birth" (Quintilian), that is, what we call "generation." All the information deemed pertinent for an encomium is applicable in the forensic speech as well. Quintilian confirms the value of such information in terms of stereotypes of honor: "Persons are regularly regarded as having some resemblance to their parents and ancestors, a resemblance which sometimes leads to their living disgracefully or honorably, as the case may be" (*Inst. Orat.* 5.10.24). Ethnic origins, too, convey stereotypical knowledge, because much can be learned from whether a person is a barbarian, Roman, or Greek. And the inhabitants of different regions have distinctive institutions and traditions, as we shall see in the next chapter. Because it is presumed that individuals reflect what is common to others of similar ethnic origins, knowledge of regional and social derivation tells the hearer vital information about a person. Of course, gender is equally important, for certain social behaviors are expected of males and others of females. Individuals are essentially gendered selves.

Thus, both the encomium and the forensic speech see generation, geography, and gender as providing important and fundamental information concerning a person's honor rating. In their presentation and calculation of that rating, both reflect the cultural conventions of what constitutes honor. According to our native Mediterranean informants, a person's honor or social worth derives from generation, geography, and gender. These fundamental sources of honor can be learned from the quite valid and significant stereotypes employed for describing individual members of a given group. In this description, speakers pay scant attention to the singular features of a unique person. Rather, what they deem worth knowing are those dimensions of persons stemming from their social embeddedness.

Education and Training

After the foundational information provided by data concerning generation, geography, and gender, the elite speaker moves on to the important area of a person's formation. Given the person's social embeddedness, the question arises, Who formed the person into the type of human he or she has become, and to what social ends? Both the encomium and the forensic defense speech instruct a speaker to comment on formation, the teachers, arts and skills, and laws or discipline learned by a person. Information about one's teachers acquaints us with others in whom the person in question continues to be embedded and whose traditions that person now embodies. A person must be similar to those responsible for one's formation. Recall the gospel axiom that well articulates this stereotype: "A disciple is not above his teacher, but every one when he is fully taught will be like his teacher" (Luke 6:40; Matt. 10:24). Unlike students today, ancient students were not expected to "think for themselves" or "question authority" or "be creative" or "develop their own opinions." Rather, students in antiquity were expected to learn and embody the traditions of their culture. It was in this way that they formed their "conscience," that is, their common awareness, the knowledge they shared with others in their social group (Malina and Neyrey 1991a, 76–80).

Knowledge of someone's acquired abilities likewise conveys vital information about that person. It aids in socially locating them and clarifying their honor rating. Noteworthy would be skill in athletic prowess, military arts, public speaking, poetry, and the like. These connote tutorial discipline, the assimilation of tradition, and not individual achievement. They are, moreover, the skills of socially prominent people, thus indicating honorable social status.

The norms of discipline to which someone submits and adapts further indicate a person's collective embeddedness. These norms reflect a form of self-control (*egkrateia*) that mirrors the social control and conformity valued in the larger society (Neyrey 1993, 138–39, 152–55). In their broadest scope, such norms of discipline *exclude* a sense of initiative, personal drive, individual criticism, and insubordination. That is, they *endorse* the group expectations of the culture that strongly forbids self-reliance and individual enterprise. Acceptance of such discipline and the norms they entail acknowledges the honor standards of the culture and signals that a person trained in them is group sensitive and group embedded. Honor is likewise claimed by mastery of honorable principles and exemplary behavior. Group norms of honor and shame continue to be the informing and formative values for assessing persons.

Accomplishments/Moral Decisions

Before cataloguing someone's deeds, the encomium instructs a speaker to make note of a person's early choices and decisions. In principle, the speaker can show that noble choices and wise decisions made in youth influenced adult behavior. The choices are either honorable or dishonorable, as they conform to a group's norms and values. In this regard, Cicero attends to a person's "habits" (*habitus*), the stable and absolute constitution of mind or body. He lists as important a person's "interests" (*studium*), "the unremitting mental activity ardently devoted to some subject and accompanied by intense pleasure" (*Inv.* 1.25.36). In both instances, we sense that change or novelty is negatively perceived; what counts is consistency and conformity to accepted values. Passions or violent feelings bespeak a sort of individualism or a threat to group traditions. At stake here would seem to be concern for motivation. Dedication to group values and the cultivation of socially accepted choices betoken a moral person, and vice versa. Plato aptly illustrates this group embeddedness and celebrates the formation of youth in group ideals and expectations:

And when they are released from their schooling the city next compels them to learn the laws and to live according to them as after a pattern, that their conduct may not be swayed by their own light fancies, but just as writing-masters first draw letters in faint outline with the pen for their less advanced pupils, and then give them the copy-book and make them write according to the guidance of their lines, so the city sketches out for them the laws devised by good lawgivers of yore, and constrains them to govern and be governed according to these. (Plato, *Protagoras* 326C, Loeb)

Youthful discipline and decisions made in regard to group expectations, then, stand out in the minds of the ancients as indicators of how a person will live and act.

Deeds of the Body

The encomium quite clearly emphasizes that a speaker should discourse on a person's beauty, strength, might, agility, and health. These traits, of course, should be evaluated and perceived in terms of the cultural values they embody; canons of bodily excellence were learned as part of the typical education at the gymnasium (Miller 1991, 121–50) and celebrated at regularly held games. A person endowed with bodily excellence would embody aristocratic ideals that reflect honorable behavior. For example, strength and power are important for athletics and warfare, both aristocratic or elite pursuits. Strength and power, moreover, are highly valued in a culture where honor is regularly claimed or defended. Beauty serves elite tastes and conforms to its canons. Yet Aristotle also defined beauty more functionally as the appropriate quality for youths, mature, and elder men to live out the social expectations of their culture:

Beauty varies with the time of life. In a young man beauty is the possession of a body fit to endure the exertions of running and of contests of strength. . . . For a man in his prime, beauty is fitness for the exertion of warfare, together with a pleasant but at the same time formidable appearance. For an old man, it is to be strong enough for such exertion as is necessary, and to be free from all those deformities of old age which cause pain to others. (*Rhet* 1.5.11, 1361b 7–15)

Health means not only absence of disease but discipline and the avoidance of excess. And so, it too implies conformity to the value of self-control.

The forensic defense speech only briefly mentions that one should note whether someone is strong or weak, tall or short, handsome or ugly, swift or slow, bright or dull. Given the importance of physiognomic descriptions (see chapter 4), these conventional clues suffice once we come to realize how much significant, stereotypical information is encoded in these labels.

Deeds of the Soul

The encomium classifies the deeds of the soul according to the four cardinal virtues. It is beyond the scope of this inquiry to examine in detail the way these four virtues embrace the specific cultural values of the Greco-Roman, Mediterranean world. But we can note that "wisdom" or cleverness (*phronêsis*) is valued in a society where risk and conflict are important, such as in military action or in honor challenge/riposte situations. Temperance or the sense of shame (*sôphrosynê*) expresses the value of self-control (*egkrateia*), the acceptance of social norms for the discipline of the body. Courage (*andreia*) is appropriate where boldness and endurance of adversity in military actions or defense of honor looms important and where obedience to a superior (father, elder, king) is celebrated. Finally, justice (*dikaiosynê*) spells out one's group obligations to the gods, parents, elders, and ancestors, as well as to patrons in patron-client relations. Temperance and justice speak to a person's group embeddedness and conformity to the group's discipline. Courage and cleverness reflect concern for honor.

The forensic defense speech indicates that a person may be labeled negatively or positively, as the case warrants. Negative labels situate one's opponents as worthy of the group's anger, envy, or enmity because of their injustice, cruelty, severity, and greed (see *Rh. Al.* 34, 1440a; 36, 1445a). Such lists of vices are signaled as noteworthy, and so reflective of social conventions. They denote dishonorable behavior, immoderately aggressive and excessive challenges to others, as well as false claims of honor.

In either case, then, the virtues extolled and the vices excoriated would be those valued according to the conventional standards of the group. They are stereotypical labels that identify actions as honorable or dishonorable. A person known for virtue, then, would be understood as someone living according to group norms and expectations. A virtuous life becomes synonymous with group embeddedness.

Deeds of Fortune

The encomium lists as deeds of fortune power, wealth, friends, fame, children, and happy death. A person thus endowed is labeled a favorite of the gods, their client and faithful devotee. Such a person enjoys ascribed honor, which is valued more than what is achieved, because it embraces the honor of the celestial patron as well. These "deeds," in particular power and wealth, serve as marks of special, even elite, status. They primarily manifest honor: (1) power, for making claims and prevailing; (2)

wealth, for conspicuous display; (3) friends or patrons, for access to resources beyond one's natural state; and (4) children, for extension of one's status through better defense, networking through marriage relationships, and the like.

In the forensic defense speech, because the character described in the speech may come from elite and nonelite levels of society, deeds of fortune are more generally described. Cicero thought it important to note whether a person was slave or free, rich or poor, famous or infamous (*Inv.* 1.25.35). These labels contain native stereotypes about qualitative categories of persons and so serve as important pieces of information about people. Quintilian instructs a speaker to comment on whether a person is rich or poor; surrounded by relations, friends, and clients; or lacking in these advantages (*Inst. Orat.* 5.10.26). But both essentially indicate how important it is to know the honor rating of a person, because this rating allows for access to wealth, power, and patronage. Ostensibly, the possession of good fortune is rather sure indication of a person's high public honor rating, while a high public honor rating assures good fortune. In short, what counts is one's group embeddedness, either in a noble kinship network or in a worthy patron-client relationship.

All in all, the most significant determinants of who or what a person is derive from outside the individual person. It is these external determinants that the ancients believed were worth knowing and noting. In short, everyone was presumed to be an "other-made" man or woman. "Self-made" persons simply did not exist. Should a self-made person of any sort emerge upon the scenes, that person would be labeled a deviant. Degenerates of that sort would have to be eliminated. In this chapter, we have frequently mentioned the various levels of embeddedness that honorable persons positively enjoy and take pride in. Persons were firmly situated within the controlling factors of generation, geography, and gender, as well as of the fictive generation characteristic of patron-client relationships. It would be simply unthinkable for persons involved in continued rootedness in a given family, group, and gender to forget this embeddedness as long as they live. Paul cites a truism when he writes: "What have you that you did not receive? If then you received it, why do you boast as if it were not a gift?" (1 Cor. 4:7). Persons who receive everything actually have no control over anything. Persons surely have no control over generation, geography, and gender. They have little if any control over who forms them, over the stages of growth they undergo, over the events and persons they encounter. For the most part, what situates a person socially befalls the person or happens to the person. Achievements flow from ascribed status and are not produced by the individual, "self-made" achiever. Hence, what ultimately counts is tradition and the persons responsible for it—the god(s) of the group, and one's ancestors, group elders, and family.

CONCLUSION

Both the encomium and the forensic defense speech are genres or broader patterns of language that derive from a social system in which persons are publicly praised or publicly praise themselves, in which persons defend and prosecute each other in a public forum. Genres derive from behavior in a social system. This holds for us, as well as for first-century Mediterraneans and other human speakers on the planet. For example, our genre "food advertisements" derives from a social system in which provisioning takes place by means of economic-based food provisioning stores, and food exchange occurs by means of fixed prices. But because literary genres derive from the social system, they do not offer direct information about the quality of persons interacting in the social system. To discover this feature, we must consider the specific requirements set out in the genre. For example, we cannot tell what people eat (why, how much, and so forth) just from some generic description of food sold for a price. If we know details (e.g., chickens sell at two dollars each), then we might conclude that people eat chickens and buy them in individual units. If the advertisement promotes frying, boiling, or roasting chickens, and the like, we can even find out how people prepare the chickens. In other words, while genre description provides general information about the social system, it is the specified parts of the genre that present the details we need to determine what type of personality is involved in the culture.

Now the specified elements of each rhetorical genre under consideration are rich in indications of the sort of persons we might expect to encounter in the first-century Mediterranean. Persons whose core self is rooted in and defined by generation, geography, and gender would clearly tend to be collectivist persons. These are group-oriented persons whose identities derive from common, localized kinship traits—and not from idiosyncratic, individually developed personality characteristics. The further fact that both the encomium and the forensic defense speech expect speakers to develop in-group, status-specific goals, attitudes, beliefs, and values, rather than individually chosen ones, again points to extremely collectivist persons.

Both Paul's apologies for not living up to cultural expectations, as well as his need to justify how and why he did in fact end up as he did, indicate a person who enjoys doing what the in-group expects. In-group refers to the collection of persons who share a common fate. Paul's in-group, of course, are those "in Christ" to be found in various localized gatherings.

The point is that Paul and his contemporaries were group-oriented, collectivist personalities. Our study of the encomium and forensic defense speeches indicate as much. And so do the applications of the elements of these genres by Luke and Paul himself. The point will be further reinforced as we turn now to a consideration of physiognomics.

4

Physiognomics and Personality: Looking at Paul in *The Acts of Paul*

Writings called *physiognômonia* ("physiognomics") contain a third source of information about persons in antiquity. The ancients believed that behavior depended upon how a living being was physically constituted; that is, function followed form. Birds cannot act like lions because the bird's physical structure totally differs from that of the lion. Birds behave as they do because they are built like birds. And lions, wolves, elephants, and dogs behave as they do because of their respective physical structures.

Physical structure determines the behavior and character of living beings. It is not surprising, then, that elephants do not fly, that moths do not roar, or that sparrows do not bark. They simply are not built to behave other than they do. While this should be obvious in regard to general anatomy and physiology, it also holds true for those traits or characteristics we might call "the nature" of the animal. For example, dogs bond with humans, are curious, loyal, sit on laps, rifle through garbage, and the like, because it is their "nature"—equally determined by physiognomy or form. So too with the respective "nature" of cats, rats, snakes, and all living beings. Each has a nature revealed in its traits and determined by its physiognomy.

Human beings are distinctive in that they exhibit a considerable range of physical shapes, hues, and structures. Yet as in the case with other animate beings, the shape of the individual human more than adequately reveals the type of personality he or she can be and explains his or her "nature." For humans, too, anatomical form determines behavior and reveals the nature of the human being in question.

Here we continue to rely on an ancient native body of knowledge that our ancient Mediterranean informants referred to as *physiognomics*. As in the previous chapters of this book, we offer here three fundamental considerations. After presenting physiognomics as described by our ancient informants, we shall apply that information to the description of Paul found in a second century A.D. document called: *The Acts of Paul.* Finally we shall evaluate this ancient native Mediterranean pattern of description in light of our larger concern to develop an adequate model of ancient Mediterranean modal persons. Thus, we shall continue to identify features of our ancient Mediterranean model of person while focusing on the figure of Paul. Here our lens is that of physiognomics, another ancient model of assessing personality.

KNOWING ONE ANOTHER

How did ancient Mediterraneans know one another? As we continue to discover, a first-century, elite, Mediterranean male might answer as follows: One gets to know a human being by observing how much he or she has *in common* with certain categories of **persons,** who have much *in common* with certain categories of **animals,** who have much *in common* with certain categories of **ethnic groups,** whose *common* traits are as fixed as the **places** in which they live, the **air** that they breathe, and the **water** that they drink (persons :: animals :: ethnic groups :: locale :: elements). Our informant might just as well begin at the other end of the spiral: One gets to know a human being by observing from what locale he or she comes, that is, where was he or she born and raised (John 1:46; Acts 22:3), then the ethnic group to which he or she belongs (Phil. 3:5; 2 Cor. 11:22), then the traits he or she has in common with certain categories of animals (Luke 13:32). One would then fit the foregoing details into rather fixed categories of persons. We maintain, then, that ancient Mediterraneans were inclined to consider persons in terms of what philosophers called genus and species. *Genus* refers to general type or sort; "generic" information looks to what is common to, shared by, and typical of a given entity in comparison with some category or class. *Species* refers to specific differences among sets of entities within a given genus category. Aristotle's famous description of a human being as "rational animal" is an instance of this sort of classification. "Animal" is the genus or general type, "rational" is the species, the specific difference.

Aristotle and his Hellenistic cultural heirs seem little concerned with knowledge of individuals. In other words, the modern historical emphasis on what is unique, distinctive, and singular about someone was not the focus of attention in antiquity. The ancient world concerned itself with general information and with generalities of the sort one finds in "wise sayings," such as "He who hesitates is lost" or "Fortune favors the bold."

The ancients clustered these generalities under headings such as *topoi* (statements on different topics), *sententiae* (wise sayings), common-places, and proverbs.

Emphasizing Differences
and Inequalities

In their assessment of their fellow human beings, elite ancients utilized a set of fixed categories, each with a limited range of descriptive, distinct features. When Paul repeated the formula that in Christ there is no "male or female, slave or free, Judean or other-ethnic" (Gal. 3:28), he made use of the common modes by which persons were identified in antiquity. As noted by ancient rhetoricians, to know a person meant to know generation, geography, and gender. Here Paul looks to gender (male/female), gener-ation-rooted social status (slave/free), and geography, because ethnic group names refer to place of origin as well as ethnicity (Judean/other-ethnic or Judeans/foreigners, for that is what "Gentiles" means). Paul claimed that in Christ, such common and expected distinctions were erased, at least regarding a person's qualification for full membership in a Messianist group. But his very assertion that such classification has lost its significance constitutes evidence that it previously existed and was quite significant.

It is important to note that these categories were regularly presented in antiquity as binary opposites. Invariably, the usual way of thinking was in terms of A/not-A, either/or, for/against, true/false, in/out, heaven/earth—with no middle term. This so-called principle of excluded middle was the prevailing logic. This should come as no surprise, because ways of dealing with probability (either/or/or/or/n) do not emerge until the end of the seventeenth century A.D. (see Gigerenzer et al. 1989). Thus, because maleness or slavehood or Greekness denote certain general characteris-tics, they are totally, radically, and essentially different from femaleness, freebornness, or barbarianness. Literally, maleness has nothing in com-mon with femaleness, slavery with freebornness, or Greekness with bar-barianness. In this case, binary opposites really form two different species. Hence, even as we insist on viewing what is "common" to a species (male, free, Greek), we must attend to what is "common" to the alternate species (female, slave, barbarian). Thus we turn our attention to these foundational categories to gain a sense of the general characteristics of each pair.

What was it like, then, for first-century Mediterraneans to assess them-selves and other human beings? From their perspective, everyone knew that qualities of gender, ethnicity (generation), and ethnically defined locale (geography) served to constitute different *species of human.* To their way of thinking, some species were patently and inevitably inferior (slave/female/barbarian), while others were superior (free/male/ Greek). And this is the way "nature" has determined it to be; it always has been so. They reasoned this way because they accepted such "facts" concerning difference among humans as coming from nature itself. As becomes obvious to anyone who pays attention, nature always supports the existence of the group, not the individual. The ancients knew this, because they simply and "scientifically" observed the world around them. Their categories derived from their perceptions, shaped by observing inequalities in three basic areas: *status* (slave/free), *gender* (male/female), and *ethnos* (Greek/barbarian). And so, even as we examine what is commonly shared with others of the same species, we must also attend to the cultural perceptions of what constitutes a species. Let us examine several of these specific differences.

Free or Slave

Ancient Mediterraneans focused their knowledge of others on distinctive nature, not idiosyncratic psyche. The elite inhabitants of that world, such as the Peripatetic and Stoic philosophers, were aware that human beings had a common nature. This common nature did not generally command their attention, but rather they focused on the radical range of categories in this nature, usually based on various inequalities, for example congenital, natural, and collective differences. One such inequality was the difference between slave and free.

The ancient Mediterranean world was one of the four or five slave cultures in world history, with social status rooted in generation or kinship. What concerns us, however, is the way that persons evaluated what it meant to be a slave, that is, What kind of person is a slave? In the Mediterranean world generally, slaves are known to be inferior or mediocre persons, and that bit of information is basically what is needed to know all about them. Veyne adequately summarizes the elite Greek perception of slavery:

> For Plato and Aristotle a just social organization is based upon inequalities: slaves, who are individuals endowed in mediocre fashion—to see this it suffices to look at them—are good only for working and obeying. (1989, 391–92)

Aristotle, for example, could state that while slaves are human beings, slavery itself is natural. The exception, of course, would be the unjust case of men who were born free and of Greek ethnicity but who were sold as slaves after their city was captured by enemies.

Ancient Mediterraneans considered it a general rule that slaves were born that way. As their physiques indicated, slaves were slaves by nature, no less than human beings were male and female or Scythian and

Campanian by nature. This "fact" was so evident to Aristotle that he felt no need to explain it. A brief note sufficed:

> The intention of nature therefore is to make the bodies also of freemen and of slaves different—the latter strong for necessary service, the former erect and unserviceable for such occupation, but serviceable for a life of citizenship. (Aristotle, *Pol.* 1.2.14, 1254b, Loeb)

Slaves are born vigorous but base beings. Exceptions to this exist, of course; it sometimes happens that slaves have offspring who are weak in body yet noble of soul. Similarly, noble persons generate ignoble offspring. But this too is "natural" because the rules of nature are "only tendential: they apply most of the time, not always. . . . Further, Aristotle thought by means of genus and species and was not in fact sensitive to individuals" (Veyne 1989, 393, citing Aristotle, *Pol.* 1.2.14, 1254b). Thus, a stereotype of "slave" existed that served adequately to characterize a person, if one cared to know about such a class of persons.

Male or Female

The very fact that our contemporary world battles against gender stereotypes indicates that such stereotypes exist and exert a powerful force on how we see the genders and what social expectations we have of each. It is axiomatic for students of antiquity that that world was thoroughly gender divided. Gender, of course, is a natural trait of mammals. However, the meanings assigned to gender, male and female roles, are cultural interpretations of biological differences, and these cultural interpretations derive from specific social systems. Ancient Mediterranean social systems shared a basic belief in kinship as the focal social institution and in patriarchy as the proper articulation of kinship. Thus, through lenses constituted of the paramount value of patriarchal kinship, ancient Mediterraneans developed clear notions of what it means to be male or female, and these notions extended to every place, object, task, and time. For example, Xenophon merely repeats the common understanding of the differences between males and females when he describes gender-specific differences in the typical household:

> Human beings live not in the open air, like beasts, but obviously need shelter. Nevertheless, those who mean to win store to fill the covered place, have need of someone to work at the open-air occupations; since plowing, sowing, planting and grazing are all such open-air employments; and these supply the needful food. Then again, as soon as this is stored in the covered place, then there is need for someone to keep it and to work at the things that must be done under cover. Cover is needed for the nursing of the infants; cover is needed for the making of corn into bread, and likewise for the manufacture of clothing from the wool. And since both the indoor and the outdoor tasks demand labor and attention, God from the first adapted

the woman's nature, I think, to the indoor and man's to the outdoor tasks and cares. (*Oeconomicus* 7.19–22, Loeb)

Space is gender divided: males live in the public ("open") arena of fields, marketplaces, and the like; females in the private ("covered") world of houses, wells, common ovens, and the like. *Tasks* likewise are gender specific: males attend to open-air tasks, such as farming and hunting, while females attend to covered tasks, such as clothing production, food preparation, and child rearing. Hence, *objects* would be male when they belong in the male sphere and pertain to male tasks (weapons, plows, and so forth), and female when they relate to female space and tasks (looms, pots and pans, and such).

The ancient Mediterranean perception of society was always vertical. People were endowed with higher or lower status by birth. Social stratification was embedded in kinship; family status ranking applied to all persons born into that family. To kill a *politês* was an action qualitatively different from killing a slave. All humans were simply not created equal, as the eighteenth-century Enlightenment would have it. Rather creation itself indicates that humans, too, are created in vertical arrangements or hierarchies that account for the qualitative difference among them. Every significant status clearly consists of a different type of human nature, with different endowments, capabilities, natural functions, and attributes. Higher status people are necessarily one's "betters." Now because human males and human females are two species, even if of the same genus, they naturally have to be ranked vertically. Although Xenophon does not articulate the notion of the inferiority or subordination of females, this feature, too, was a commonplace in ancient poetry and philosophy. The Hellenistic Aristotelian, Theophrastus (fourth to third century B.C.), reflects much of the gender stereotype in his remarks on the household:

> For Providence has made man stronger and woman weaker, so that he in virtue of his manly prowess may be more ready to defend the home, and she, by reason of her timid nature, more ready to keep watch over it; and while he brings in fresh supplies from without, she may keep safe what lies within. In handicrafts again, woman was given a sedentary patience, though denied stamina for endurance of exposure; while man, though inferior to her in quiet employments, is endowed with vigor for every active occupation. In the production of children both share alike; but each makes a different contribution to their upbringing. It is the mother who nurtures, and the father who educates. (*Oeconomica* 1.3.4, 1343b–1344a, Loeb)

Greek or Barbarian

When Paul spoke in his letter to the Romans of "Judeans and Greeks" (Rom. 1:16; 2:9–10; 3:9), he followed the typical ancient custom of distinguishing people in terms of ethnos and place of origin, with prejudice against those who were different from the writer or speaker. Normally the elite ancients who used such terminology distinguished between "Greeks and Barbarians." "Barbarians" (literally, "bearded people") in this dichotomy refers to all other ethnic groups or foreigners, to "Gentiles." Greeks, says Aristotle, should rule over barbarians (*Pol.* 1.2, 1252b). Euripides adds: "Right it is that Greeks rule barbarians, not that alien yoke rest on Greeks, mother. They be bondsmen, we be freeborn folk" (*Iph. Aul.* 1400–1401, Loeb). Thus, Greek is to barbarian as free is to slave as male is to female; the former in each case is the naturally superior status. Livy, moreover, states that hostility between Greeks and barbarians is rooted in nature and thus eternal:

> The Aetolians, the Acarnanians, the Macedonians, men of the same speech are united and disunited by trivial causes that arise from time to time; with aliens, with barbarians, all Greeks wage war and will wage eternal war; for they are enemies by the will of nature, which is eternal. (*Ab Urbe Condita,* 31.29.15, Loeb)

The principle clearly emerges: The superior ethnic group distinguishes itself from all others, who are thereby inferior. As Windisch has noted:

> *Hoi barbaroi* are the other peoples who are different in nature, poor in culture, or even uncultured, whom the Greeks hold at arm's length, and over whom they are destined to rule, esp. such national enemies as the Persians and the Egyptians. (1964, 547)

Even Romans might find themselves in the midst of "barbarians" and despise their otherness, as did the aristocrat Ovid in his exile. It is with cultural alarm that he describes having to live side by side with "barbarians," whose appearance, dress, and speech is different from and inferior to his:

> For with us dwell without distinction the barbarians, occupying even more than half of the dwellings. Even should you not fear them, you may loathe the sight of their bodies covered with hides and with their long hair. Even those who are believed to derive their descent from the Greek city wear Persian trousers instead of the dress of their fathers. They hold intercourse in the tongue they share; I must make myself understood by gestures. Here it is I that am a barbarian, understood by nobody; the Getae laugh stupidly at Latin words. (*Tristia* 5.10.29–38, Loeb)

It is important to keep in mind that first-century members of the house of Israel felt concerning all other peoples the way Greeks felt about barbarians. At least, this is what Luke implies when he tells us what Peter says to non-Israelites: "You yourselves know how unlawful it is for a Judean to associate with or to visit anyone of another ethnic group" (Acts 10:28).

Elite or Nonelite

In ultimate analysis, the prevailing perspective was that only free males who manifested superior qualities in a significant way—the only males worth knowing—were the well born of the dominant ethnic group. In addition to the distinction between male/female and free/slave, the ancients were acutely aware of the social status of persons as an index of personhood. We previously noted how significant it was for Luke to indicate that Jerusalem elites perceived Peter and John as "uneducated, common men" (Acts 4:13). In regard to Rome, for example, P.A. Brunt has noted: "From first to last Roman society and politics were aristocratic" (1976, 169). He concludes that Roman elites therefore looked for similar aristocratic local magnates to win them over and enfranchise them because these elites had much in common. And it does seem that ancient Mediterranean legislation was essentially and primarily concerned with the well born and their problems. Elite problems had largely to do with their landholdings and the equipment and personnel on these holdings. Thus Buck notes in regard to Roman law:

> There is a bias towards the kind of land held by the upper classes: the big farm with a large staff, a large farmhouse and many outbuildings; the large ranch with big flocks and herds, and exuberant herdsmen. There is very little directly referable to the small farm with its handful of goats. In fact the scarcity of references to goats, the poor man's animal, is so marked as to be almost surprising. (1983, 5)

Ordinary Roman people, the *plebs* (as well as the nonelites of other ethnic groups), looked, smelled, talked, gestured, and walked like a different species of human being. Ammianus Marcellinus, for example (28.4.28–34), says as much of the plebs of his day (fourth century A.D.). And this perception can be replicated in the remarks of others about the *hoi polloi,* the masses or the country folk.

Similarly in Second Temple Israelite law, the "economic" problems involved were those of "the household." The household refers to the larger unit composed of an extended family, its slaves, lands, and other holdings—not the holdings of a single individual. Households were in the charge of

> farmers who were free and who owned their land. In fact the entire economics of Judaism in its initial statement addresses only the social world formed by this "household." Time and again we shall find no economics pertaining to commercial, professional, manufacturing, or trading, let alone laboring, persons and classes. "The household" is a technical term, and landless workers, teachers, physicians, merchants, shopkeepers, traders, craftsmen and the like cannot, by definition, constitute, or even affiliate with, a household. (Neusner 1990, 52)

The direction of society, then, lies with the group and especially with the elite elements of the society.

PHYSIOGNÔMONIA

The ancients developed a theory and a body of literature dealing with how to understand the nature of human beings in terms of their gender, their group and place of origin, and their appearance. The way a person looked allowed the informed observer to discern and interpret the character of the person in question. This body of literature was called in Greek *physiognômonia,* which we transliterate as *physiognomics.* Countless ancient authors employed the stereotypical principles available in the physiognomic treatises: Maximus of Tyre, Dio Chrysostom, Lucian, Apuleius, Julius Pollux, Phrynichus, Sextus Empiricus, Marcus Aurelius, Plutarch, Aulus Gellius, Galen, and Clement of Alexandria (Evans 1941). Elizabeth Evans (1935), later followed by J. Couissin (1953), has demonstrated how in the iconistic descriptions of the Roman emperors in the pages of Suetonius's *The Lives of the Caesars,* of Ammianus Marcellinus, as well as in the compilation called the *Historia Augusta,* a regular part of the schemata of those biographies was more or less influenced by the doctrines of the physiognomists on the interpretation of character from physique.

Thus, modern students of ancient physiognomics have available a rich bank of primary documents that can readily provide data from our native Mediterranean informants. The modern conversation on this material is quite advanced and is readily found in scholarly literature.

What Was Physiognomics?

Let us start with an anecdotal definition. Aulus Gellius tells the story of how Pythagoras "physiognomized" (*ephysiognômonei*) young men who presented themselves for his instruction. Aulus Gellius defines this verb:

> That word means to inquire into the character and dispositions of men by an inference drawn from their facial appearance and expression, and from the form and bearing of their whole body. (*Attic Nights* 1.9.2, Loeb)

When considering a person, the ancients thought that there was really nothing inside that did not register on the outside (see discussion below of *charaktêr*). Moreover, the only things to be found inside a person were different fluids, such as blood, yellow bile, black bile, and phlegm, whose blending formed the externally perceptible character (see Evans 1941, 107 n.60). Physiognomics is the study of what "registers on the outside," which in turn tells us what is on the inside. Physiognomics, then, is the study of human character on the basis of how people look and act.

To facilitate the process of assessing others and properly presenting oneself, writers and speakers in the Mediterranean tradition developed a set of physiognomic stereotypes. A succinct definition of "physiognomics" can be found in Pseudo-Aristotle's *Physiognomics,* a work dating to before the first century B.C. This treatise offers a set of stereotypes of human character based on

> the natural and acquired character traits that affect the signs studied by physiognomists . . . a person's movements, postures, colors, facial expressions, hair, type of skin, voice, flesh-tone, parts of the body and overall physique. (Ps.-Aristotle, *Physiognomics* 806a, 22–33, our translation)

This is clearly one of the most direct ways to get to know other persons, to present oneself properly, and to describe others for maximum effect. And the theoretical basis of this "science" is quite logical. Clearly in the Peripatetic mold, Ps.-Aristotle explains:

> It is especially in the creations of nature that one can see how body and soul interact with each other, so that each is mainly responsible for the other's affections. For no animal has ever existed such that it has the form of one animal and the disposition of another, but the body and soul of the same creature are always such that a given disposition must necessarily follow a given form. (*Physiognomics* 805a, 7–15, Loeb)

Thus, if one recognizes "the form," one can discern the "disposition" that must necessarily follow. The task, then, is pragmatically to observe the dispositions (*dianoiai*) that invariably correlate with specific forms. This gives salience to the old sayings, "Birds of a feather flock together" and "A man is known by the clothes he wears" or "the company he keeps."

The motive behind this "science" is eminently practical. For negative reasons, to deal with unfamiliar persons, one must have some idea of how they will act, lest one be taken in by them, swindled, and dishonored. The remarks of S. D. Goitein, who notes the importance of this scrutiny and presentation in the medieval Mediterranean, hold true a fortiori for the ancient world:

> The preoccupation with the character of an individual . . . should not surprise us. It was conditioned by the exigencies of life. The dickering and haggling that accompanied any transaction required a quick perception of the nature of the person with whom one was dealing. In view of the endless troubles caused by the difficulties of communication and transport, by an unstable economy, and by the general insecurity, businessmen had largely to rely on the ability, honesty, and dedication of the person to whom they entrusted their goods and money. The intense competition in social and

communal life, requiring constant rubbing of shoulders with (real or imaginary) friends and enemies, forced everyone to check whether he had made the right choices. In short, watching character was not a mere pastime. (1988, 189–90)

Positively, to have maximum impact on others, one must know how to present oneself before public scrutiny. Consequently, such knowledge of others and the presentation of the public self were extremely important. Furthermore, a number of ancient authors took up the task of describing various categories of persons in physiognomic terms with the purpose of showing their readership how to have some impact on an audience. Clearly it was important to know how to describe the character and dispositions one wanted to present in terms of the external traits typical of the character in question. Such physiognomic presentation of character and dispositions was the concern of biographers, historians, actors, playwrights, storytellers, mimes and, of course, rhetors.

Even for ancient physiognomists, the descriptive "forms" were quite limited in number. For example, Ps.-Aristotle's *Physiognomics* begins by noting that other physiognomists have employed three "methods" (*tropous*) in the science of physiognomics:

> For some base the science on the genera of animals, assuming for each genus one form and disposition for the animal. On these grounds they have supposed one type of body for the animal and then have concluded that the man who has a body similar to this will have a similar soul. A second class have pursued the same method, but have not based their conclusions entirely on animals, but upon the genus man itself, dividing him into races, in so far as they differ in appearance and in character (for instance Egyptians, Thracians and Scythians), and have made a corresponding selection of characteristics. A third class have made a collection of superficial characteristics [*tôn êthôn tôn epiphainomenôn*], and the dispositions which follow each—the passionate man, the fearful, the sexual and each of the other affections. (*Physiognomics* 805a, 21–32, Loeb)

This author's own treatment begins with the surface characteristics of the human body—that is, face, hair, skin, voice, and so forth—that lead him to suggest physical vignettes of certain kinds of men, such as the brave man or the coward, the man of easy disposition, the orderly man, the shameless man, the high-spirited or low-spirited man, and the like (806a, 28–808b, 30). He next considers the activities and characteristics of animals, such as the masculine lion, who "in character is generous and liberal, magnanimous and with a will to win" (809b, 14–36), and the feminine panther, whose "character is petty, thieving, and generally speaking, deceitful" (809b, 37–810a, 9).

The descriptive forms used by ancient physiognomists can be categorized into four general areas: gender types, geography and ethnic types, animal types, and anatomical types, which are described below.

Gender

We have already noted some preliminary observations of the ancients concerning gender. Now, however, we turn to explicit statements on this topic in the physiognomic literature itself. Ps.-Aristotle insists that we begin our understanding of unequal forms by attending to gender:

> the first division which must be made in animals is into two sexes, male and female, attaching to them what is suited to each sex. Of all the animals which we attempt to breed, the females are tamer and gentler in disposition than the males, but less powerful and more susceptible to rearing and handling. This being their character, they have less spirit than the males. (*Physiognomics* 809a, 28–35, Loeb).

He goes on to note that females have a more evil disposition than males and are more forward and less courageous: "The males are in every respect opposite to this; their nature is as a class braver and more honest, that of the female being more cowardly and less honest" (809b, 11–14). Or again, ". . . the male sex has been shown to be more just, braver, and speaking generally, superior to the female" (814a, 9–10).

The anonymous physiognomist who authored the Latin *De physiognômonia liber* (André 1981) made his compilation in the fourth century A.D. from writings by Loxos (before Ps.-Aristotle), Ps.-Aristotle, and Polemo of Smyrna (died about A.D. 145). This author considered the following as male traits: "violent, impulsive, without rancor, generous, open, not to be deceived or duped by trick or ruse, bent on vanquishing by merit, and magnanimous" (André 1981, 52). The female traits, on the other hand, include the following: "clever, prone to anger, harboring hate, both merciless and envious, without resistance to fatigue, docile, deceitful, resentful, inflexible and timid" (André 1981, 52–53). The commentators who noted the differences between males and females did so largely to shame the male, should he manifest female characteristics. There seems to have been little or no physiognomic interest in females as such. After all, elite males had little to do with females that mattered in public life.

We can observe the importance of underscoring gender differentiation of offspring from birth, a replication of the Mediterranean trait of marking off the world in terms of gender. The gender differences take on a moral quality, for very many ancient writers considered such characteristics as God-created and God-willed: "For Providence made man stronger and women weaker . . . and while he brings in fresh supplies from without, she may keep safe what lies within" (Theophrastus, *Oeconomica* 1344a, 4, Loeb). Xenophon likewise invests this distinction between male/public and female/private with moral value.

> Since both the indoor and the outdoor tasks demand labor and attention, God from the first adapted the woman's nature, I think, to the indoor and the man's to the outdoor tasks and cares. For God made the man's body and mind more capable of enduring cold and heat, and journeys and campaigns; and therefore imposed on him the outdoor tasks. To the woman, since God has made her body less capable of such endurance, I take it that God has assigned the indoor tasks. . . . Now since we know what duties have been assigned to each of us by God, we must endeavor, each of us, to do the duties allotted to us as well as possible. . . . And besides, the law declares those tasks to be honorable for each of them wherein God has made the one to excel the other. Thus, to the woman it is more honorable to stay indoors than to abide in the fields, but to the man it is unseemly rather to stay indoors than to attend to the work outside. If a man acts contrary to the nature God has given him, possibly his defiance is detected by the gods and he is punished for neglecting his own work, or meddling with his wife's. I think that the queen bee is busy about just such other task appointed by God. (*Oeconomicus* 7.22–23, 29–30, Loeb)

God ascribes activities and duties to each gender in terms of the body given each, and the polis reinforces these gender distinctions in its legal customs and codes.

The perceptions of the authors of the physiognomic literature, we maintain, reflect the popular gender stereotypes that were widely known in antiquity. For example, the perspective of Xenophon quoted above differs little from that of the typical Hellenist, Philo of Alexandria, who offered the following stereotype to his audience:

> Market-places and councils-halls and law-courts and gatherings and meetings where a large number of people are assembled, and open-air life with full scope for discussion and action—all these are suitable to men both in war and peace. The women are best suited to the indoor life which never strays from the house, within which the middle door is taken by the maidens as their boundary, and the outer door by those who have reached full womanhood. (*Spec. leg.* 3.169, Loeb)

His ideal description of the gender division of space (male and female space, men's and women's quarters) is itself but one example of this topos. And it implies a systematic division of all things into gender-related categories: persons, space, tasks, and things. According to typical gender expectations in antiquity, males represent the family to the outside; females keep the family intact on the inside. Males control everything in the family that goes to the outside; females are in charge of what stays on the inside, even while producing for public sale. Males defend the family from the outside; females maintain its integrity on the inside and to the public. The Mediterranean gender division of labor carries over quite emphatically into all spheres of life.

The viewpoint, of course, is that of the elite male. Implicit in it is the problem that bedevils all males in a gender-divided world: how to keep their females in line so as not to cause public shame for their kinship group. For as the saying had it: "Every woman has loose morals; the virtuous woman has just escaped notice" (*Life of Secundus the Philosopher* 1, Aune 1988, 114 as cited in Perry 1964). In addition, males had to know precisely what was expected of males and females to avoid anything that might qualify a male even remotely as a female. Male and female seem to have been considered equivalent to two different species of human, two different natures, akin to slave and nonslave (see Aristotle, *Pol.* 1.2, 1252b). And this was the point of gender information for physiognomics. Human beings, like the rest of the animate world, consisted of two genders, and each gender had its own constitutive nature, indicated by its radically different form.

After gender, human beings could get to know others in three ways: ethnologically, zoologically, or anatomically. In other words, one could learn the typical traits of persons depending on where they came from, just as domestic animals were categorized by place of origin. Moreover, it was understood that because of their form, persons reveal traits in common with animals. Now animals have the traits they do because of their physique; traits follow physique just as dispositions follow form. Dogs always behave like dogs; lions, like lions. Persons with the form of certain animals will have the dispositions of those animals. Finally, close observation of human beings indicates that behavioral traits correspond with the total shape of one's physique, one's total anatomy.

> The most favorable part for examination is the region around the eyes, forehead, head and face; secondly, the region of the chest and shoulders, and lastly that of the legs and feet. (Ps.-Aristotle, *Physiognomics* 814b, 2–8, Loeb)

We shall now consider the three remaining categories of physiognomic knowledge: locale or geographical origin of one's ethnic group, similarities with animals, and description of physique.

Geography and Ethnic Types

Let us begin by recalling the simple observation that people in the New Testament are frequently and typically identified in terms of either some polis, locale of origin, or ethnic group, which is itself a geographically oriented label:

Jesus of Nazareth (Matt. 21:11; John 1:45; Acts 10:38)

Jesus the Nazarean (Matt. 2:23; Luke 18:37; John 18:57; Acts 2:22)

Jesus the Galilean (Matt. 26:69)

Peter the Galilean (Mark 14:70; Luke 22:59)

Judas the Galilean (Acts 5:37)

Disciples called Galileans (Acts 1:11; 2:7)

Paul of Tarsus (Acts 9:11; 21:38; 22:3)

Joseph of Arimathea (Matt. 27:57; John 19:38)

Simon of Cyrene (Matt. 27:32; Mark 15:21; Luke 23:26)

Corinthians (Acts 18:8; 2 Cor. 6:11)

Jerusalemites (Mark 1:5; John 7:25)

Romans (John 11:48; Acts 2:10; 16:21, 37; 28:17)

Samaritans (Matt. 10:5; Luke 17:16; John 4:9)

Aquila the Judean, a native of Pontus (Acts 18:2)

Lydia of Thyatira (Acts 16:14)

Philip of Bethsaida (John 1:44; 12:21)

Andrew and Peter of Bethsaida (John 1:44)

This sort of labeling implies that knowing the locality from which persons came can provide very important information about them.

The point behind such designations is that just as animals may be categorized by genus and difference, so too human beings. Perhaps the most significant generic classification of human is according to ethnic grouping: Just as species of an animal genus are known from the places from where they come (e.g., Arabian horses, Irish setters, Rhode Island Reds), so too various types of humans can be adequately known from their place of origin. Finally, just as animals might have their configuration of species traits (e.g., playful as a Yorkshire terrier, mean as Brazilian red ants), so too humans. Thus an individual hog's qualities derive from looks, breeding, and geography (*boni seminis suis animadvertuntur a facie et progenie et regione coeli,* that is, "the good ones are noted by looks, breeding and region under the sky," Varro, *Econ.* 2.4.4). When commenting on Varro, Charles Guiraud points this out for other animals (1985, *ad loc.*), while Liliane Bodson, in her research into zoology in antiquity, underscores these features (1982). Animals are basically known from their place of origin; knowledge of native region entails information about character and physique.

In general, we may say that the traits of a living being depend on the nature (genus and specific difference) of the being in its natural environment. Ptolemy illustrates this well-known perspective:

> a more *general destiny takes precedence* of all particular considerations, namely that of *country of birth,* to which the major details of a geniture are naturally subordinate, such as the topics of the form of the body, the character of the soul and the variations of manner and customs; it is also necessary that he who makes his inquiry naturally should *always hold first to the primary and more authoritative cause,* lest misled by the similarity of genitures, he should unwittingly call, let us say, the Ethiopian white or straight-haired, and the German or Gaul black-skinned and woolly-haired, or the latter gentle in character, fond of discussion, or fond of contemplation, and the Greeks savage of soul and untutored of mind. . . . (*Tetrabiblos* 4.203, Loeb, italics added)

Thus according to Ptolemy, while the general always supersedes the particular, the primary cause of differentiation or particularization is *geography,* in the sense of an ethnic group's location. Physical location on the earth is subject to influence from the sky, and both celestial influence and physical location shape features of the ethnic group. To know any region of origin is to know all individuals from that region—both physically and culturally! Ptolemy spells out this insight:

> For if the seed is generically the same, human for example, and the condition of the ambient the same, those who are born differ much, both in body and soul, with the difference of *regions [chorôn].* (*Tetrabiblos* 1.8, Loeb; emphasis added)

Especially when examining the ethnic origins of persons, it is always important to attend to the geographical location of their ethnic group. Ethnic types are created and fixed by the nature of places. The differences among people derive largely from ethnic characteristics that are rooted in the water, soil, and air native to the ethnic group. In antiquity, geography essentially entailed knowledge of ethnic groups situated in some locality that shaped them to be as they were. Obviously the presumption was that mobility was minimal. Knowledge of some natural environment always involved information of interpenetrating physical and social features.

Further, the ancients typically believed all beings are composed of a mixture of four basic elements: earth, air (wind, spirit), fire, or water. These mixtures measured character: too much heat means inertia; too little air means slavery. But the factor that determines the varying amounts of each element in individuals directly relates to geography and the region of the world from which they come. Aristotle, for example, noted concerning the element of "air" or spirit:

> Let us now speak of what ought to be the citizens' natural character. Now this one might almost discern by looking at the famous cities of Greece and by observing how the whole inhabited world is divided up among the nations. The nations inhabiting the cold places and those of Europe are full of spirit but somewhat deficient in intelligence and skill, so that they continue comparatively free, but lacking in political organization and capacity to rule their neighbors. The peoples of Asia on the other hand are intelligent and skilful in temperament, but lack spirit, so that they are in continuous subjection and slavery. But the Greek race participates in both characters, just as it occupies the middle position geographically, for it is both spirited and intelligent; hence it continues to be free and to have very good political institutions, and to be capable of ruling all mankind if it attains constitutional unity. (*Pol.* 7.7, 1327b, Loeb)

While "cold" and "hot" are characteristic of certain geographical regions, they in turn denote the abundance or absence of "spirit" (air), which indicates a capacity to rule or be ruled. Thus character can be known from location, since locality is indicative of the varying degrees of the basic elements. If Aristotle can be said to be representative of the viewpoint that all persons are composed of the four basic elements, Pliny the Elder perceives all in terms of "hot" and "cold," and "dry" and "wet." Naturally each by itself or in combination produces various characteristics in human groups.

> It is beyond question that the Ethiopians are burnt by the heat of the heavenly body near them, and are born with a scorched appearance, with curly beard and hair, and that in the opposite region of the world the races [Northern Europeans] have white frosty skins, with yellow hair that hangs straight; while the latter are fierce owing to the rigidity of their climate but the former wise because of the mobility of theirs; and their legs themselves prove that with the former the juice is called away into the upper portions of the body by the nature of heat, while with the latter it is driven down to the lower parts by falling moisture; in the latter country dangerous wild beasts are found, in the former a great variety of animals and especially of birds; but in both regions men's stature is high, owing in the former to the pressure of the fires and in the latter to the nourishing effect of the damp. (*HN* 2.80.189, Loeb)

Of course, the ideal lies in the golden mean, the balance of the four elements and the perfect combination of hot/cold and dry/wet. The ideal physical mean connotes an ideal moral character as well, as Pliny continues:

> Whereas in the middle of the earth, owing to a healthy blending of both elements, where are tracts that are fertile for all sorts of produce, and men of medium bodily status, with a marked blending even in the matter of complexion; customs are gentle, senses clear, intellects fertile and able to grasp the whole of nature; and they also have governments which the outer races

never have possessed, any more than they have ever been subject to the central races, being quite detached and solitary on account of the savagery of the nature that broods over those regions. (*HN* 2.80.189–190, Loeb)

As one might expect, Pliny's "central races" all happen to be Mediterranean; they have the proper blend of heat and cold, dampness and dryness. Their geographical location at the center of the inhabited earth (*oikoumene*), itself in the center of the cosmos, betokens their innate superiority, especially their natural capacity to rule. This "scientific" fact conveniently supports the imperial policy of Rome and the myth underpinning it (see Winkes 1973a, 905–9).

At the risk of belaboring this point, we think it important to cite a rather lengthy section of Hippocrates's tract "Air, Water and Places," in which he indicates the type of "character" that springs from specific "places." After discussing the differing characters of Europe and Asia by virtue of "place," he focuses on the tribes of Europe which likewise differ in stature, shape, and courage according to their respective "place":

Inhabitants of a region which is mountainous, rugged, high, and (not) well watered, where the changes of seasons exhibit sharp contrasts are likely to be of big physique, with a nature well adapted for endurance and courage, and such possess not a little wildness and ferocity. The inhabitants of hollow regions that are meadowy, stifling, with more hot than cold winds, and where the water is hot, will be neither tall nor well made, but inclined to be broad, fleshy, and dark-haired; they are dark rather than fair, less subject to phlegm than to bile. Similarly bravery and endurance are not by nature part of their character, but the imposition of law can produce them artificially. . . . Such as dwelling in a high land that is level, windy, and watered, will be tall in physique and similar to one another, but rather unmanly and tame in character. As to those who dwell on thin, dry and bare soil, and where the changes of the seasons exhibit sharp contrasts, it is likely that in such country people will be hard in physique and well-braced, fair rather than dark, stubborn and independent in character and temperament. For where the changes of the seasons are most frequent and most sharply contrasted, there you will find the greatest diversity in physique, in character, and in constitution. . . . [Where] the land is bare, waterless, rough, oppressed by the winter's storms and burnt by the sun, there you will see men who are hard, lean, well articulated, well braced and hairy. Such natures will be found energetic, vigilant, stubborn, and independent in character and temper, wild rather than tame, of more than average sharpness and intelligence in the arts, and in war of more than average courage. (24.1–40, Loeb; see Plato, *Laws* 5.747d)

Geographical Stereotypes

It should be clear, then, that physiognomic literature provides a complete explanation of how the characteristics of various ethnic groups derive from the places they inhabit, the air they breathe, and the water they drink. The value of airs, waters, and places for ethnic qualities became common knowledge among elites and points of honor among nonelites as well (see Aujac 1966, 270–73). The sky overhead, with its constellations and comets, were factors in the formation of human "nature" as well (see Malina 1993a, 1995a). And just as ethnic groups have their own geographical location, they likewise display geographically rooted ethnic-stereotyped features and characteristics by which other groups might assess them. For example, Cicero observes how the Carthaginians are fraudulent and liars because their ports are visited by too many merchants; the Campanians are arrogant because of the fertility and beauty of their land; and the Ligurians are hard and wild because they are just like all other people who struggle to make mountain soil productive (*Agrarian Laws* 2.95). Josephus, in turn, notes how Tiberians have "a passion for war" (*The Life* 352) and how Scythians "delight in murdering people and are little better than wild beasts" (*Against Apion* 2.269).

Geographical stereotypes are quite traditional in the Mediterranean. For example, in the book of Genesis, we find Joseph telling his brothers to lie to the Pharaoh about their occupation and not admit to being shepherds, "for every shepherd is an abomination to the Egyptians" (Gen. 46:34). But it was not only to Egyptians that shepherds were an abomination. The fourth-century A.D. astronomer/astrologer Firmicus Maternus gives us traditional lore when he notes that thanks to the stars under which they are born, it is inevitable that an ox herder, cattle driver, or shepherd "will be a brawler and a popular agitator, who always rouses the rabble with turbulent seditions, inflaming the spirits of the people with loud and furious contentions, an enemy of quiet and peace, one who desires civil and domestic strife with single minded intensity" (*Mathesis* 8.6.6, Tuebner). Obviously all of these shepherd attributes fit Israel in Egyptian estimation. From the New Testament period, some of the more interesting geographical stereotypes would include the bromide about Cretans as untrustworthy, shifty, indolent gluttons (Titus 1:12); the observation that in "the seamanship of its people . . . the Phoenicians in general have been superior to all peoples of all times" (Strabo, *Geography* 16.2.23, Loeb); and the assertion that "this is a trait common to all the Arabian kings," that they do "not care much about public affairs and particularly military affairs" (*Geography* 16.4.24). And as we noted previously in Vergil's *Aeneid*, Aeneas deduces from the behavior of Sinon, one Greek, that all Greeks are devious liars: "Know one and you know them all!" (*Ab uno disce omnes,* 2.65). From his vantage point, soaring like an eagle in the sky, Lucian's Sky-man lets loose a number of stereotypes as he observes people on the earth below:

Whenever I looked at the country of the Getae I saw them fighting; whenever I transferred my gaze to the Scythians, they could be seen roving about
on their wagons: and when I turned my eyes aside slightly, I beheld the
Egyptians working the land. The Phoenicians were on trading-ventures, the
Cilicians were engaged in piracy, the Spartans were whipping themselves
and the Athenians were attending court. (Lucian, *Icaromenippus* 17, Loeb)

Finally, "these are the marks of the little-minded man. He is small limbed,
small and round, dry, with small eyes and a small face, like a Corinthian or
Leucadian" (Ps.-Aristotle, *Physiognomics* 808a, 30–33). All ethnic groups,
therefore, are perceived as sharing certain general character traits by
virtue of the locale from which they spring.

In conclusion, consider Polemo's (A.D. 88–144) description of the typical Corinthian and what he could conclude from the eyes:

> For I once saw a Corinthian endowed with smallish eyes and these deep set.
> They were between small and big in size, grey, dry, blinking, with eyebrows
> protruding over the cheeks and empty space below the eyebrows. The re-
> gion around the eyes had a black and blue look like from a bruise striking
> the area. He was, therefore, impudent, crass, shameless, rebellious to such
> an extent that he gave trouble to the authorities. He was a man who op-
> posed others, a hater of the pious, bold in shameless deeds, never ceasing
> doing evil to his colleagues, prone to drunkenness, impatient. (*Physiog-
> nomics* 138; see also André 1981, 77)

Thus, knowing a person's place of origin ("Corinthian"), one could in-
voke a stereotype of what people are like who derive from there. And so
one may safely conclude ("he was therefore . . .") that his or her character was of a distinctive sort (". . . impudent, crass, shameless, rebellious . . .").

Polemo also offers a range of standard, geographically based stereotypes of nations as follows (236–44): first, the nations of the world (chapter 31), followed by a consideration of Northerners (chapter 32), Southerners (chapter 33), Easterners (chapter 34) and Westerners (chapter
35) and concluding with a focus on "Greeks and their pure race" (chapter
36). He begins by noting:

> It follows from the indices and signs of this discipline that as often as you
> judge any race or a people of the world on the basis of these indices, you
> will judge them correctly. However you will find that some signs typical of
> a people are negative and lead them to deviance, while others are positive,
> correcting the deviance. For example you will scarcely find keen insight
> and excellence in letters among the Egyptians; on the other hand keen in-
> sight is widespread among the Macedonians; and you will find among
> Phoenicians and Cilicians the pursuit of peace and pleasure; and finally you
> will be offended by Scythians, a treacherous and devious people. (chap. 31,
> 236).

The geographical indices of north, south, and east and west are related to character: to "deviance" or its correction. The same observation about geographic location is made in the anonymous treatise on physiognomics: "Egyptians are shrewd, tractable, given to levity, rash, ever concerned about sex," but Celts or Germans are "untractable, strong, savage," while "Thracians are vicious, lazy, drunkards" (André 1981, 56).

When Polemo describes the peoples of the north, south, and east and west, he tends to give us a brief description of the physical traits caused by the distinctive climate of the region, and then a catalogue of the character traits "natural" to that locale. For example, in Polemo's description of Northerners, after a description of physique due to climate ("blond and red hair, fair skin, etc."), he notes that they are "quick to anger, quick to judge, inconsiderate, sincere, slow to learn" (chap. 32, 238). Comparably, Southerners ("black skin, kinky hair, etc.") in turn "act kindly, with ready wit and memory . . . possess propensities to pleasure, scheming, lying, greed and theft" (chap. 33, 238). In regard to Easterners and Westerners, he enunciates the principle that those who live closer to the sea are like Southerners, while those farther from the sea are like Northerners.

> The inhabitants of India are not very distant from Southerners because they are close to the sea and there is nothing of the Northerner in their land. . . . Similarly Iberians, located between Northerners and Southerners, have a most moderate temperament and mental ability and are beautiful of countenance (chap. 34, 240).

Thus he considers "wet" (versus "dry"), as well as "cold" (versus "hot"), as direct indicators of character.

Polemo concludes this section with the observation that "the most pure of all is the people that is moderate in its whole physique," as he moves on to the Greeks, "whose forms are pure and without any ethnic admixture" (chap. 36, 242). They fit the mean in every respect: stature, build, color, and so forth. The only qualities Polemo lists are "fully alert, quick to learn . . . strong and powerful . . . with eyes containing much light" (chap. 36, 242–44). Just as the balance of the four elements resulted in virtue and nobility, so the median locale will produce the best people, with the proper mixture of wet/dry and cold/hot.

Geocentrism

By our standards, Polemo's ethnic divisions clearly underscore the unsurprising ethnocentrism of learned ancient Mediterranean writers, which we label "geocentrism." By this term, we wish to attend to the complex of motifs in antiquity known as either the "omphalos myth" (see Terrien 1970) or the notion of a "mother *polis*." The fact is all human beings are oriented (see Tuan 1977). As a rule, people take their original bearings, the place in which they were born and raised and continue to live, as the center of all directions. After all, life proceeded from that place of origin—their life no less than that of their ancestors. The view that place is the original center of life for oneself and one's ethnic group was symbolized by the image of the center as the navel of the social body. This is "geocentrism" replicated in ethnocentrism—the belief that my ethnic group represents normative human nature. To the Greeks, Delphi was the navel of the universe (Agathemerus 1.2), a tradition celebrated by Pindar (*Pyth.* 4.74, 6.3), Aeschylus (*Cho.* 40, 166; *Eum.* 1036), and Plato (*Resp.* 4.427bc), and later by Strabo (*Geography* 9.3.6) and Pausanias (*Descr. Greece* 10.16.3). Archaeological investigations have uncovered a marble object there that is identified as the very navel itself. Alternately, Jerusalem served the same function for the Judeans, as the following passage indicates:

> Just as the navel is found at the center of a human being, so the land of Israel is found at the center of the world . . . and it is the foundation of the world. Jerusalem is at the center of the land of Israel, the Temple is at the center of Jerusalem, the Holy of Holies is at the center of the Temple, the Ark is at the center of the Holy of Holies and the Foundation Stone is in front of the Ark, which spot is the foundation of the world. (*Tanhuma,* Kedoshim 10, cited in Smith 1978, 112. For an older example, see Jubilees 8:14; Judges 9:37; Ezek. 5:5; 38:12; see Hanson 1996.)

Each ethnic group, then, might be expected to locate itself in the center of the world, just as it contrasts itself with all other peoples in its verbal references to itself (Judean and Other Ethnic Groups; Roman and barbarian, Greek and barbarian—in each case the contrasting element means "foreigner").

In addition to the "omphalos myth," a certain city might be labeled a "metropolis" (*mêtropolis*), that is, a "mother polis." This reference indicates not only that the polis in question spawned daughter poleis or colonies, but that it held the central place of power, wealth, and prestige in the region. The title, often bitterly contested between nearby poleis (Magie 1950, 1:1636), was proudly displayed by poleis such as Miletus— known as "First Settled City of Ionia, Metropolis of Many Great *Poleis* in Pontus and Egypt and in Many Places of the Inhabited World" (Magie 1950, 1:1636 and 2:11496, n.19), Tarsus (Dio Chrysostom, *Or.* 33.17; 34.7; *Geography* 14.5.13), and Antioch (*Geography* 16.2.5). Jerusalem was given similar honors by Philo, the Alexandrian:

> As for the holy city, I must say what befits me to say. While she, as I have said, is my native city she is also the mother city [*mêtropolis*] not of one country Judaea but of most of the others in virtue of the colonies sent out at diverse times to the neighboring lands Egypt, Phoenicia, the part of Syria

called the Hollow and the rest as well as the lands lying far apart, Pamphylia, Cilicia, most of Asia up to Bithynia and the corners of Pontus, similarly also into Europe, Thessaly, Boeotia, Macedonia, Aetolia, Attica, Argos, Corinth and most of the best part of Peloponnese. (*Gaius* 281, Loeb; see *Flaccus* 46)

It is important to note that in the perception of Israelites of the first century A.D., there was no forced dispersion of Judeans across the Mediterranean and the Middle East. In other words, there was no "diaspora." As Philo indicates, Judeans around the Mediterranean formed "colonies." Now whether rooted in an "omphalos myth" or the claim to be a "metropolis," the geography of a polis translated into an assumption of intellectual or moral superiority, hence character. This is exactly what the physiognomists meant when they treated locale. They were quite convinced that geography and locality determined group features that were necessarily expressed in individual personal character.

A fundamental cultural correlate of geocentrism was the in-group/outgroup perspective. In-group belonging and commitment are rooted in the perception of solidarity born of a common fate and rooted in similarity with others, specifically with one's family, extended family, neighborhood, town or city section, and ethnic group. In-group members are treated with loyalty, openness, allegiance, and support. Those falling outside the in-group boundaries belong to the out-group. With the out-group, dealings are indifferent, even hostile. For all practical purposes, ethnically out-group persons are, once more, a different species of being. Yet in-group and out-group lines were not all ethnically based, because even within the same in-group, members of a gender or age group might form a sort of in-group over against the other sex or age group(s). Mediterraneans knew that in-group boundaries were of varying arrangements and qualities. Thus Plutarch advised:

> when differences arise against brothers, we must be careful especially at such times to associate familiarly [*plesiazein*] with our brothers' friends, but avoid and shun all intimacy with their enemies, imitating at this point, at least, the practice of Cretans, who, though they often quarrelled with and warred against each other, made up their differences and united when outside enemies attacked; and this it was which they called "syncretism" [*sygkrêtismos*]. (*On Brotherly Love* 490B, Loeb)

It was expected, then, that those of similar geographical origin would harbor in-group feelings toward one another, especially when absent from their place of origin and even when long departed from it. For it was the place of origin that endowed group members with their distinctive ethnic characteristics.

The belief that geography and locale determine the character of persons who come from a given region or polis becomes an important feature of physiognomic theory when it comes to forming scenarios of interactions between first-generation followers of Jesus and the larger Hellenistic world. Paul speaks of "Judeans and Other Ethnic Groups." Well, then, what did these "Other Ethnic Groups" think of themselves? The topic merits closer consideration. In this case, we examine what Roman authors have to say of the great city of Rome. Pliny demonstrated his geocentrism when he considered Europe as the significant part of the world and Italy at the center of Europe. Rome, of course, was the center of Italy:

> To begin then with Europe, nurse of the race that has conquered all the nations, and by far the loveliest portion of the earth, which most authorities not without reason have reckoned to be not a third part, but a half of the world, dividing the whole circle into two portions by a line drawn from the river Don [Tanaus] to the Straits of Gibraltar [Gadatinum]. (Pliny, *HN* 3.1.5, Loeb)

Besides dividing the world into two parts, of which Europe is "by far the loveliest portion," in another place he embroidered on this geocentric perception:

> I am well aware that I may with justice be considered ungrateful and lazy if I describe in this casual and cursory manner a land [*Italia*] which is at once the nursling and the mother of all other lands, chosen by the providence of the gods to make heaven itself more glorious, to unite scattered empires, to make manners gentle, to draw together in converse by community of language the jarring and uncouth tongues of so many nations, to give mankind civilization, and in a word to become throughout the world the single fatherland of all the races. But what am I to do? The great fame of all its places—who could touch upon them all? and the great renown of the various things and peoples in it give me pause. . . . The Greeks, themselves a people most prone to gushing self-praise, have pronounced sentence on the land by conferring on but a very small part of it the name of Great Greece! (Pliny, *HN* 3.5.39–42, Loeb)

Pliny's concern for geography is only a cover for his claim for the virtue of the Roman people: "The one race (*gens*) of outstanding eminence in virtue among all the races in the whole world is undoubtedly the Roman" (*HN* 7.40.130). To prove it would not be difficult: "There is a countless series of Roman examples (of men of intellectual excellence), if one chose to pursue them, since a single race (*gens*) has produced more men of distinction in every branch whatever than the whole of the other lands" (7.30.116; for similar sentiments see Cicero, *De Haruspicum Responsis* 9.19; Vegetius, *Epitome* 1.1). In Pliny's perspective, the question is not Nathanael's ethnocentricism: "Can anything good come out of

Nazareth" (John 1:46), but rather, Can anything good come from any place other than Rome!

Ethnicity as Civilization

Thus, we can begin to draw some conclusions from this physiognomic study of place, geography, and locale. When the author of Acts has Paul boast that he was from "Tarsus in Cilicia, a citizen of no low-status polis" (Acts 21:39), a claim is made about the kind of person Paul is, his character, virtue, and excellence. On the broadest scale, this is what was implied in the earlier discussion of "Greek/barbarian." Whether the binary opposition is "Greece" versus "barbarians," or "Rome" versus "others," or "Judeans" versus "others," the implication is the same: An individual who belongs to the highlighted ethnic group and stems from the locale where the group resides "naturally" participates in the virtue and excellence of that ethnos. Such a person is "civilized," in contrast to all other races, nations, and places; all others are simply uncivilized foreigners, and this by happenstance of birth!

It is true that upstart Rome was originally "barbarian" when compared to civilized Athens or Macedonia. But after its conquest of Hellenic regions, it became the purveyor of "Hellenism." Hellenism stood for Greco-Roman civilization. And so to be "Romanized" was to share in the Hellenism spread throughout the Mediterranean region. This is what Pliny was referring to when he noted that Rome was

> chosen by the providence of the gods to make heaven itself more glorious, to unite scattered empires, to make manners gentle, to draw together in converse by community of language the jarring and uncouth tongues of so many nations, to give mankind civilization, and in a word to become throughout the world the single fatherland of all the races. (*HN* 3.5.39–40, Loeb)

This Roman oikoumene was the civilized world. Paul Veyne has noted:

> Republican Rome, that people who had had as its culture that of another people, Greece, did not feel this culture as strange, but simply as civilization. Likewise, in the Empire and outside its frontiers, Greco-Roman civilization was civilization itself; one did not Romanize or Hellenize, one civilized. (1989, 411)

This is what Philo of Alexandria implied when writing of Caesar Augustus's conquests in the Alps and in Illyria. He stated how the *princeps* "had healed the disease common to Greeks and barbarians . . ." (*Gaius* 145). What in fact had Augustus done? Philo spells it out as follows:

> This is he who reclaimed every state [*polis*] to liberty, who led disorder into order, and brought gentle manners and harmony to all unsociable and brutish nations, who enlarges Greece [*Hellas*] with numerous new Greeces

and hellenizes [*aphellenisas*] the outside world [*barbaroi*] in its important regions . . . . (*Gaius* 147, Loeb)

We must not fail to observe that there is a difference in places, and that some localities beget better men and others worse; and all civilized people must take this into account. Some places are subject to strong and fatal influences by reason of diverse airs and waters or winds and other sky features, or again, from the character of the food given by the earth, which not only affects the bodies of men for good or evil, but produces similar results in their souls (see Plato, *Laws* 5.747d).

Animal Types

The physiognomic literature is replete with descriptions of animals' traits that should help one understand humans who look and act like the animal in question. Because physiognomics operates on the principle that the outer form adequately reflects the inner soul, Ps.-Aristotle observes: "It is also evident that the forms of the body are similar to the functions of the soul, so that all the similarities in animals are evidence of some identity"—and this includes rational animals (*Physiognomics* 808b, 27–30, Loeb). Suetonius was especially given to the use of animal types in his descriptions of historical personages. For example, his moral portrait of Augustus ascribes to the ruler the same traits and contrasts as a lion (Evans 1935, 65). And the physical portrait of Julian by Ammianus Marcellinus (25.4.22) is composed of features of the lion, as well (Evans 1935, 72–74; see Winkes 1973a, 902–5; 1973b for examples of portraits).

Something of this sort of characterization is known to readers of the New Testament. For example, Jesus labeled Herod Antipas a "fox" (Luke 13:31–32), presuming that his audience knew the character of foxes. Similarly, without further qualification, Jesus called the hostile people whom his disciples would face "wolves" (Matt. 10:16; Luke 10:3), and he denounced his enemies as "serpents" (Matt. 23:33). A consideration of the qualities popularly attached to these animals in the first-century Mediterranean would indicate the types of persons involved.

What was a fox like? What might be presumed in the popular imagination? Ps.-Aristotle tersely remarked that foxes are of bad character (*Physiognomics* 812a, 17), while Polemo reports at length: "The fox is wily, deceitful, coy, evasive, rapacious, shrewd, playful" (*Physiognomics* 174, Loeb). The wolf, according to Polemo, is "bold, treacherous, vicious, plundering, greedy, harmful, deceitful, offering help in order to harm, helpful to friends" (172). The anonymous physiognomist likewise offers a description of a wolf, with proper applications to human being:

> The wolf is a rapacious animal, irascible, deceitful, bold, violent. People like this animal are as follows: hooked nose, eyebrows swept upward, joined

and bushy, small eyes closed, somewhat recessed, small, round head, hairy
body, long hair, short and bowed legs. Men of this type are crafty, impious,
blood-thirsty, quick to anger, vicious to the extent that they refuse what is
given or offered them, but steal what is not given. (André 1981, 136–37)

Finally the anonymous physiognomist describes a serpent and indicates
what people are like who resemble it.

> The serpent is a cruel, harmful, insidious animal, terrible when it decides
> to be, quick to flee when afraid, gluttonous. People like this animal are as
> follows: small, thin, round head, small, round, shining eyes, long, thin neck,
> well defined mouth, tallish body, narrow chest; they will move their heads
> quickly and easily. Such men are murderers, bold, timid, devoted to evil-
> doing. (André 1981, 137)

Polemo noted a similar stereotype: "The serpent is hypocritical, wise,
harmful, fearful, quick to flee, often friendly, quick to change, of baser
character" (188).

Thus, when Jesus compared people in his world with certain animal
types, he can be said to describe their character in terms of the cultural
stereotype of that animal. And this was considered adequate and pertinent information about people.

Anatomical Types

Because "a given disposition must necessarily follow a given form"
(Ps.-Aristotle, *Physiognomics* 805a, 15), the physiognomic literature spends
considerable time correlating anatomical features with human qualities.
As previously noted:

> The most favorable part for examination is the region around the eyes, fore-
> head, head and face; secondly, the region of the chest and shoulders, and
> lastly that of the legs and feet. (Ps.-Aristotle, *Physiognomics* 814b, 2–8, Loeb)

It was common practice in analysis to begin with the eyes, illustrating the
proverb that the eyes are the door or gateway to "the heart" or character.
Thus Cicero observes concerning a man's looks:

> She [nature] has so formed his features as to portray therein the character
> that lies deep within him; for not only do the eyes declare with exceeding
> clearness the innermost feelings of our hearts, but also that which is called
> the countenance [*vultus*], which can be found in no living thing save man,
> reveals the character [*mores*]. (*De legibus* 1.26–27, Loeb)

In another place Cicero notes, "For every action derives from the soul,
and the countenance is the image of the soul, the eyes its chief indicators"
(*Orat.* 3.221). "Shame resides in the eyes," Aristotle notes (*Problems* 31,
957b). Along the same lines, the anonymous physiognomist considers
the study of the eyes as fundamental to the whole enterprise: *Nunc de*

oculis disputandum est, ubi summa omni physiognômoniae constituta est
("now we discuss the eyes where the sum total of all physiognomy is situated," André 1981, 66; see parallels gathered by the editor, André 1981,
142). This perspective is further verified by the sheer space (that is, some
20 percent or more) that most physiognomists devote in their writings to
the eyes. Yet as the summary from Ps.-Aristotle indicates, all parts of the
anatomy are duly treated.

If one can move from physical anatomy to moral character, one can
equally go from moral and personal characteristics to how a person must
have looked and in fact did look. For example, Ps.-Aristotle gives anatomical descriptions of the following types: the brave man, the coward, the
man with easy disposition, the insensitive, the shameless, the orderly, the
high spirited, the effeminate, the acid tempered, the sentimental, the gentle, the mock-modest, and so forth (*Physiognomics* 807a–b). He lists as the
physical characteristics of "the brave man":

> stiff hair, an erect carriage of body, bones, sides and extremities of the body
> strong and large, broad and flat belly; shoulder-blades broad and far apart,
> neither very tightly knit nor altogether slack; a strong neck but not very
> fleshy; a chest fleshy and broad, thigh flat, calves of the legs broad below;
> a bright eye, neither too wide opened nor half closed; the skin on the body
> is inclined to be dry; the forehead is sharp, straight, not large, and lean, nei-
> ther very smooth nor very wrinkled. (807a, 31–807b, 4, Loeb)

The perspective is frontal, with special attention to the hair, neck, head,
and eye.

The anonymous physiognomist offers twenty-five such profiles as well
(André 1981, 121–32). Then, too, ancient historians and biographers as well
as mimes and mask-makers used the truisms of physiognomics to describe
and represent their characters (André 1981, 19–24), while imperial descriptions were fashioned in terms of physiognomic stereotypes (Evans 1935;
Winkes 1973a, 1973b). There can be little doubt that the famous depiction
of Paul in *The Acts of Paul* was likewise crafted in terms of anatomical physiognomic stereotypes. We turn now to a consideration of that depiction.

THE PERSON OF PAUL
IN *THE ACTS OF PAUL:*
DESCRIPTION AND CHARACTER

The Acts of Paul is a document written by a presbyter in Asia Minor
in the late second century A.D. to edify Christians and perhaps to prop-
agate a particular assessment of Paul. Tertullian tells us that for his trou-
bles, the author of the document was deposed from church office for

propagating a false view of Paul and of the role of women in the church (see Schneemelcher 1992, 2:1214).

We read in the segment labeled "The Acts of Paul and Thecla" how Onesiphorus, a resident of Iconium, went out along with his wife and children to meet Paul. Titus had told him "what Paul looked like," so that he might recognize him. Standing along the royal road to Lystra, he measured all who passed by in accord with Titus's description.

> And he saw Paul coming, a man small of stature, with a bald head and crooked legs, in a good state of body, with eyebrows meeting and nose somewhat hooked, full of friendliness; for now he appeared like a man, and now he had the face of an angel. (*The Acts of Paul* 3:2, Schneemelcher 1992, 2:1239)

Given what we have learned about physiognomy, we can be sure that this is no mere physical description of Paul nor an exact historical remembrance of him. It contains, rather, a sketch of Paul's "character" or person. The description of Paul is no terser or fuller than comparable descriptions of persons according to physiognomic canons. What kind of person are we to imagine Onesiphorus met? What does this description tell him about Paul?

On the basis of Paul's external features, Onesiphorus knows his character: "Greeting, thou servant of the blessed God!" (*The Acts of Paul* 3:4). This evaluation of Paul stands in immediate contrast with that of the two "hypocrites" traveling with Paul, Demas and Hermogenes. Because Onesiphorus did not greet them as servants of the blessed, they were vexed. But the host appropriately remarked, "I do not see in you any fruit of righteousness." Thus, Onesiphorus is not simply looking at Paul's external features but from them he discerns Paul's character, "a righteous person."

Two recent studies of the description of Paul in *The Acts of Paul* can guide us in our initial investigation. In a crisp, three-page article, Robert Grant (1982) argued that the description of Paul does not precisely match any in the physiognomic manuals we possess. Rather, Grant argues that this description is based on Greek poetry and rhetoric. He cites seven similar examples from ancient literature (Archilochus, Erotian, Dio Chrysostom, Galen, a Scolion on Theocritus, Herodes Atticus, and Philostratus). And because these tend to describe a "general," he concludes that Paul was so characterized because he, too, was an administrator and was in the process of being treated as "a general of God."

Grant bases much of his argument on the comparison of Paul with a fragment of Archilochus (eighth or seventh century B.C.). Although there are variations in the versions of this description of a general, Grant presents us with a composite picture:

> I love not a tall general nor one long-shanked,
> nor with splendid curls or partly sheared.
> Let me have one who is short and bow-legged,
> firm on his feet, full of heart.
>
> (Grant 1982, 2)

This description of the preferred "general" shares some traits with Paul. Both are "short" (*mikron*), not "tall"; they each have bent legs, either "bow-legged" (*rhoikos*) or "crooked" (*ankylos*). Whereas Archilochus does not love the man who is fussy about his hair, Paul is bald or shaven (*psilon*). But Paul's head and face are described more fully, "with eyebrows meeting and nose somewhat hooked," and he is said to enjoy "a good state of body" (*euektikon*). While the general is "full of heart" (*kardiês pleôs*), Paul is "full of grace" (*charitos plêrê*). And while the general must be "set firm on his feet" if he is to command and fight, Paul engages in blessings, first of Onesiphorus and then of others. Paul, moreover, is described as "smiling" (*emeidasen*), hardly the demeanor of a general.

Grant next cites a description from Herodes (second century A.D.), which is reported by Philostratus, about a young Celtic warrior of exceptional height:

> His hair grew evenly on his head, his eyebrows were bushy and they met as though they were but one, and his eyes gave out a brilliant gleam which betrayed his impulsive temperament; he was hook-nosed, and had a solidly built neck, which was due rather to work than to diet. His chest, too, was well formed and beautifully slim, and his legs were slightly bowed outward, which made it easy for him to stand firmly planted. (Philostratus, *Lives of the Sophists* 552, Grant 1982, 2)

This description proceeds in orderly fashion from the top of his head to his feet. In this, it differs from the report of the general whose hair and legs alone were in view. This Celt enjoys a good head of hair, as opposed to the bald Paul, but like Paul, he too has joined eyebrows, a hooked nose (*grypon*), a well-formed chest, and bowlegs (*knêmên mikron es ta exô kyrtoumenên*).

The strength of Grant's brief argument lies in these two descriptions, one of a general and the other of a warrior. He does not pursue the hints of those who study the ancient physiognomic literature in regard to the typical quality of these descriptions, nor does he finally tell us anything about the "character" of Paul that is encoded in this sort of description. This deficit was remedied in part by the study of Abraham Malherbe (1986), who explicitly mined the physiognomic manuals and descriptions of honored figures for parallels to the portrait of Paul in *The Acts of Paul*.

Malherbe does not rest his analysis on complete descriptions, as Grant did (Archilochus, Philostratus), but searches for mention of similar features and what they might communicate. One of Malherbe's strongest pieces of evidence is Suetonius's description of Augustus, which he found in Patricia Cox's study of biography in late antiquity (Malherbe 1986, 173; Cox 1983, 14):

> He (Augustus) was unusually handsome and exceedingly graceful at all periods of his life. . . . He had clear, bright eyes. . . . His teeth were wide apart, small, and ill-kept; his hair was slightly curly and inclining to golden; his eyebrows met. His ears were of moderate size, and his nose projected a little at the top and then bent slightly inward. His complexion was between dark and fair. He was short of stature . . . but this was concealed by the fine proportion and symmetry of his figure. (Suetonius, *The Lives of the Caesars* 2.79.1–2, Loeb)

Suetonius elaborates on the head and face of Augustus, with passing mention of his overall size and figure. But in that, Augustus and Paul can be seen to share smallness of stature, hooked noses, and meeting eyebrows, as well as an overall appearance of well-proportioned figures.

Malherbe then articulates the type of character that might be intimated through these features. Meeting eyebrows were considered a mark of beauty (Philostratus, *Heroicus* 33.39), and hooked noses suggested either royalty (Plato, *Resp.* 5.474D; Pollux, *Onomasticon* 2.73) or magnanimity (Ps.-Aristotle, *Physiognomics* 811a, 36–38). Malherbe is at pains to argue that the description of Paul does not unflatteringly portray him as ugly, for many of the same features are found in accounts of Heracles, who was "short" (*mikron*), dark, and with a hooked nose (*grypon,* Clement of Alexandria, *Protrepticus* 2; Plutarch, *Antonius* 4.1). Paul's baldness is then explained in terms of his shaven head, in accordance with the vow referred to in Acts 18:18 and 21:24.

Malherbe's study invites an even closer examination of the description of Paul in terms of the physiognomic literature. He has alleged a number of parallels for comparison and plausibly argued that "character" is being portrayed through the physical features described. Taking into account all the formal categories contained in the physiognomic literature, we turn now to the description of Paul.

Gender

It is no minor matter that Onesiphorus waits for "a man" (*andra*), because gender constitutes an important part in the presentation and perception of persons in antiquity. This gender consideration will subsequently play a significant role in the presentation of the heroine of the story, a certain Thecla, who mimics male behavior. Males demonstrate maleness by their courage (*andreia*) and their aggressive public behavior, in particular their frank and bold public speech (*parrhêsia*). In the case of Paul, when Thecla visited him in prison, "Paul feared nothing but comported himself with full confidence in God" (3:18). "Confidence" or *parrhêsia* is the mark of a courageous male. It may be that Grant's insistence that Paul is portrayed as a military general owes something to the general character of maleness. Because in antiquity the ideal male was often a warrior, and because great and noble males display courage (*andreia*), warriors and generals included, the maleness of characters described in Suetonius and Plutarch is often measured in terms of military traits. Yet maleness may be measured in other terms as well. These include physical traits that befit leaders, generals, warriors, and other public figures. If Paul is an "ideal male" in any sense that his culture would recognize, then his maleness would be communicated by characteristic male traits, such as "courage" and "boldness." Maleness, not the role of warrior or general, is the character trait being communicated here.

Geography and Ethnicity

As we previously noted, geographical origins and ethnicity play an important role in the presentation of a person. Readers would find it important to know that Onesiphorus is from Iconium (*The Acts of Paul* 3:1), as is Thecla (*The Acts of Paul* 3:26). But concerning Paul, although the narrative is silent, readers may be presumed to have the popular knowledge about Paul such as is found in the Acts of the Apostles or his letters. According to his ethnos, he is a "Hebrew . . . Israelite . . . descendant of Abraham" (2 Cor. 11:22) or "of the people of Israel, of the tribe of Benjamin, a Hebrew born of Hebrews" (Phil. 3:5). According to geography, he is "a Judean, born at Tarsus in Cilicia, but brought up in this polis" (Acts 22:3).

When Thecla's would-be husband, Thamyris, brings Paul before the proconsul, he begins his accusation with the charge: "We do *not* know whence he is" (*pothen estin, The Acts of Paul* 3:16). This lack of knowledge of Paul's geographical origins is linked in the narrative with lack of knowledge of his person or character. For example, Thamyris questions Paul's associates, Demas and Hermogenes, about him; they lie as they reply: "Who this man is, we do not know" (3:12). Likewise the proconsul asks: "Who are you?" (3:16). If Thamyris or the proconsul knew "from where he is," they would know much about Paul.

We can confirm the importance of knowing "from where" a person is by reference to a parallel inquiry in the Fourth Gospel. Jesus' accusers charge that "he made himself the Son of God" (John 19:7). When conducting his *cognitio* of this accusation, Pilate begins by asking the relevant question: "Where are you from?" (*pothen ei sy,* John 19:9). In the course of the Fourth Gospel, knowledge of whence Jesus comes (*pothen*) and whither he goes (*pou*) has been a major issue in assessing his identity and character. Outsiders either do not know (3:8; 8:14; 9:29) or mistakenly think they know (6:41–42; 7:27–28). Many times Jesus proclaims the correct answer, namely, that he comes down "from the sky" (6:38) or that he descends "from the sky" and ascends back there (3:13; 6:62). Insiders like the blind man accurately deduce the true "whence" of Jesus because of his power to heal (9:30). And finally, the reader is told that Jesus comes down from God and eventually returns to the sky (13:1–2). Readers can answer Pilate's question; they know who and "from where he is," namely, a person whose parentage traces to none other than God and whose "place of origin" is nothing less than the sky.

Thus, although the personages in the story, Thamyris and the proconsul, do not know either Paul's place of origin or his ethnic stock, they judge these features to be critical information in their assessment of his character. The implied reader, however, may be presumed to know that Paul is a Judean colonial who was born in Tarsus, no insignificant polis.

Anatomy and Character

In our survey of the studies of Grant and Malherbe, we have seen that the most important and dominant vehicle for portraying Paul is his anatomical description. Titus told Onesiphorus "what Paul looked like" (3:2), a phrase that deserves closer attention. The Greek reads *potapos estin têi eideai ho Paulos,* which emphasizes "what sort of appearance or outward shape" Paul had. The term *eidea* refers to the generic form of someone or something. It is this generic form that classifies entities within a genus and indicates their general nature. Thus, Onesiphorus is not only "looking" (*etheôrei,* 3:3) for Paul but expecting a certain kind of person as well. Later, when Thecla is drawn to Paul, the narrator states that she had "only heard his word" but "had not yet seen Paul in person" (3:7). Again the Greek is informative: *oudepô ton charaktêra Paulou hôrakei,* literally, "she had not yet seen or observed his character."

The Greek term "character" (*charaktêr*) derives from the process of minting coins. "Character" is the impression stamped on a slug from the carvings on the stamping die. The die leaves a similar impression on each coin. Not only should the die and the coin have the same "character," but each coin minted from that die should bear the same "character." This implies that some objects will be similar and share the same features or form. Thus, "character" pertains to what is shared by a group, common to many or typical of many. It is not singular, unique, and peculiar to one individual.

The term extends by metonymy to the ways in which people are classified and recognized in terms of some "characteristic." The standard Greek lexicon (Liddell, Scott, and Jones 1968) defines the Greek word "character" as "type or character (regarded as shared with others) of a thing or of a person, rarely of an individual nature." Thus "character" points us in the direction of some commonly shared set of features, a stereotype by which groups are typed and recognized (see Ignatius of Antioch, *Magnesians* 5.2; Plato, *Phaedrus* 263B). For example, in antiquity and up to rather recent times, ethnic groups each had common, characteristic clothing, so persons were known by the clothes they wore. Thus in Aeschylus's *Suppliant Maidens,* the king does not recognize the women approaching him because "your apparel is not that of the women of Argos, nor yet of any part of Hellas" (236–37).

Persons, moreover, can be recognized by their common, characteristic speech. Slogans such as "Peace" and "War" serve as the "character" whereby political parties are recognized (Aristophanes, *The Peace* 220). Different ethnic groups have different, characteristic languages, which serve as their "character" (Herodotus, *Histories* 1.57 and 142; Diodorus of Sicily, *Library of History* 1.8.4), but the distinctiveness of the Greek language lay in its pure vocabulary and its Greek idiom (*ton Ellênikon charaktêra,* Dionysus of Halicarnassus, *Pomp.* 3). It is proverbial in Greco-Roman comedies that "a man's 'character' (*charaktêr*) is revealed by his speech" (Menander, fragments 72 and 143; Terence, *The Self-Important* 384). Furthermore, people can be distinguished by their common, characteristic "way of life," which can be adopted by others. Thus Jason instructed his Judeans to go over to "the Hellenic way of life" (*pros ton Ellênikon charaktêra,* 2 Macc. 4:10), that is, adopt Greek clothing, diet, and behavior, presumably including nude games in the gymnasium.

It was a truism in ancient Mediterranean society that appearances can be deceptive (see Pilch 1992). Medea laments that she has no norm for "character" to tell good from bad people, but her lament only proves the point of external "characters" for evaluating people:

> O God, you have given to mortals a sure method
> of telling the gold that is pure from the counterfeit;
> Why is there no mark engraved on men's bodies [charaktêr sômati],
> By which we could know the true one from the false one.
> (Euripides, *Medea* 516–19, Loeb)

The outward, external features of anything observed normally serve as reliable clues for judging a person or thing. But when dealing with a liar or hypocrite, the externals fall short and prove unreliable (see also Seneca, *Epistulae* 65.1–4). Yet in normal situations, "character" should prove trustworthy. In *The Acts of Paul,* Onesiphorus was not deceived by the hypocrites Demas and Hermogenes; he did not see in them any fruit of righteousness, as he did in Paul (3:4).

In sum, the term "character" expressed a group's commonly shared, characteristic features, which served to classify a person or thing as part of that group. In time, the term was extended to types of persons from various groups. Theophrastus's work, *Characteres,* describes the ethos of persons, that is their behavioral characteristics along with physical features (see Diogenes Laertius, *Lives* 5.45). At times, ancient authors focused on behavioral characteristics. Thus Polybius remarks that it is the "current coin" (*charactêros touto nomisteuomenou*) in Greece and among the Aetolians to take bribes (*Histories* 18.34.7), pointing to a moral designation as a group label (e.g., Cretans in Titus 1:12). Epictetus, moreover, speaks about people who, like coins, bear the imprint of various emperors, who themselves embody various virtues, that is, "qualities which make him a human being." Thus, there are coins with the imprint of Trajan, which Epictetus will keep, but others with the face of Nero he discards (*Discourses* 4.5.16–17). Extending the metaphor to persons, Epictetus will embrace persons who have the "character" (*charaktêra*) of being "gentle, generous, patient, affectionate" (4.5.17), but reject them if they are "choleric, furious, querulous" (4.5.18).

However, while the term "character" refers to behavioral features in certain contexts, it always points to outward, physical aspects, even if implicitly. From external features, persons might be designated as belonging to certain ethnic groups in given localities, such as Libya, Egypt, Cyprus, or Ethiopia (Aeschylus, *Suppliant Maidens* 277–86), but *not* from Argos. It might indicate the features of a face (Josephus, *Ant.* 13.322), whereby a son is recognized as the offspring of a certain father (see Herodotus, *Histories* 1.116).

In *The Acts of Paul,* when Thecla hears Paul's voice, although she has not yet seen his "character," the author is concerned with his physical appearance. This physical appearance will offer clear indication of his behavioral or "ethical" qualities as a virtuous person. The narrator has already given the reader both a physical description of Paul and indications of the kind of person he is, and so it remains for Thecla to see and appreciate what the readership already knows.

Physical Description and Character

Physiognomics provided culturally precise information that correlates a person's looks ("character") with ethical traits one might expect of that person. Consider the physiognomic features that are noted relative to Paul in *The Acts of Paul.*

Eyes

Many physiognomic descriptions give considerable emphasis to a description of the eyes: (a) color, (b) position in the face (protruding or hollow set), and (c) activity (blinking, laughing, straining, and so forth). Polemo, for example, devotes a third of his work to the subject of eyes (Foerster 1893, 1.107–70; see also Ps.-Aristotle, *Physiognomics* 811b, 15–28 and 812a, 38–812b, 13; Pliny, *HN* 11.141–45). While instructing orators, Cicero placed primary emphasis on the eyes as communicators of one's message:

> Everything depends upon the countenance, while the countenance itself is entirely dominated by the eyes. . . . For a delivery is wholly the concern of the feelings, and these are mirrored by the face and expressed by the eyes . . . but it is the eyes that should be used to indicate the emotions, by now assuming an earnest look, now relaxing it, now a stare, and now a merry glance . . . and nature has given us eyes, as she has given the horse and the lion their mane and tail and ears, to indicate the feelings of the mind. (*Orat.* 3.221–23; see also Quintilian, *Inst. Orat.* 11.3.75–76)

But if Cicero instructs orators to adapt their eyes to their emotions, the author of *The Acts of Paul* does not present Paul dissembling with his eyes: "Paul, who had eyes only for the goodness of Christ, did them no evil, but loved them greatly" (3:1). Although we do not know the color of Paul's eyes or their position in his face, the narrator tells us that Paul has turned his gaze from many things to focus on only one, the goodness of Christ. For that is what *apoblepôn* means. Thus, Paul is not like the hypocrites and flatterers, Demas and Hermogenes, with whom he converses; his gaze is fixed on "goodness" (*agathosêsên*), which he generously shares with others. At the very minimum, then, he is not envious as was Thamyris (3:15). Nor did he have an "evil eye" to harm anyone (see Neyrey 1988a; Elliott 1990, 1994). As the document states, "he did them no evil, but loved them greatly." His gaze, then, is benevolent and full of benefaction.

Voice

Ps.-Aristotle distinguishes between two types of voices, indicative of two types of character. High-pitched voices suggest angry or annoyed persons, whereas deep voices indicate an easy temperament, even a courageous one (*Physiognomics* 807a, 13–18; see also 813a, 31–813b, 7). He goes on to link the two types of voices with two types of characters, the brave and the cowardly:

> The brave animals have deep voices, and the cowardly high-pitched voices, the lion and the bull, the barking dog, and the brave cocks are all deep-voiced; whereas the deer and the hare are shrill-voiced. (807b, 18–22, Loeb)

The narrator does not specifically describe Paul's voice. But when he comments in one place that Paul "sought to make sweet to them all the words of the Lord" (3:1), he is hardly "angry or annoyed," which characterize a high-pitched voice in the lore of the physiognomists. And when he later speaks boldly before the proconsul (3:17), he displays "courage" and so his voice would be perceived as deep and easy, as brave men should speak.

Concerning speech, Aristotle states that three things require special attention: "First, the sources of proofs; secondly, style; and thirdly, the arrangement of the parts of the speech" (*Rhet.* 3.1.1, 1403b, 2–6). "Style," of course, means "delivery." Yet concerning "delivery," no treatise had yet been written (3.1.5, 1403b, 37–40). However, if one were to discourse on "delivery," one should consider the following:

> Now delivery is a matter of voice, as to the mode in which it should be used for each particular emotion; when it should be loud, when low, when intermediate; and how the tones, that is, shrill, deep, and intermediate, should be used; and what rhythms are adapted to each subject. For there are three qualities that are considered: volume, harmony, rhythm. (3.1.4, 1403b, 28–34)

The author of the rhetorical treatise labeled *Rhetorica ad Herennium* expanded on Aristotle's terse comments by listing three possible "tones" to be used: conversation, debate, and amplification.

> The Tone of Conversation is relaxed, and is closest to daily speech. The Tone of Debate is energetic, and is suited to both proof and refutation. The Tone of Amplification either rouses the hearer to wrath or moves him to pity. (*Rh. Her.* 3.13.23)

Even the "conversational tone" can be further specified:

> Conversational Tone comprises four kinds: the Dignified, the Explicative, the Narrative, and the Facetious. The Dignified, or Serious, Tone of Conversation is marked by some degree of impressiveness and by vocal restraint. The Explicative in a calm voice explains how something could or could not have been brought to pass. The Narrative sets forth events that have occurred or might have occurred. The Facetious can on the basis of some circumstance elicit a laugh which is modest and refined. (*Rh. Her.* 3.13.23; see further 3.14.24)

Thus another part of the face and body could be schooled to communicate its message through tone.

This understanding of voice may be the background necessary for evaluating the description of Paul's speech:

> He sought to make sweet [*eglykainen*] to them all the words of the Lord, of the doctrine and of the interpretation of the Gospel . . . and he related to them word for word the great acts of Christ. (3:1)

We suggest that, according to the rules of the treatise *Rhetorica ad Herennium,* Paul should be perceived as speaking in a conversational, narrative tone. For the dignified tone, the speaker should "use the full throat but the calmest and most subdued voice possible" (3.14.1), whereas in the narrative tone, varied intonations are necessary, "now sharpness, now kindness, now sadness, now gaiety" (3.14.3).

The ancients, moreover, regularly spoke of someone speaking "sweet words" (Sir. 12:16; 27:23; see Nestor in Homer, *Iliad* 1.247–49). Thus Paul's voice is described in such a way as to convey information about his sincerity, kindness, and truthfulness. It was, of course, proverbial that flatterers speak "honey words" either for gain or to deceive (Prov. 24:26; Theophrastus, *Characteres* 2). But because Demas and Hermogenes have already been described as "full of hypocrisy and flattery" (*hypokriseôs gemontes, kai exeliparoun,* 3:1), the narrator contrasts Paul with them, demonstrating that his speech is sincere, truthful, and beneficial. As hard as his companions labor to disguise their speech, all the more does Paul speak kindly, truthfully, and openly.

(Smallness of) Stature

According to the data we possess, men tend to be perceived as either tall, medium, or short. In the ancient papyri from Egypt, for example, we find "iconistic" descriptions of persons, both men and women, who are described as of "medium height" (*mesos, Select Papyri* 1.12, 27, 28, 29) or "medium or less" (Evans 1969, 39–40). Evidently in these descriptions, identifying characteristics play an important role, and so the general remarks about height, skin color, hair, and especially scars are to be taken literally as significant clues about the type of person in question. In other descriptions, however, the designation of a man as "tall" or "short" may not be realistic or accurate and may actually be intended to convey information about character, rather than stature. In terms of a gender-divided world, it was axiomatic that "the male is larger and stronger than the female, and the extremities of his body are stronger, sleeker, better conditioned and more fit for every function" (Ps.-Aristotle, *Physiognomics* 806b, 32–35).

Generals and warriors are often portrayed heroically as "tall" (*megas*). Herodes describes a certain Celtic warrior as "Heracles," who was "as tall as a tall Celt, about eight feet high" (Philostratus, *Lives of Sophists* 552). Evans (1935, 52–55; 1969, 6) mentions the frequency with which physiques are described in general terms, like *forma eximia, corpus ingens* ("slight in form," "large-bodied"; see Tacitus, *Annals* 13.8 and 15.53). Generally, tall stature is related to the virtue of courage (*andreia*) and is natural in aggressive males who command armies and rule empires (Evans 1969, 53–54).

Yet it is also true that certain men are portrayed as "small of stature" (*mikron*). This includes even generals, as the examples of Archilochus (Grant 1982, 2) and Augustus (Malherbe 1986, 173) indicate. But just as "tall" is consonant with the virtue of courage and with specific social roles, such as warrior, so too "short" may be suggestive of or correlate with other virtues and civic positions. Many Greek heroes were short or small (Malherbe 1986, 174). Such persons might be engaged in tests of strength, such as Heracles (Clement of Alexandria, *Protrepticus* 2.42); thus their virtue will appear different from the warrior caste.

In describing animals, Ps.-Aristotle begins his presentation of them by focusing on what differentiates them in respect to "bravery and cowardice, justice and injustice" (*Physiognomics* 809a, 27–29). In the case of animals, then, size correlates with "virtue" or disposition. But the outstanding clue to interpreting size is found in the physiognomic theory of humors. The theory of humors is about body fluids: blood, yellow bile, black bile, and phlegm. These fluids blend in a variety of ways duly indicated by externally perceptible character configurations. Excess in body size can lead to a person's "accomplishing nothing" if the humors are out of proportion. In general, "excessively small men are quick" because the blood travels over a small area, and so impulses arrive quickly at the seat of intelligence (813b, 7–9); "excessively large men are slow" because the blood must travel further and arrive later at the seat of intelligence. Hence, "blood" or humorous fluids must be taken into account to assess a person.

Ps.-Aristotle further remarks that "small men *with dry flesh and complexion,* which is due to the heat of the body" never accomplish anything (813b, 12–13). But "small men *with moist flesh and complexion* due to coldness do accomplish their purpose" (813b, 20–22). Hot or cold, when correlated with large and small, indicate character and suggest success or failure in public roles (Lloyd 1964, 100–102). What matters is some balance in the factors of wet/dry and hot/cold, not merely the person's size (Evans 1969, 10).

When we turn to the description of Paul in *The Acts of Paul,* we note that he is presented as "short" or "small" (*mikron tôi megethei,* 3:3). But Paul is also presented as a man who accomplishes things. If we apply Ps.-Aristotle's measure that short men who accomplish things have a balance of hot and cold, moist and dry, then we might conclude that Paul is appropriately "balanced." If any one of the humors predominates, then the man is sanguine (too much blood) or phlegmatic (too much yellow bile). The ideal situation consists of a proper mixture or blending of the humors. Indeed "health" might be defined as the "balanced equilibrium" (*isonomia*) of such combinations as wet/dry, cold/hot, but "the single rule (*monarchia*) or predominance of one among them causes disease" (Alcmaeon, quoted by Evans 1969, 17; see Seneca, *De Ira* 2.19.1–20.4).

Thus, while Paul is short, he accomplishes his tasks; therefore, he must enjoy a balance of humors. He is therefore a "healthy" person. Given the accounts of his infirmities in his letters (2 Cor. 10:10; Gal. 4:13–16), his illnesses must be due to external factors such as physical intrusions or infections. They do not derive from physical debility. So much for our physiognomic conclusion.

Baldness

Greek dictionaries contain four terms for "bald," and each of them has a rather different connotation. (1) The term most suitable for a man who has lost his top hair is *phalakros* (see Herodotus, *Histories* 4.23); yet he might be described as (2) *madaros,* that is, a man whose external coat of hair is singed or plucked off, or (3) *psednos,* that is, a man who is thin on top with scanty covering, or finally (4) *psilos,* that is, a man stripped of hair, even with a shaved head (Liddell, Scott, and Jones 1968, 2024).

Hair and the lack of it is another important physiognomic datum. Ps.-Aristotle, moreover, considers hair an index of virtue or vice. "Soft hair shows timidity and stiff hair courage" (*Physiognomics* 806b, 7–8). He bases this on the observation that deer and sheep, the most timid of animals, have the softest hair, whereas lions and boars, the bravest of animals, have very stiff hair. He further correlates this with the regions of the world where people inhabit: "Those living in the north are brave and stiff-haired, and those in the south are cowardly and have soft hair" (806b, 16–19). "Those with very woolly hair are cowardly; this applies to the Ethiopians . . . hair which curls at the ends tends toward stout-heartedness; witness the lion among others" (812b, 30–35; see also Pliny, *HN* 11.94.229–231). In another place he remarks about the color of hair: "Those with tawny-colored hair are brave; witness the lions. The reddish are of bad character; witness the foxes" (812a.15–18; see also Polemo, chaps. 40–41, 248–50).

In the case of Paul, we have only the brief note that he was "bald" (*psilon têi kephalêi,* 3:3). As Malherbe notes (1986, 175), there has been considerable variation on the translation of this word when *The Acts of Paul* has been rendered into other languages. The Armenian version portrayed Paul with curly hair, whereas the Syriac version presents him with scanty hair, and the Latin translation as shaven. All of these variations are borne out by Ernst von Dobschütz's investigation of the iconography of Paul in the early church (1928, 1–20; see also Ricciotti 1953, 151–59). The term *psilos,* we noted above, connotes the absence of hair on the head due to some human action, either stripping or plucking or shaving (see Aristophanes, *Thesmophoriazusae* 227). This would support the view of those who interpret Paul's "bald" head in terms of his numerous vows to shave his head (Acts 18:18 and 21:24). In this case, then, his "baldness" would be a mark of piety (*eusebeia*), which is a part of the virtue of justice (*dikaiosynê*). Whereas Onesiphorus did not see any "fruit of righteousness" in the hypocrites, Demas and Hermogenes, he did in Paul (3:4). The "shaved" head was sufficient evidence.

Crooked Legs

At the end of his physiognomic treatise, Ps.-Aristotle summarizes the zones of the body that deserve consideration:

> The most favorable part for examination is the region round the eyes, forehead, head and face; secondly, the region of the breast and shoulders, and lastly that of the legs and feet. (*Physiognomics* 814b, 2–7, Loeb)

His perspective is clearly vertical, starting with the head and descending to the feet. This ranking of the bodily parts itself communicates information, at least that the head is most important and the legs and feet least significant. Although he comments on sinewy legs, he says nothing about bowleggedness (810a, 30–36; see Polemo, chaps. 8–10, 204–6).

There seems, moreover, to be no consistent term for the bowleggedness that is ascribed to Paul. Philostratus describes a Celtic warrior whose legs bent outward (*knêmên mikron es ta exô kyrtoumenên* (*Lives of Sophists* 552), whereas Archilochus does not favor a general whose legs drift outward (*oude diapepligmenon*) but prefers one who is "bandy-legged" (*rhaibos*, Dio Chrysostom, *Or.* 33.17). Paul has crooked legs (*agkylon tais knêmais*, 3:3). The clearest examples of bowleggedness, moreover, describe a warrior or a general. And the explanation given in praise of this trait lies in the ability of such persons "to stand firmly planted" (Philostratus, *Lives of Sophists* 552; Dio Chrysostom, *Or.* 33.17) or to be "set firm on their feet" (Archilochus, fragment 58).

Any inquiry concerning Paul's bowleggedness invariably entails information about the kind of person Paul was supposed to have been. The comparative material that describes a general and a warrior suggests a fearless person who could stand his ground. Later in the narrative, Paul is presented as just this sort of person, who speaks boldly to the group "concerning continence and the resurrection" (3:5). When standing before the proconsul, he speaks fearlessly in defense of the God of Christians who authorized him (3:17). Indeed "Paul feared nothing, but comported himself with full confidence in God" (3:18). Thus, Paul's bowleggedness would seem to be indicative of a person who stands firmly (*asphalôs bebêkôs*); it is as much an index of manly courage as of military prowess.

Good State of Body

Paul is said to enjoy "good health" when he is described by the Greek term *euektikos* (other Greek terms for "health" or "healthy" are *euexia, hy-*

giês, hygieinos, and *anosos*). As we have seen more than once in the progymnasmata genre above, the ancients regularly divided the goods pursued by and befalling humans into two categories, those of the body and those of the soul. Among the latter, Plato, for example, lists the four cardinal virtues (wisdom, temperance, justice, and courage), while among the former he groups health, beauty, strength, and wealth. Health "holds the first place among these" (*Laws* 1.631C). Aristotle listed "health" among the elements of "happiness":

> good birth, plenty of friends, good friends, wealth, good children, plenty of children, a happy old age, also such bodily excellences as health, beauty, strength, large stature, athletic powers, together with fame, honor, good luck and virtue. (*Rhet.* 1.5.4, 1360b)

He defines "health" as that "excellence of the body . . . a condition which allows us, while keeping free from disease, to have the use of our bodies" (1.5.10, 1361b). Like Plato, he too balances the goods of the body with those of the soul, listing among the former "health, beauty, and the like" (see also Cicero, *Inv.* 2.59.177; *Rh. Her.* 3.6.10). "Health," he continues, "is productive both of pleasure and of life, and therefore is thought the greatest of goods" (*Rhet.* 1.6.10, 1362b). As we have previously noted, the authors of progymnastic treatises considered "health" one of the praiseworthy "deeds of the body," along with beauty, strength, agility, and might.

Hermogenes: "beauty, stature, agility, might"

Aphthonius: "beauty, swiftness, strength"

Theon: "health, strength, beauty, quick sensibility"

"Health," then, is usually described and evaluated as an elite and aristocratic value. It was cultivated by gymnastic exercises in the formal education of the polis elite. These were the persons destined for civic roles, such as warriors or statesmen. The right ordering of the body signaled to some an ordered relation of a person to society (Plato, *Resp.* 4.444B). Thus when Paul is presented as a person who enjoys a "good state of body," this constitutes a praiseworthy characteristic indicative of his social status as *politês* of the polis of Tarsus, and the gymnastic training such status entailed. This might well be an elaboration of Paul's own claims in 1 Cor. 9:24–27 that he was schooled in the athletic exercises common to the gymnasium.

Meeting Eyebrows

A commonplace among the ancients, we noted, was that the eyes are the windows of the soul (Cicero, *De legibus* 1.26–27; Quintilian, *Inst. Orat.*

11.3.75). They are the gauge by which one can read a person's sense of honor (Aristotle, *Problems* 31, 957b, 183). The eyebrows, too, are a source of characterization because "they mould the expression of the eyes and determine that of the forehead" (*Inst. Orat.* 11.3.78). Living creatures express emotion and character in the upper part of the face when they contract, raise, or smooth the eyebrows. When the brow is knitted (*synophyomai*), the face expresses frowning (Euripides, *Alc.* 777). Hence, according to some authors "meeting eyebrows," which result from an action of the face, suggest a person easily vexed or hard to please (Ps.-Aristotle, *Physiognomics* 812b, 25).

However, when the eyebrows naturally meet, we should expect a different character. In several places, portraits of warriors contain "meeting eyebrows" (*synophrys*). Suetonius presents Augustus in this way: "His teeth were wide apart, small and ill-kept; his hair was slightly curly and inclining to golden; his eyebrows met" (*The Lives of the Caesars* 2.79.2). Philostratus likewise presents a young Celtic warrior as a figure with "bushy eyebrows," which "met as though they were one" (*Lives of Sophists* 552; see also Dio Chrysostom, *Or.* 33.53). A radiant young maiden is described as having dark black eyebrows that practically meet (*Anacreontea* 16.16; see also Theocritus, *Bucol.* 8.72). Our data indicate, then, that "meeting eyebrows" might suggest either beauty (Malherbe 1986, 173 n.23) or manliness. In the case of Paul, it would seem that the description of him as a person with "meeting eyebrows" was intended to suggest manliness, especially when coupled with other courageous features, such as his crooked legs.

Nose Somewhat Hooked

Noses, when described, are contrasted either as "hooked" (*grypos*) or "snub" (*simos*) noses. Thus, in passing Aristotle remarks:

> The aquiline [*grypotês*] and the snub [*simotês*] nose not only turn into normal noses by not being aquiline or snub enough, but also by being too violently aquiline or snub arrive at a condition in which they no longer look like noses at all. (*Rhet.* 1.4.12, 1360a)

Plato adds an interpretative element to this by calling the snub nose "piquant" (*epicharis*), but the hooked nose "right royal" (*basilikon, Resp.* 5.474D; see Pollux, *Onomasticon* 2.73). In Xenophon's *Cyropaedia,* although a small man is told to marry a small woman, a man with a hooked nose (*grypos*) is told to wed a woman with a snub nose (*simê*), for "[y]our own nose is so hooked; and hookedness (*grypotês*), I assure you, would be the proper mate for snubbiness (*simotêta*)" (7.4.21). In the small sampling of documents we possess, males tend to have hooked noses, but females snub ones (see Terence, *Self-Tormentor* 1061). When Ps.-Aristotle examines animal noses, he characterizes them accordingly:

Those that have thick extremities to the nostrils are lazy; witness cattle. Those that have a thickening at the end of the nose are insensitive; witness the boar. Those that have a sharp nose-tip are prone to anger; witness the dog. Those that have a circular nose-tip, but a flat one, are magnanimous; witness the lions. These that have a thin nose-tip are bird-like; but when it is somewhat hooked [*epigrypon*] and rises straight from the forehead they are shameless; witness ravens; but those who have an aquiline [*grypên*] nose with a marked separation from the forehead are magnanimous; witness the eagle. (*Physiognomics* 811a, 28–38 Loeb)

Thus the human nose described as "aquiline" (literally, "eagle-like") might suggest to the ancients just that, the eaglelike quality of magnanimity. In general, then, it seems that a "hooked" nose denotes a male described as handsome and virtuous, whereas the man with a snub nose is simian and shameful.

Yet Paul is not said to have a "hooked" nose, so much as a "long nose." The term that describes his nose is not *grypos* or *epigrypos* but *epirrhinon,* which the dictionary translates as "with a long nose" (Liddell, Scott, and Jones 1968, 654). This same term occurs in Pseudo-Lucian's description of a person similar to Paul:

I was met by a Galilean with receding hair and a long nose [*epirrhinos*], who had walked into the third heaven and acquired the most glorious knowledge. (*Philopatris* 12, Loeb)

Yet, if the choice of noses is either snub or hooked, then Paul in *The Acts of Paul* should be thought of as having the latter, another index of his manliness, even of his generosity.

Full of Friendliness

This translation of *charitos plêrês* as "full of friendliness" does not capture all that is culturally encoded here. Minimally Paul appears physically "attractive" to those who look at him, which is a common meaning of *charis* or "grace" (Homer, *Odyssey* 2.12 and 6.237; Prov. 3:22; 4:9; Sir. 26:13). Thus the Israelites are said to have found "favor" or "pleasantness" in the eyes of the Egyptians (Exod. 3:21; 11:3; 12:36). "Beauty," of course, is a relative thing. Aristotle described the beauty appropriate to the three states of a man's life. In a young man, beauty means athletic ability: "the most beautiful are naturally adapted for contests of strength and speed." But for a man in his prime, "beauty is fitness for the exertion of warfare." And finally, for an old man, beauty means sufficient strength to do what is necessary and freedom from deformities (*Rhet.* 1.5.11, 1361b).

But this particular turn of phrase probably suggests that a pleasant exterior reflects a virtuous or pleasant character. Biblical authors, for example, often describe persons as "full of" either virtue or vice. Elymas, the magician, is "full of all deceit and villany" (Acts 13:10; see Sir. 1:30; 19:26); other persons are said to be "full of rage" (Isa. 51:20; Acts 19:28) or "full of wickedness" (Nahum 3:1; Ezek. 7:23; Job 10:15). Yet people might be filled with virtue: Jesus is described as "full of grace and truth" (John 1:14), and Josiah's heart is "full of godliness" (*eusebeias,* 1 Esdras 1:23).

The presentation of Paul in *The Acts of Paul* seems to have much in common with that of Stephen in Acts 6. Both are said to be "full of" something praiseworthy: Paul is full of "grace" or pleasantness, and Stephen is "full of" "wisdom" or "grace and power." Both, moreover, are said to have "the face of an angel," that is, of the sky servants of God:

Paul   "Now he appeared like a man, and now he had the face of an
              angel." (*The Acts of Paul,* 3:3)

Stephen   "the Council saw that his face was like the face of an angel."
              (Acts 6:15)

The point is that an "angel face" has little to do with the chubby cherubs of traditional Christian devotion. In antiquity, angels were divine sky servants, invariably male, carrying out the divine will with power and might (see Malina 1995a, 61–65). When visible, they shone brilliantly. In Israelite and much later Jewish writings, we learn that angels were like flames, made of the element fire in its purest form. These writings contain the mention of someone looking like an angel (Billerbeck 1922–1961, 2:665–66), which generally means a brilliant demeanor or a powerful appearance. In the vindictive book of Esther, for example, the heroine came before the Persian king and addressed him: "I saw you, my lord, like an angel of God. . . . For you are wonderful, my lord, and your countenance is full of grace" (15:13–14). When Paul is said to be "full of 'grace,'" this is probably intended to characterize him as an attractive person, radiating confidence and power.

Thus, to look "like an angel" would mean to look like God's sky servant, radiantly appealing, intent on a mission, and powerful of purpose. It could signal a person with a significant public role who conveys the impression of being the agent of a very powerful patron. For people who are "full of grace" can be said to enjoy divine benefaction and patronage. The mother of Jesus is "favored" (Luke 1:28), as is the deacon Stephen, who is "full of the holy spirit" (Acts 6:3), "full of faith" (6:5), and "full of grace and power" (6:8).

And we should not dismiss the note of "friendliness" in the phrase. The first thing that Paul does upon seeing Onesiphorus is to "smile" (*emeidiasen*). We note with some surprise that "smiling" is rarely noted in the

Bible. People "laugh," but that term seems to occur often in situations where people "laugh at" another, either in mockery or as a response to a challenge (Job 22:19; Ps. 51:6). "Laughter" is occasionally linked to deception (Sir. 13:6) and might require a lie to cover it up (Gen. 18:12–15). But there is no deception in Paul's "smile," in spite of the slander in *The Acts of Paul* 7:8 that he teaches deceptive and subtle words; for he is portrayed in contrast to the hypocritical flatterers, Demas and Hermogenes (3:1; 4:1).

DESCRIPTION AND CHARACTER: WHAT KIND OF PERSON IS PAUL?

What, then, would an ancient hearer or reader make of the description of Paul in *The Acts of Paul*? As what sort of person is he portrayed? At this point we wish to summarize the information about Paul that derives from the physiognomists' craft applied to the foregoing depiction of Paul's "character." We remain entirely dependent on our native Mediterranean informants for our categories and clues. From what the physiognomists describe as their project and from what they have presented in their works, we might fairly conclude what follows.

"An Ideal Figure"

Our ancient Mediterranean informants, the physiognomists, reasoned from what a person looked like to the type of character the person possessed. And those who used the physiognomists reasoned from behavioral traits that they knew or sought to portray to the way a person must have looked. This tight correlation between looks and personality was a truism in the cultural catalogue of the period. Robert Grant argues that the description of Paul was not dependent upon any known physiognomic manual but upon a popular description in poetry and rhetoric of a military figure and general named Archilochus (Grant 1982, 1–2). Archilochus, he has shown, was very well known by Greco-Roman as well as Christian authors in antiquity (Grant 1982, 2). In one sense, Grant begs the issue. Indeed Archilochus was a popular figure, perhaps a type, but what made his physical description suit him? Did "Archilochus" or his portrayer create the type, or was "Archilochus" portrayed and recognized according to an already established type? This study would suggest that Archilochus did not really look as he was described but rather was described according to what he was thought to have been and done. Writers and readers were schooled in stereotypes and learned to portray individuals according to the conventions of their times.

Yet Grant makes an important point, namely, that Paul is presented according to a type that would be readily recognized. But what type? We would argue that the portrait of Paul, while consonant with a general or military figure, is first and foremost that of a noble or ideal male. He is essentially masculine and virile according to the conventions of antiquity. But military prowess was only one aspect of maleness. By arguing this, we accept the parallel with Archilochus as valid for interpretation but would stress the typical expectations of a virile male, an ideal masculine figure.

The ancient historian Livy presents a description of Scipio that can support our interpretation of the figure of Paul. A figure in Livy's narrative awaits Scipio, but he has already formed in his mind a caricature of the great leader:

> The Numidian had already been filled with admiration for the man in consequence of his reported achievements, and had conjured up in mind *an ideal figure* [*speciem*], tall and stately. But greater still was the reverence that possessed him for the man in his presence; and while Scipio had great natural dignity [*natura multa maiestas*], long hair added charm, as did a general appearance not due to studied elegance, but *truly masculine and soldierly* [*virilis vere ac militaris*]. (*Ab Urbe Condita* 28.35.5–7, Loeb; emphasis added)

"Military" or "soldierly" appearance is itself one way of attesting to the maleness of a person. As we shall see, there are other ways of portraying the "ideal figure" of a male.

Ideal Male

We previously sketched the cultural expectations for an ideal male in antiquity. He is first and foremost a public figure who appears in public places (e.g., marketplaces, civic forums) and performs public acts (e.g., public speaking). Ideal public figures might be prominent in polis affairs—athletes or warriors and generals. Boldness and courage are the hallmark of a virile male, both of which are displayed in public in the various arenas where males gather and vie for honor.

Although Paul may share many traits with males whose maleness is linked with military prowess (see also 2 Cor. 10:3–5; Rom. 13:12), his maleness here is not dependent on things military. There are other traits mentioned and celebrated that suggest "virility" and "masculinity," which have nothing to do with "military" affairs. For example, Paul is an accomplished public speaker: he delivers a speech to the Christ-adherents assembled in Onesiphorus's house (*The Acts of Paul* 3:5–6), a forensic defense before the governor Castellius (3:17), and public addresses in a host of Greek and Asian poleis. Even the slanders of his enemies ("sorcerer," "deceiver," 3:15, 20) confirm that Paul is a powerful and persuasive public speaker.

Moreover, Paul's "maleness" is portrayed by his courage and confidence (3:18). Of "courage" (*andreia*) Aristotle says:

> To courage it belongs to be undismayed by fears of death and confident in alarms and brave in face of danger, and to prefer a fine death to base security, and to be a cause of victory. It also belongs to courage to labor and play a manly part. Courage is accompanied by confidence and bravery and daring, and also by perseverance and endurance. (*Virtues and Vices* 4.4, 1250a, 44–1250b, 6, Loeb)

When Thecla attends Paul chained in prison and facing judgment and possible death the next day, he is described as a man who "feared nothing, but comported himself with full confidence in God" (3:18). He plays his "manly part," as Aristotle says, by being "undismayed by fear of death"; he displays confidence (*parrhêsia*) as well as endurance. But Paul is hardly a warrior or general facing a battle, except in metaphorical terms. Furthermore, his confidence is a hallmark of citizens of ancient democratic *poleis* (Polybius, *Histories* 2.38.6). *Parrhêsia,* public confidence in speaking the truth, was becoming only to males, not to females (Aristophanes, *Thesmophoriazusae* 520–43) or male slaves (Demosthenes, *Or.* 9.6). Paul's courage and confidence, then, are a factor in his getting a hearing for his public proclamation of the gospel, that is, his fulfillment of a public role characteristic of an ancient, honorable male. He is a very "virile" and "masculine" person.

Paul, moreover, is portrayed as a heroic male who possesses the virtue of "justice" to a high degree. Among the ancients, "justice" consisted of three parts:

> The parts of justice are piety, fair dealing, and reverence: piety towards the gods, fair dealings towards men, reverence towards the departed. (Menander Rhetor, 1.361.17–25)

This statement reflects the old tradition found also in Aristotle:

> First among the claims of righteousness (justice) are our duties to the gods, then our duties to the spirits, then those to country and parents, then those to the departed; and among these claims is piety [*eusebeia*], which is either a part of righteousness or a concomitant of it. (*Virtues and Vices* 5.2–3, 1250b, 17–24, Loeb)

Paul knows and acquits himself of his duties to God when he speaks fearlessly on behalf of this God to the governor (3:18). Although we have no record of his fulfillment of his duties to his own family, Paul generously gives his outer garment to Onesiphorus's children to be sold to buy food for this refugee family, which once offered Paul lodging in their house (3:23). In terms of Paul's duty to the dead, we are presented with a splendid description of mourning for the presumably dead Thecla (3:23–24). Paul mourned Thecla, fasting for six days in an open tomb on the roadside, praying on bended knee for her. Whereas it belongs to a warrior or general to display "courage," it becomes an honorable citizen to be loyal and faithful in the execution of his duties, that is, to demonstrate "justice" or "righteousness."

What kind of person is Paul, then? He is clearly an ideal male figure. The composite of his various physical features suggests a certain kind of person. His benevolent eyes are fixed on goodness; his voice, with a conversational tone, evokes sincerity, kindness and truthfulness. His stature, although short, is that of an active person who accomplishes much; he has "balanced" humors, a sign of excellence. His shaved head denotes piety to God. His crooked legs, although ideal for a military figure, suggest a fearless person who stands his ground. Paul's body is in good shape and healthy, which may suggest a relatively high status associated with gymnastic training. His meeting eyebrows suggest manliness and beauty; his longish nose, virtuousness and handsomeness. Being full of grace indicates a favored person suitable for a public role. His physical features, then, indicate the kind of person he is: masculine, fearless, pious, virtuous, truthful, benevolent, but above all, fit for public life. This information may be intended to flesh out the claims made in the Acts of the Apostles that Paul was a Roman citizen (Acts 16:37; 22:25–28). Paul's "character" would indicate what a typical good citizen looked like and how he acted. The physiognomic description of Paul, then, serves as the only information about him in *The Acts of Paul,* yet by contemporary standards, it is more than adequate. This is all the ancients thought necessary to know about him, providing all the vital clues to the kind of person he was.

CONCLUSION: PHYSIOGNOMICS AND FIRST-CENTURY PERSONS

We have now presented a third source of native information for describing persons, along with the encomium and the forensic defense speech. Thus we have a substantial body of information from ancient Mediterranean informants about their standard manner of perceiving and describing a person. We conclude this chapter with further reflections on this third model and the kinds of information it provides. Admittedly physiognomics strikes modern, psychologically oriented Westerners as shallow and unreliable. But the ancients themselves obviously accepted it as an adequate cultural expression of their way of perceiving the world. It served imperial historians and artists with clues and categories for portraying the elite of the Greco-Roman world. It served public speakers and imperial officials with ways of gauging the people with whom they interacted. It was a requisite body of information used by physicians when dealing with their patients (Evans 1945).

Physiognomic knowledge is a way of knowing persons from how they look and how they act. It is knowledge based on externals and outward appearances. It requires that the knower accumulate an extensive set of stereotypes concerning the animal world and the characteristics of its inhabitants. If physiognomy were in vogue today, the main place to learn about people would be a zoo! Yet there were no zoos in antiquity. Physiognomists and the elites they instructed learned about animals anecdotally, that is, from stories, rather than from observation. Even when Romans later attended games in the arena, they knew how animals would act from the stories they learned. The ancients inevitably described what they observed to fit what they already knew, both of animals and of people who looked like various animals. If it is anything, traditional society is constant and certain in its constancy. Physiognomic knowledge was a priori knowledge, not open to adjustment or alteration.

Knowledge of the nature of anything, of course, reflects cultural presuppositions about how animals and persons functioned. In the Hellenistic period, "natural" (*kata physin*) refers to the cultural perception of the objective, unchanging situation as it has existed for as far back as anyone can remember (usually three generations, at most). Because the culture strongly valued stability and constancy, any deviation from what has always been perceived as the usual way was unnatural. It is the usual, customary way that is natural. Thus Paul would have nature (meaning culture) dictate hairstyles in Corinth (1 Cor. 11). And, as we have seen, Romans are superior by nature, while "barbarians" (bearded tribal peoples) and slaves (physically strong, sturdy non-Greeks and non-Romans) are inferior by nature.

The point is, physiognomists are concerned with the nature of human persons and this nature, which is known from externals, is unchanging, stable, and constant. Nature correlates with qualities that are internal, yet all internal qualities may be known rather easily from external traits and behaviors. Both internal qualities and the external features that mediate and reveal them are characteristic of types of beings. These types of beings get stamped with their characteristics due to their generation in fixed geographical locations and as a given gender. Animals belong to the same genus when they breed true. Thus, genus identity derives from generation, while species differences are due to geography. This is no less true for humans, although within their various geographically based types, they do have specific characteristics, discernible by comparison with animals.

Stereotypes and Collectivist Knowledge

Physiognomics is knowledge of collectivities. We might call it collectivist or "sociologistic" knowledge. It stands in sharp contrast to the psychological perspective we moderns bring to bear in understanding persons with their distinctive and individualistic biographies. For the first-century Mediterraneans, biography is not about personal development— that necessarily was the same for everyone born at the same social ranking and in the same location. Biography would concern itself about what befell a person, what happened to a person, or what was a person's fate. The distinctive features of a person's life are all outside the person and have an impact from the outside. These features really have no effect on the person; they do not change a person; they do not "make a person grow." Biography only demonstrates how a person stayed the same, endured, or persevered in face of outward influences.

In sum, human "nature" as defined by first-century Mediterraneans was the outcome of their commonly shared intellectual and cultural interpretation of human being. This interpretation derived from (a) current cultural assessments of *gender* and *gender-based* roles, coupled with (b) a stereotypical, essentially ethnocentric appreciation of a person's *place of origin,* along with (c) the perceived quality of the primary *groups* in which a person was always embedded. Thus we are describing a group-centered or sociocentric way of understanding a collectively oriented human being. Ancient Mediterraneans would claim to know another person quite well on the basis of this "sociologistical" model. For them, knowledge of a person's gender, place of origin, ethnic characteristics, and social status provided all the important information to know that person very well. Most of this knowledge was to be found in how a person looked and acted. None of these features changed, nor could they change. Hence, a person must have manifested from childhood all the adult traits one would later reveal, and to know an adult adequately, one could gain all useful knowledge from information about a person's childhood.

Individual persons were known primarily in terms of a set of group characteristics (generation, gender, geography, animal type, or physical type). The implied characteristics themselves offer a sampling of the ancient Mediterranean elite code of values and system of classification, that is, elite stereotypes. An individual might fit the stereotype expected of his or her family, gender, geography, animal type, and physical type, and thus easily communicate his or her group-shared character. On the other hand, a person may not fit the stereotype. This is also significant information because it indicates that the person in question is not measuring up to cultural and social expectations and so stands apart as a degenerate, a deviant from the group.

Distinctive Features of
Physiognomic Description

Physiognomic descriptions of persons in antiquity do not necessarily contain pieces of information different from those expressed through forensic defense speeches or encomia. All three agree on the importance of having knowledge of a person's origins (parents/ancestors and place of birth). All three presume that the new person will be a chip off the old block; the blood lines and family history contribute solid and reliable information about the identity of the latest expression of that heritage.

Nor do any of the three native Mediterranean models expect change and development in a person. Change in antiquity presumes some form of deviance. Ideally individuals would fulfill their destinies; they would live lives worthy of their inherited status. The child ideally is a miniature of the adult; it exhibits in childhood its breeding, which is predictive of its future. It will act according to its nature or essence.

Yet physiognomy differs from descriptions of persons in forensic defense speeches and from what ancients called "lives" (*bioi*) primarily in that it relies on explicit stereotypes as predictive of behavior. As the physiognomic tradition has often affirmed, function follows form, or behavior follows a given nature. If one knows the nature of a being, one knows how it will act. If it does not act according to its nature, then one must look for external influences, visible or invisible. A reader of *The Acts of Paul* knows all there is to know of Paul's "personality" from the initial description. The narrative that follows the description illustrates some, but by no means all, of the culturally worthwhile features of Paul. Readers could infer how Paul would act from the way he is described. And vice versa: If one knew what Paul did, one could readily describe how he had to look! All ancient iconography relies on this principle.

Both the way of knowing persons through stereotypes as well as the stereotypes on which physiognomy draws derive from the traditional lore, popular perceptions, and commonplaces of the ancient world. The collection of writings in the Bible as well as the literature of the Greco-Roman world describe persons in terms of that extensive and convenient body of stereotypes shared by ancient Mediterraneans.

What, then, do we know about persons described in such documents? From the native Mediterranean perspective, we know everything that the ancients deemed worth knowing. We are presented with an assessment of persons in terms of the cultural code of the group responsible for the document, according to the group's expectations of an honorable or shameful person, or both. What do we not learn about persons from this type of description? We learn virtually nothing about their idiosyncratic and distinctive individuality, their psychological development and uniquely personal history, their feelings and their uniqueness. For even their uniqueness is expressed in such stereotypes as virginal birth, divinity, or stellar apotheosis. We know nothing about them as distinct and autonomous individuals, precisely because "individualists" were either extremely rare in antiquity, so as not to be noted at all, or deemed socially deviant, hence to be discounted as not worthy of attention.

5

Ancient Mediterranean Persons in Cultural Perspective

Our journey has taken us through three native sources of information about how persons were perceived and portrayed in the ancient Mediterranean world. The authors of the progymnastic, rhetorical, and physiognomic literature serve us adequately as native informants concerning those features believed to be important to know about a person. Our journey through these documents, moreover, has more than adequately indicated that their authors lived in and attest to collectivist societies populated with nonindividualist, group-oriented persons. In contrast, modern Western societal forms stand at the individualist end of the spectrum, promoting individualist persons who view themselves and others "psychologically." As we have seen, however, collectivist, group-oriented, ancient Mediterraneans shared a scenario in which they viewed themselves "sociologically" in terms of generation, gender, and geography, with constant concern for public awards of respect and honor. This scenario suggests that (a) Paul and his audience perceived human beings quite differently from the way Euro-Americans do, hence (b) they thought quite differently about who a person might be and what might be the expected range of human behavior.

This suggestion should not be too surprising because even a number of biblical scholars who use the historical-critical method of biblical interpretation have regularly raised suspicions about the rather odd personality types described in biblical books. Those who have adopted literary methods find an even more esoteric range of persons in those documents. Yet we would contend that historical-critical and literary methods alone do not produce fair assessments of the persons depicted in the New Testament. We submit that to be a considerate and fair reader of Paul (or any other writer of the period), the modern Bible interpreter must acquire scenarios depicting what first-century native Mediterraneans considered "good knowledge of their status system and of what it takes to make it" (Ogbu 1981, 420). In this chapter, our goal is to describe such a scenario of the collectivist, group-oriented person of Paul's time and place (see Elliott 1993).

GROUP-ORIENTED PERSONS

To begin with, we note that all people the world over use the word "I," and those who use this word with meaning make reference to their "selves." But the dimensions of this "I" are not the same in all cultures. We follow Triandis in describing the "self" as all the statements a person makes that include the word "I," "me," "mine," and "myself." This description indicates that all aspects of social motivation are included in the self. Attitudes (e.g., I like . . .), beliefs (e.g., X has attribute X, in my view), intentions (e.g., I plan to do . . .), norms (my in-group expects me to do . . .), roles (my in-group expects people who hold this position to do . . .), and values (e.g., I feel that . . . is very important) are aspects of the self. Thus

> the self is coterminous with the body in individualist cultures and in some of the collectivist cultures. However, it can be related to a group the way a hand is related to the person whose hand it is. The latter conception is found in collectivist cultures, where the self overlaps with a group, such as family or tribe. (Triandis 1990, 77–78)

Thus "I" can be thought of either in terms of individualist or collectivist cultures. Depending on the type of social system in question, the word "I" will mean quite different things at each end of the individualist-collectivist spectrum.

Individualism, roughly speaking, means that individual goals precede the group's goals. In contrast, collectivism suggests that group goals naturally precede individual goals. As a cultural orientation, American individualism was, and still is, a way of being a person that is totally alien to all of the scenarios of the ancient Mediterranean world. Even in the contemporary world, individualism can be found only among the affluent, socially and geographically mobile segments of society. Individualist cultures as a whole, moreover, have developed only where Enlightenment values have permeated society and agriculture has become the occupation of the extremely few. The contemporary version of the individualistic self has emerged rather late in human history. It surely was not available in the first-century Mediterranean (see Duby and Braunstein 1988). Hence, to imagine persons of that time and place in terms of contemporary Euro-American personal experience would be highly inadequate, if not ethically questionable, to say the least. If we wish to be historically and culturally accurate in understanding collectivist models of personality, we must turn to native models of that understanding, which are adequately presented in the rhetorical, progymnastic, and physiognomic literature surveyed in this book. Failure to use the native descriptions of our ancient Mediterranean informants will inevitably result in errors of anachronism and ethnocentrism.

Perhaps to be complete, we ought to note that anthropological comparisons indicate that contemporary hunter-gatherer peoples likewise fall along the individualist side of the continuum, while modern agricultural primitives fall along the collectivist. So Triandis postulates stages in the emergence of individualist and collectivist understandings of person: (1) proto-individualism in ancient hunter-gatherer societies, (2) collectivism in agricultural societies (presumably from sedentarization that began some nine thousand years ago), (3) elite neo-individualism in the post-agricultural societies beginning in sixteenth-century Renaissance city-states, (4) and the common neo-individualism of the individualist cultures underpinning the Industrial Revolution. The primary reemergence of ancient individualism can be found in the neo-individualism that marks the industrialized regions of Europe and the United States. The United States—meaning immigrant, northern European United States—in nearly all examples is emphatically individualist, with all the typical traits of an exaggerated, overblown individualist culture.

In today's world, Triandis observes that 70 percent of the world's population remains collectivist, while the remaining 30 percent is individualist (1990, 48). As a matter of fact, individualism seems totally strange, esoteric, incomprehensible, and even vicious to observers from collectivist societies (note the critiques of Pope John Paul II 1993; 1995). Again, Triandis notes that what is of most importance in the United States, namely, individualism, is of least importance to the rest of the cultures of the world (1990, 50). Further, in the face of the modern anomaly of individualism, Clifford Geertz has tried to develop a definition of it as it appears in current U.S. usage. He describes that individual as

> a bounded, unique, more or less integrated motivational and cognitive universe, a dynamic center of awareness, emotion, judgment and action organized into a distinctive whole and set contrastively both against other such wholes and against its social and natural background. (Geertz 1976, 225)

He too notes that this way of being human is, "however incorrigible it may seem to us, *a rather peculiar idea* within the context of the world's cultures" (italics added).

Now the point of all the foregoing observations is to demonstrate that

any self that we might encounter in the New Testament, whether Jesus of
the Synoptic tradition or Paul or anyone else, should be understood as a
collectivist self or as a group-oriented person and *not* as an individualist
self. To understand the persons who populate the pages of the New Testament, we must *not* consider them as individualists. The personal, individualist, unique, self-concerned focus typical of contemporary North
American and north European experience was simply not available in
antiquity. And even if it had been, it would have been of no concern to
first-century Mediterraneans. Given their cultural experience, such self-
concerned individualism would have appeared deviant and detrimental to
other group members. It would have impaired the group's ability to survive. Behavior that indicated self-concern might be noticed but disdained
and negatively sanctioned. If those people were not individualists, what
or how were they?

For people of that time and place, the most elementary unit of social
analysis is not the individual person considered apart from others as a
unique being. Rather, it is the collectivist person, the group-embedded
person, the person always in relation with and connected to at least one
other social unit, usually a kinship group. Contrast, for example, how an
American and Paul might explain why they regard someone as abnormal.
First, the American will look to psychology, childhood experiences, personality type, or some significant event in the past that affects an adult's
dealing with the world. Biography in the United States tends to consist of
a description of an individual's psychological development in terms of singular events involving a unique person passing through the psychological stages of life. Hence, an "abnormal" person in the United States is assessed as one who is psychologically "retarded" or deviant because he or
she is "neurotic" or "psychotic" as a result of "having been an abused
child," and the like. The collectivist Mediterranean person, however, is
not psychologically minded but rather anti-introspective. "Character"
consists of outward features; hence, a person can be known by external
features alone. For elite ancients, as we have seen, basic personality derives almost entirely from generation, geography, and gender—from ethnic characteristics rooted in the water, soil, air, and sky native to the ethnic group. Being "abnormal" for them would mean not measuring up to
the social and cultural expectations or stereotypes that constitute the
identity of such persons. A Mediterranean such as Paul, for example,
would label someone as "abnormal" and mean by that "she was a sinner,"
"he submits to Satan," "he was possessed." Such designations of abnor-
mality indicate that "the person is in an abnormal position because the
matrix of relationships in which he is embedded is abnormal" (Selby
1974, 15). The problem is not within a person but outside a person,
namely, in faulty interpersonal relations. There really is nothing psycho-

logically unique, personal, and idiosyncratic going on within a person at all. All people in a family (generation) and in a distinctive polis or region (geography) are presumed to have the same experiences and very similar qualities. If any distinctions hold, they are regional and gender based, as we have seen.

Thus we might paraphrase Geertz and suggest the following definition of a group-oriented or collectivist person as follows:

> Our first-century person would perceive himself or herself as a distinctive whole *set in relation* to other such wholes and *set within* a given social and natural background; every individual is perceived as embedded in some other, in a sequence of embeddedness, so to say. (Malina 1993b, 68)

This abstract notion of embeddedness has been clearly expressed in the remark of Plutarch, which we cited earlier in this book:

> The nurse rules the infant, the teacher the boy, the gymnasiarch the youth, his admirer the young man who, when he comes of age, is ruled by law and his commanding general. No one is his own master, no one is unrestricted. (Plutarch, *Dialogue on Love* 754D, Loeb)

"No one is his own master!" Further, this might be illustrated by the value placed on concern for others in one's in-group:

> Our sacrifices are not occasions for drunken self-indulgence—such practices are abhorrent to God—but for sobriety. At these sacrifices prayers for the welfare of the community must take precedence over those for ourselves; for we are born for fellowship, and he who sets its claims above his private interests is specially acceptable to God. (Josephus, *Against Apion* 2.195–96, Loeb)

Plutarch and Josephus aptly illustrate what we mean by a collectivist person "set in relation" to others and "set within" a given social background. Thus we describe such persons as strongly group-oriented or group-embedded persons. These are persons who define themselves almost exclusively in terms of the groups in which they are embedded. Their total self-awareness emphatically depends on such group embeddedness.

When we surveyed the progymnastic, rhetorical, and physiognomic writings and analyzed the presentation of Paul in light of the native models of person in those writings, we worked at a very concrete level. Now we step back from those native models and reflect in a more abstract and general fashion on the kind of person we have identified as typical of Mediterranean antiquity, the group-oriented or group-embedded person. What follows is inevitably less vivid and detailed than the previous, document-based analysis. We still draw, however, on the native models and ancient data about Paul in what follows to provide an anthropological profile of that same group-oriented person.

Embeddedness

We have frequently observed that ancient Mediterranean people identified and defined themselves as situated and embedded in various other
persons with whom they formed a unity of sorts. Embeddedness is a
social-psychological quality describing that dimension of group-oriented
persons by which all members of the group share a common perspective.
This means that the individual person shares a virtual identity with the
group as a whole and with its other members. The individual does not
sense a division or opposition between himself or herself and the group
in which he or she came to be embedded, usually by socialization following birth. A group-embedded person may be separated from the group,
but that person carries within values and voices that echo many years after the person might be transplanted to some new location. Previously we
suggested the following example: the formation and thorough enclosure
of the person in the social reality of the group might perhaps be likened
to the formation and enclosure of an embryo in the womb, but in this instance, life in the "womb" is a mode of social-psychological being in the
group.

If we were to inquire about what held such groups together, we would
find that their social glue was a version of what we would call loyalty or
solidarity or group attachment ("love"), and was symbolized by blood,
birth, or fictive birth. Ancient Mediterraneans considered themselves embedded in a range of in-groups with varying degrees of loyalty: in family,
fictive family (teacher and disciple, faction, work group, patronage), village, polis, and the like. Let us look more closely at the range of such
groups.

Family

Family (or kinship) refers to that social institution concerned with naturing and nurturing human beings. As far as we know, all societies deal
with the social meaning of the biological processes of reproduction and
its outcomes. All societies are much concerned with the subsequent social support humans require for a meaningful existence, from birth to
death. "Family" or "kinship" in all of its forms derives from distinctive cultural interpretations of those biological processes and those outcomes.
The dominant and focal social institution for most people in the first century was the family, whether the immediate patriarchal household of father, mother, married children, unmarried children, slaves, and servants,
or the imperial patriarchal household at the center of the *oikoumene,* or
fictive kin groups such as burial clubs. Males, for example, are known in
terms of their father and his extended family. Note that when people are

first introduced in New Testament documents, we commonly read that they are the "son of so-and-so":

Simon, son of John (Matt. 16:17)

James and John, sons of Zebedee (Matt. 4:21)

Levi, son of Alphaeus (Mark 2:14)

Bartimaeus, son of Timaeus (Mark 10:46)

Although Jesus' genealogy serves a variety of purposes, it primarily functions to proclaim his embeddedness in the clans and traditions of Israel (Matt. 1:1–16; see Malina and Rohrbaugh 1992, 24–26). In fact, one of the dominant self-describing terms of the Jesus of the Fourth Gospel is his insistence on being son of God, who is his Father (John 2:16; 3:35; 5:17; 6:57; 8:16; 10:15; 12:49). Identity, however, resides not just in one's father but in one's father's father, their clan, and ultimately in the etiological ancestor of the extended family (see Hanson 1989). John the Baptizer's identity greatly depends on appreciation of the fact that his father is a priest of the division of Abijah and his mother a daughter of Aaron (Luke 1:5). Barnabas is a Levite (Acts 4:36); Paul, a Benjaminite (Phil. 3:5). The acknowledged father of Jesus, Joseph, is of the house and family of David (Luke 1:27). For different reasons, it is important for Gentiles to be labeled as the "offspring of Abraham" (Romans 4; Galatians 3), as well as for Judeans to claim Abraham as their father (John 8:33, 39). Membership, protection, and other benefits can be rightfully claimed on the basis of such kinship.

Similarly, females are known in terms of another person, generally a male member of their family. First, a female is embedded in her father's family and so is known in relation to him:

Rebekah, daughter of Bethuel (Gen. 24:24)

Judith, the daughter of Beeri the Hittite (Gen. 26:34)

Aseneth, the daughter of Potiphera, priest of On (Gen. 41:45)

Zebidah, the daughter of Pedaiah of Rumah (2 Kings 23:36)

Nehushtah, the daughter of Elnathan of Jerusalem (2 Kings 24:8)

But when married, females then become embedded in their husbands:

Milcah, the wife of Nahor (Gen. 24:15)

Anah, the daughter of Zibeon, Esau's wife (Gen. 36:14)

Abigail, the widow of Nabal of Carmel (1 Sam. 30:5)

Joanna, the wife of Chuza (Luke 8:3)

Aquila, with his wife Priscilla (Acts 18:2)

Herodias is known to us as the wife of two men, first Philip and then Herod (Mark 6:17).

A household in antiquity certainly differed from the typical nuclear family common in the United States. It included married sons and their wives and families, as well as a host of slaves, servants, and retainers. Moving up the social ladder, households would correspondingly contain a greater variety of people needed for its proper functioning. The "household of Caesar" (Phil. 4:22) comprised a host of civil servants, bureaucrats, slaves, and the like. In the eyes of the ancients, a "household" was the normal kinship group. It formed the primary grouping in which persons were embedded. Yet there were other groups patterned after the household, which we might call fictive kin groups or fictive family.

Fictive Family

The followers of Jesus described themselves as a household, for example, "the household of faith" (Gal. 6:10). We would call their grouping a fictive family. Such a fictive family is unlike a normal family in that it is not based on "naturing" or biological reproduction. Rather, it is concerned with "nurturing" or social support, concern, interest, help, and the like. Consequently, "fictive family" in antiquity designates a group that has the structure and many of the values of a patriarchal family: a central person who is like a father, with members who treat each other like siblings. The teacher, faction founder, head of a trade guild, or patron of a club (collegium) had the father role, while the disciples, faction followers, and clients were like siblings. Through discipleship, faction membership, and clientelism, a person entered another, secondary set of kinlike relationships.

Thus, early Christian groups constituted fictive families or fictive kin groups. They were a "household of faith" (Gal. 6:10) and addressed one another as "sister" and "brother" (see Mark 3:31–35). A bishop who could honorably manage his own household was thereby qualified to preside over the household of the church (1 Tim. 3:4–5). Comparable fictive-family identity would describe association in other groups, such as the Pharisees' *haburah,* a close-knit group of companions. In antiquity, fictive families were significant groupings in which persons found themselves embedded. We consider several more such fictive kin groups.

Teachers and Disciples

Teachers and disciples formed another set of fictive kinship relations. For the relation of teachers and disciples was very much like that of father and son. Disciples were subsequently known as the followers of the teacher in question. We saw in regard to the encomium and the forensic defense speech that "education" was really about formation in humanity, and its goal was socialization, one of the chief goals of families. Thus, education constituted an important piece of information about a person, for it indicated whether that person was in fact trained in a group's understanding and appreciation of virtue and honor. Just as Luke was quick to point out that Paul was a disciple of Gamaliel (Acts 22:3), so other ancient persons were identified in terms of their mentors or teachers. For example, Achilles was the student of Chiron; Alexander, of Aristotle; and Cicero, of Posidonius. The same pattern emerged after the New Testament period in later Pharisaic scribalism, called rabbinism. Not only did disciples study with specific teachers, but they thereby entered certain gatherings or groups of disciples called "schools," thus taking on the identity, ideas, and behavior of the tradition emerging from such a "school." By doing this, an individual person's identity was encapsulated in group identity. To know the teacher or mentor was to know the disciple.

Factions and Coalitions

When we consider a person's membership in a faction or coalition, we consider another area of embeddedness. Richard Horsley and John Hanson have called our attention to groups at the time of Jesus that clustered around social-crisis leaders called "prophets" and around persons with plans for Israel's social restoration called "messiahs" (1985, 110–34, 160–89). Various figures recruited followers to join them, such as Theudas (Acts 5:36), Judas the Galilean (Acts 5:37), and a certain Egyptian (Acts 21:38). John the Baptizer obviously gathered a large group of followers, among whom was Jesus. There even seems to have been some competition and rivalry between John's disciples and those of Jesus (see Mark 2:18 and John 4:25–30). Such groups, recruited by a central person for some specific purpose, are called factions. Factions are types of coalitions that generally disappear once the purpose for which they were formed is realized (Malina 1988b, 14–16). Given different recruiters, or different purposes, or both, we might expect disputes among factions.

We hear of competition between two factions in the synagogue: one group acclaims itself as "disciples of Moses," in opposition to another group who are "disciples of Jesus" (John 9:28). The New Testament, of course, contains many references to members of groups such as the Pharisees, Sadducees, or Herodians. Although we occasionally know the name of this or that Pharisee (e.g., Nicodemus, John 3:1), the ancient writers thought it sufficient simply to indicate that this or that person was a Pharisee (Mark 7:1; 10:2; Luke 7:36; 11:37; 18:10). The point is that people recruited into factions or other coalitions became embedded in them to such an extent that they took their major identity as disciples or followers of the central personage of the group. Jesus, of course, is a case in point. At times it seems that Paul also expected the members of his churches to act in the same way, that is, to consider themselves as his disciples. After all, he claimed to be their "father" (1 Cor. 4:14–15; 2 Cor. 11:3) and "founder" (1 Cor. 3:10).

In this regard, it would be interesting to pursue references in the New Testament to "Herodians" (Mark 3:6; 12:13). Were these members of a monarchist group that supported the interests of the Herodian family? What of "the synagogue of the Freedmen, and of the Cyrenians and of the Alexandrians, and of those of Cilicia" (Acts 6:9)? Are these people gathered together and identified in terms of shared language or colonial solidarity or some other specifying feature? The point is that collectivist persons tend to form few but abiding in-group relations and to take their identity from such relationships.

Work Groups, Collegia, and Synagogues

A fourth area of embeddedness might be one's work group or an association of similar tradesmen. This should be immediately evident from the way persons are identified in the New Testament:

Simon and Andrew, fishermen (Matt. 4:18)

Zacchaeus, tax collector (Luke 19:2)

Simon, a tanner (Acts 10:6)

Lydia, a seller of purple goods (Acts 16:14)

As Rohrbaugh has shown (1991b, 125–49), when artisans and merchants were allowed in a polis, they tended to live together in the same quarter and on the same street. Paul, for example, sought lodging with other workers of leather (Acts 18:3). Silversmiths, who presumably lived together in a certain quarter of Ephesus, united as a group against Paul (Acts 19:24–27). These tradesmen and artisans gathered together to form their own associations, such as burial organizations and dining clubs (collegia), ethnic social-aid groups (synagogues), and the like. The ancient world was populated with many types of groups and associations gathered around specific crafts and trade. Sons were socialized to learn their fathers' trade, with its shared viewpoints and social relations. Thus, when we know the trade of an individual, we know a significant piece of information about him. This presumes, however, that we know the cultural meaning of being such an artisan or tradesman.

Patron and Clients

People might also be embedded in a web of patron-client relationships (see Elliott 1987; Malina 1988b). Because a person received goods, influence, or other favors from a patron, he or she became a client and was then known as "the friend of so-and-so." In return for favors received, the client owed loyalty and commitment. The accusation against Pilate in John's description of Jesus' degradation ritual makes mention of this feature: "If you release this man, you are not Caesar's friend; every one who makes himself a king sets himself against Caesar" (John 19:12). The core of Pilate's identity, then, rests in his being known as Caesar's loyal client, that is, his "friend."

The U.S. myth of the Western frontier idealizes American independence and individualism. But nothing could be more foreign to the first-century Mediterranean, where individuals were constantly reminded that they stood in some sort of dependent relationship, whether to parents, landlords, kings, gods, or God. When ancient Mediterraneans speak of "freedom," they generally understand the term as both freedom from slavery to one lord or master, and freedom to enter the service of another lord and benefactor (Malina 1978, 62–76; Martin 1990, 22–35). For example, individuals are reminded that in regard to their own selves, "you are not your own" (1 Cor. 6:19). The sense of actually belonging to another, meaning that another person directs and determines what one does, is expressed in various ways. Paul insists that the Corinthians "were bought with a price" (1 Cor. 6:20; 7:23). This means that through Christ Jesus, individuals are now property of God: they are his slaves. In other places Paul stresses how individuals are freed from being slaves of sin and death and have become slaves of God, slaves of righteousness (Rom. 6:16–22). Although the language of freedom is used, adherents of Christian groups become free to join the service of a faithful and noble Lord. In fact, the premier confession of the very prophet of freedom is "Jesus is Lord" (Rom. 10:9; 1 Cor. 12:3; Phil. 2:11). A "lord" in the ancient world was a person who had total authority and control over another person and everything that other person had. Of course, to recognize another as lord is to express one's total embeddedness in that person. Moreover, Paul himself is always "slave" or "servant" of God or "steward of God's mysteries." Freed from slavery, individuals become the clients of a new patron; they are embedded in a new set of social relationships, which defines their identity.

This same point can be illustrated by reference to the way ancient biographies describe a person's behavior as fulfilling stereotypical roles with no particular attention paid to psychological developmental stages apart from raw physiological growth periods, such as childhood and adulthood (1 Sam. 2:26; Luke 2:52). What is important is the influence exerted on the persons in question either by their *genius,* or patron spirit, or by an enemy spirit. A Mediterranean such as Paul ascribes failures in his behavior to the influence of an evil power over him: "Satan hindered us" (1 Thess. 2:18). Other people violate all social norms of behavior because they are under the power of an "unclean spirit" (Mark 5:2–5). Josephus tells us that in a battle outside Bethsaida Julias, his horse, stumbled in a marshy spot, and he broke his wrist: "And my success on that day would have been complete had I not been thwarted by some demon" (*The Life* 402, Loeb).

The Polis

For elite males it seems that next to the kin group, the prevailing awareness of group embeddedness was situated in their membership in the polis, that is in their being a *politês* (a "citizen" of that social unit). Paul of Tarsus, Philo of Alexandria, and the like, are all instances of such designations. Obviously the significance of the person in question derives from the significance of the polis. As we noted previously, nonelite village people, such as Jesus of Nazareth, do not have the exalted aura of "citizen"; hence they derive their honor from family or occupation, as previously described. But others, such as Paul, are to be valued more highly because they were born in a "metropolis" or in "Tarsus, no low-status city." For as we have seen, geography is a primary contributor to the identity of a person, along with gender and generation.

Socialization, Tradition, and Loyalty

Group-oriented persons must in some way assimilate the code of behavior governing the roles and statuses of the geographic group in which they were embedded. This process of assimilation is what handing on traditions is about. In collectivist cultures, tradition is of paramount concern.

Deference to the group, admission of its past greatness, and confession of the superiority of its ancestors are all evident in the reverence given to what the Romans called the *mos maiorum,* the customs of the ancestors. Roman ancestors were called *maiores natu,* those greater than us by the fact of birth. Romans, like collectivist peoples in general, were culturally constrained to attempt the impossible task of living up to the traditions of those necessarily greater personages of their shared past. The traditions handed down by former members of the group are presumed valid and normative. Forceful arguments might be phrased as: "We have always done it this way!" *Semper, ubique, ab omnibus!* ("Always, everywhere, by everyone!") "The old ways are the best ways." This would be true of ideas, social structures, cultural values, as well as crafts and trades. While there were some significant technical innovations, these were considered of little social interest in the first century.

Paul appeals to just this point when he prefaces his accounts of the Eucharist (1 Cor. 11:23) and the resurrection (15:3) with an appeal to traditional authority, "I hand on . . . what I received." He expects the church to "maintain the traditions even as I have delivered them to you" (1 Cor. 11:2), and he is critical of behavior that flouts them (1 Cor. 14:33–36). The Pharisees on occasion criticize Jesus precisely because he did not adhere to the "tradition of the elders" (Mark 7:3–5; see Malina 1988a; Neyrey 1988c; Pilch 1988; Hanson 1993). Hence, we find the exhortation to "stand firm and hold to the traditions which you were taught by us, either by word of mouth or by letter" (2 Thess. 2:15; see 3:6). Likewise, the chief duty of Timothy is "follow the pattern of the sound words which you have heard from me" and "guard the truth" (2 Tim. 1:13–14; 3:14).

Evidently the group holds the past in great esteem. Anthropological studies of "time" indicate that people in the United States view time quite differently from those of other cultures, in particular peasant societies, past and present (Malina 1989, 4–9). Whereas we tend to be future oriented, they give corresponding value to the past. Rituals and ceremonies, for example, function in such cultures to confirm the values and structures of the past and make them relevant in the present (Malina 1986a, 140–43; 1994c; Neyrey 1995, 200–201). The preferred model of time in the ancient world was one of social devolution, with the distant past imagined as the golden age, succeeded by a silver age, a bronze age and the like (see Aratus, *Phenomena* 36–136). The best of all times existed in the distant past and everything subsequent has been degenerating, coming apart. In contrast, moderns might be said to espouse a developmental model in which everything is evolving toward some future perfection ("It's getting better all the time," as the popular song has it).

The value placed on the greatness of the past and on constant tradition shows up in the repeated injunction that disciples imitate their masters. Paul tells the Corinthians, "Be imitators of me as I am of Christ" (1 Cor. 11:1). Paul himself imitates Christ by embodying the hymn quoted in Philippians (2:6–12). Like Jesus who gave up equality with God in obedience to the deity, he forgoes the former value found in the law and seeks only to be conformed to the dying and risen Jesus (Phil. 3:7–10, 17). Clouds of past witnesses in Hebrews 11 illustrate the meaning of "faith" for imitation, and incomparable Abraham is often held up as a model of faith in Galatians 3 and Romans 4. And of course, Jesus commands his disciples to be like him by "denying themselves." The ancient self was a collectivist self, an individual embedded in a family. Self-denial means leaving one's family, siblings, and land—the dearest features of a first-century person's life. This is what taking up the cross (or yoke) and following Jesus entails (Mark 8:34; see Malina 1994b). The disciples must be like the master, either in acts of service (John 13:13–16) or in imitation of the master's fate (John 15:18–20). The best one might hope for is to try to live up to the model presented, that is, the social expectations to which one is socialized. Group-oriented people, then, tend to be oriented to the past and to hope to embody the traditions of their ancestors. They strive to imitate those great ones and to live up to the expectations created by those past cultural figures.

Sanctions and Rewards:
Duties, Piety, and Virtues

The prevailing system of sanctions and rewards, of course, will manifest how individuals are embedded in others and how they are socialized into traditional roles and values. After all, it is sanctions and rewards that protect the process of socialization. What is of primary concern in this regard is the socialization of individuals into the values, duties, and piety of their respective kinship or fictive kinship groups. This area would form the general code of social formation or "education." Here we take up issues stemming from gender and generation, namely, the social expectations of gender identity and birth into a particular family or clan.

Duties

The majority of persons in ancient Mediterranean collectivist cultures did not have any rights in any modern legal sense. Human rights were a thing of the future, emerging in Western history during the Enlightenment period. But these ancient persons surely did have duties. Where roles and status are perceived as ascribed by God and part of "nature," these entail reciprocal social expectations. Because family is the dominant social institution of the ancient world, we consider only the kinship obligations into which persons are socialized. It comes as no surprise that sons and daughters, both of whom are embedded in their father, are enjoined to "honor" parents. The importance of this is manifested by its important place in the Ten Commandments: "Honor your father and mother" (Exod. 20:12; Deut. 5:6; Mal. 1:6; Eph. 6:1–3). Honor is manifested by obedience to one's father (Gen. 27:8, 13, 43; 28:7; Col. 3:21; Eph. 6:1) and by the support given an aged parent (Sir. 3:11–16). Alternately, the biblical authors censure all forms of disrespect to one's father and record a variety of ways in which this figure can be dishonored: cursing one's father (Exod. 21:17; Lev. 20:9; Prov. 20:20; 30:11); shaming him (Prov. 28:7); dishonoring him (Deut. 27:16; Mic. 7:6); robbing him (Prov. 28:24); mocking him (Prov. 30:17); striking him (Exod. 21:15); and disobeying him (Prov. 5:13). A father is particularly shamed by a rebellious son (Deut. 21:18–21) and by an unchaste daughter (Deut. 22:21; see Gen. 19:31–35; Lev. 21:11, 19; and Deut. 27:20). It is the duty of children to treat a father honorably—in the specific ways in which that culture defined respect and honor. By the first century, lists of household duties formally expressed reciprocal duties among the various members of a family (Eph. 5:21–6:9; Col. 3:18–4:1; and 1 Pet. 2:13–3:7; see Elliott 1986, 66–73). A husband must treat his wife with the respect owed blood relatives, even though she may not be his kin. She in turn must show loyalty to the male in whom she is now embedded, transferring to him the loyalty formerly owed her father. Children are to obey their parents, in particular their fathers; and slaves must obey their masters. Needless to say, we would expect obedience to be greatly praised, and it is (Mark 14:36; Rom. 5:19; Phil. 2:7–8; Heb. 5:8). Thus duties, especially those that define roles within the primary institution of the family, were clearly articulated and inculcated.

Piety

As we saw earlier in this study in our discussion of what the ancients meant by "justice," one owed loyalty to the gods, one's parents, and the dead. Devotedness to these personages was labeled in Greek as *eusebeia* and in Latin as *pietas*. These words cover what we moderns generally call "religion." A religious, faithful, devoted person was *eusebês* or *pius*. Scholars regularly discuss eusebeia/pietas in terms of religious loyalty and devotion to the gods, but we focus on what the ancients surely considered of equal significance: religious devotion to elders, parents, and family. After all, ancient Mediterraneans did not learn how to separate family and religion, just as they never separated politics and religion (Malina 1986c, 1994c).

Performing one's duty to parents and family was no less *eusebeia* than that directed to the gods or God. This is recognized by authors such as Plato (*Resp.* 10.615C) and Lucian (*Somn.* 10), and is recorded in numerous ancient inscriptions (Moulton and Milligan 1976, 265; Foerster 1971, 175–85). In the New Testament, children and grandchildren are instructed to see to the needs of their widowed mothers and grandmothers; this devoted loyalty is called "piety" (1 Tim. 5:4). In a more general exhortation, the author of 2 Peter lists the ideal virtues a pious person should have, including "self-control, steadfastness, piety, brotherly affection and love" (1:6–7; see Neyrey 1993, 154–55). Where family looms as the major institution and where people are known in ways that replicate embeddedness in the family group, their respect for and devotion to the family is celebrated as a major virtue, piety.

Faithfulness, Loyalty, Altruism

We are so accustomed to translating the word *pistis* as "faith," referring to religious creed, that we tend to miss its basic meaning of "faithfulness" or "loyalty." Faithfulness and loyalty are owed to the basic personages in whom one is embedded, namely, God and one's kin group. Furthermore, given a person's embeddedness in family and other social groups and the constant awareness of prescribed duties toward those in whom one is embedded, it is not surprising to learn how concern for others, especially group members, is valued here. In this regard, we recall the previously quoted remark of Josephus that "sacrifices and prayers for the welfare of the community must take precedence over those for ourselves; for we are born for fellowship, and he who sets its claims above his private interests is specially acceptable to God" (*Against Apion* 2.195–96, Loeb). Faithfulness or loyalty, then, emerges as a distinct value among group-oriented persons.

Group orientation indicates that individuals should always "seek the good of the neighbor" (1 Cor. 10:24) and not pursue selfish objectives. "Selfish" objectives might be those dictated by one's *particular* group interest (for example, the good of one's immediate family) rather than larger group interests, such as the good of the whole clan or tribe. "Selfishness" here is not individualist selfishness but collectivist selfishness, an unwillingness to put other families before one's own! At Corinth, such group-oriented selfishness, which was rooted in the greater prestige and social rewards that individuals brought their in-group, seems to have bucked the sense of accountability to the larger group, either by an unseemly marriage (5:1–2), by eating proscribed foods (8:1–2, 7–11), or by self-indulgent behavior at the Eucharist (11:21–22). Paul points out how the incestuous marriage harms the group by sort of oozing out and permeating the reputation of the whole group, much like leaven permeates and ferments dough (5:6–8). And the unscrupulous eating of meats offered to idols causes scandal to some, destroying the weak person for whom Christ died (8:11). Promoting the interests of one's own in-group or advancing one's own status expectations, then, offends the larger group. Self-indulgent behavior at the Eucharist profanes the ceremony so much that "it is not the Lord's supper that you eat" (11:20). Other people at Corinth luxuriated in their charismatic gifts, a behavior Paul sought to moderate for the sake of the good of the group. Prophecy is better than tongues, for it "builds up" the group, whereas the speakers in tongues "edify" only their own in-group (14:3–4). Yet both prophecy and tongues should be regulated and made subject to controls for the sake of the larger group, its "edification" (14:26–33). Evidently group self-centeredness is the nemesis of the other-centered orientation that looks to the whole or larger group.

Embeddedness and Loyalty

We conclude this section, "Socialization, Tradition, and Loyalty," by recalling that first-century Mediterranean persons were fundamentally embedded in groups, primarily kinship and fictive kinship groups. As such, they were not individualists. Rather they were group-oriented persons living in collectivist cultures. As they went through the genetically based stages of psychological awareness, they were constantly shown that they existed solely because of and for the sake of the group in which they found themselves. Without that group, they would not have any identity (Foster 1961; Selby 1974). Such persons perceive themselves as always interrelated with other persons, while occupying a distinct social position both horizontally (with others sharing the same status, ranging from center to periphery) and vertically (with others above and below in social rank).

Group-oriented persons, moreover, internalize and make their own what others say, do, and think about them because they deem it necessary, if they are to be human beings, to live out the expectations of others. Such persons need to test this interrelatedness, which draws attention away from their own egos and toward the demands and expectations of others who can grant or withold reputation or honor. Group-oriented persons rely on others to tell them who they are ("Who do people say that I am?" Mark 8:27). Consequently, from this perspective, modern questions of "consciousness" (did Jesus know he was God? did Jesus have faith?; see Fitzmyer 1994, 85–87) make no sense. For such questions are posited with the freight of individualistically oriented persons in mind, and not in terms of the group-oriented persons of antiquity, who depend on others to tell them who they are, what is expected of them, and where they fit.

Thinking in Stereotypes

Persons socialized into group-oriented societies invariably make sense of other people by assessing them "sociologically" rather than "psychologically." In other words, people in collectivist cultures appraise others in terms of the stereotypes they share with their in-group. As we noted previously, this means that an individual person assesses everything on the basis of reasons, values, symbols, and modes of assessment typical of the group in which the person has been embedded. By contemporary Euro-American standards, such "sociological" thinking is essentially based on prejudice, because one thinks in terms of the prejudgments and biases, positive and negative, handed on by the group. One is never expected to question these prejudgments, and given social experience, even contrary evidence is selectively overlooked or considered nonexistent because it is absolutely impossible (like a "good Samaritan," a contradiction in terms, as in Luke 10:29–37). Such thinking is stereotypical thinking.

Stereotypes are general categories (such as food, clothing, society, and the like). Thinking in stereotypes is but another form of thinking in generalities, that is in rather inclusive conceptions. Stereotypes, in fact, condense reality into perceivable units because human beings cannot hold a wide range of details in mind at once. And human beings need to have reliable cognitive maps of the world in order to make sense of and interact with others. The process of socialization outfits human beings with the cognitive maps shared by their groups in order to make meaningful social, human living possible. Of course, with these cognitive maps, humans learn to assess and evaluate the territories involved. Stereotypes indicate that someone or something is honorable or shameful, approved or disapproved, normal or deviant. This is just what we saw in the previous chapter regarding gender expectations and geocentrism. While we may not wish to share the ancient Mediterranean prejudices inherent in their stereotypes (we surely have enough of our own prejudices), for the moment let us consider how stereotypes function for group-oriented people.

Experiencing life in terms of stereotypes means to approach everyday reality with its persons and things by using general conceptions rather than by taking time to construct customized designs. Stereotypes are like maps, recipes, models, or menus. Living by means of stereotypes is like touring a city by looking at a map rather than by visiting the actual city with its distinctive layout and architecture. It is like dining by reading a recipe rather than by actually eating the food prepared from a recipe. Stereotypes simplify real-world persons and groups, while allowing us to prescind from the rich reality that persons and groups actually evidence. Thus through stereotypes we approach persons in terms of what they presumably have in common with others of their group or category, while submerging any individual features they might actually have. We noted how gender, generation, and geography form the basis for stereotypical thinking in the physiognomic literature. Such stereotypical perceptions yield fixed or standard mental pictures that various groups commonly hold of each other. These standard mental pictures represent the expectations, attitudes, and judgments of those harboring the stereotypes. Because individuals find themselves inserted into various groups by birth, family ties, and the wider ranging links already forged by their elders, group-oriented personalities take group embeddness of human experience as primary. Such people find it overpoweringly obvious that they are embedded in groups, that they always represent the groups into which they have been inserted, and that other people are thus embedded, as well. The stereotypes group-oriented persons commonly use to describe themselves and others relate to that embeddedness. In what follows, we present some basic stereotypes by means of which first-century Mediterraneans understood themselves and others. These stereotypes are basically discernible from the negative or positive labels attached to a given group, place, trade, and the like.

Character Stereotypes

The physiognomic writings more than amply illustrate the stereotypical approach to persons characteristic of the ancient Mediterranean. Recall Aristotle's remark:

> Let us now speak of what ought to be the citizens' natural character. Now this one might almost discern by looking at the famous cities of Greece and by observing how the whole inhabited world is divided up among the nations. The nations inhabiting the cold places and those of Europe are full of spirit but somewhat deficient in intelligence and skill, so that they continue comparatively free, but lacking in political organization and capacity to rule their neighbors. The peoples of Asia on the other hand are intelligent and skillful in temperament, but lack spirit, so that they are in continuous subjection and slavery. But the Greek race participates in both characters, just as it occupies the middle position geographically, for it is both spirited and intelligent, hence it continues to be free and to have very good political institutions, and to be capable of ruling all mankind if it attains constitutional unity. The same diversity also exists among the Greek races compared with one another: some have a one-sided nature, others are happily blended in regard to both these capacities. (*Pol.* 7.6.1–2, 1327b, Loeb)

Fuller explanation of how the characteristics of various ethnic groups derive from the places they inhabit, the air they breathe, and the water they drink is clearly set forth in the Hippocratic corpus and becomes common knowledge among elites as well as points of honor among nonelites (see *Hippocrates* Air, Water and Places, 1.70–137).

Ethnic and Other Stereotypes

Over the course of time, certain ethnic groups or subgroups were labeled with some negative or positive trait, and these labels became common currency in the region. For example, Josephus describes the Tiberians as having "a passion for war" (*The Life* 352), and of the Scythians he says, they "delight in murdering people and are little better than wild beasts" (*Against Apion* 269). Cretans have become well-known prevaricators thanks to the negative stereotype recalled by the author of Titus (1:12). Alternately, Strabo throughout his *Geography* identifies characteristic traits of various peoples. Of one ethnic group he writes, "in the seamanship of its peoples . . . the Phoenicians in general have been superior to all peoples of all times" (16.2.23); of another, "this is a trait common to all the Arabian kings" that they do "not care much about public affairs and particularly military affairs" (16.4.24). Individual members of an ethnic group were presumed to share the traits of the group. To know one Greek, for example, is to know all Greeks, for it is quite proper to generalize on the basis of a sampling of one (Vergil, *Aen.* 2.65).

With their unsurprising ethnocentrism, ancient Mediterraneans divided the peoples of the world into "us" and "them." Greek writers in general spoke of "Greeks and Barbarians" (e.g., Strabo, *Geography* 1.4.9), whereas Paul the Judean spoke of "Judeans and Greek" (Rom. 1:16; 1 Cor. 1:24; Gal. 3:28; Col. 3:11) or "circumcised and uncircumcised" (Gal. 2:7–8). Such typing is found extensively in Acts 14:1; 18:4; 19:10, 17; and 20:21. Certain behavior followed from this stereotyping: "Judeans have no dealing with Samaritans" (John 4:9); "It is unlawful for a Judean to associate with or visit anyone of another nation" (Acts 10:28). What of the Latins? What did they think of the Greeks, whose civilization they deemed superior? In his book on slavery in antiquity, Patterson cites with approval the data amassed by classicists:

> The Greek classicist Nicholas Petrochilos has made a special study of Roman attitudes toward Greeks, and his findings fully suppport my argument. The Romans, he shows, soon developed a set of stereotypes about the Greeks, which centered on what they considered to be the six main failings of the Greek character: (1) *volubilitas,* a tendency to prefer formal facility in speech to substance; (2) *ineptia,* a proclivity for inappropriate or excessive behavior, a readiness to elaborate on subjects of which they knew nothing; (3) *arrogantia* and *impudentia,* related according to Cicero to "irresponsibility, deceitfulness and an aptitude for flattery"; (4) deceitfulness, singled out as a particularly unpleasant trait; (5) a weakness for excessive luxury and ostentation. But it was the sixth quality that the Romans most despised: *levitas.* Embracing "aspects of instability, rashness and irresponsibility," it connoted "absence of good faith, honor and trustworthiness" and was "a prominent element in the popular conception of Greek character." Cicero, in a celebrated case, tried to win support for his plea by impugning the credibility of the Greek witnesses on this basis, and Petrochilos comments that "*levitas* here is that lack of credibility which is the consequence of subordinating standards of honor and duty to personal and unworthy motives, and it is attributed by Cicero to the Greeks as a people." (Patterson 1982, 90)

Besides ethnic stereotypes, the ancients regularly evaluated others in terms of geography, trade, and social groupings. For example, Jesus and Paul are known by a geographic stereotype, the evaluation of which depends on the public perception of the place. Paul comes from an honorable place—"Tarsus, no low-status polis" (Acts 21:39)—but Jesus from a dishonorable one—"Can anything good come out of Nazareth?" (John 1:46). Poleis, moreover, were the residences of elites (Matt. 11:8; Luke 16:19); Judean peasants were derogatorily labeled by urban elites as *'am ha'aretz* (see Acts 4:13). Moreover, polis differs from polis in wealth, prestige, and the like, all of which would accrue to persons who lived there.

Furthermore, persons might be known by their trades, crafts, or occupations. People have fixed ideas of what it means to be a worker in leather, a landholder, a steward, or a worker in stone or wood. Only trouble could arise if an artisan displayed wisdom or performed mighty deeds that do not belong to the role of artisan (Mark 6:1–6; John 7:15).

Moreover, as we noted previously, people were evaluated according to their social groupings or factions, such as Pharisees or Sadducees or as Stoics or Epicureans (Neyrey 1990a, 129–34). Ancient readers would either know the content of this group stereotype or be provided with a brief summary of the term (Acts 23:6–8). Paul presumes such information when he identifies himself to the Philippians as a Pharisee (Phil. 3:5). By way of illustration, the essential information one needs to understand the label Pharisees or Sadducees can be reduced to a single issue: (a) "the Sadducees say there is no resurrection, nor angel, nor spirit; but the Pharisees acknowledge them all" (Acts 23:8; see Acts 4:1–2; Mark 12:18). Alternately, Mark records another stereotype of the Pharisees:

> For the Pharisees, and all the Judeans, do not eat unless they wash their hands, observing the tradition of the elders; and when they come from the market place, they do not eat unless they purify themselves; and there are many other traditions which they observe, the washing of cups and pots and vessels of bronze (7:4; see Matt. 23:25–26; Neusner 1976).

When explaining Sadducee and Pharisee, Josephus described them using the stereotypes of Epicureans and Stoics respectively (*The Jewish War* 2.162–65; *Ant.* 13.297–98; 18.12–17). Membership in such groups was not a matter of personal, individual choice. Rather it depended on group-oriented criteria such as (1) family or clan (Sadducees), (2) place and/or group of origin (Jesus's faction recruited in Galilee, in and around Capernaum; Pharisee settlements), (3) inherited craft/trade (scribes). Each of these groups, moreover, tended to associate only with its own, thus constantly reinforcing its evaluative stereotype of itself and others.

Stereotypes and Social Roles

We should examine one other set of stereotypes, namely, social roles. Social roles deal with recurrent social expectations. It was presumed that people with certain roles in society would carry out those roles in keeping with society's expectations. What roles ought we consider? Let us start with general roles in the broader society. Within the family, father and mother had clearly defined roles: the father was begetter and protector; and the mother, nurturer and provider. Readers are reminded of the brief discussion of the rights and duties of parents and children, mentioned earlier. Within the political arena, we know of the roles of kings, governors, proconsuls, and other municipal officials. Roman elite society was structured into a clear *ordo,* or series of roles and statuses; a comparable structure existed in ancient armies. Each person in these social structures was expected to fulfill a clearly defined set of social expectations. Likewise, in the temples of the various poleis we find highly differentiated roles, such as high priests, ordinary priests, and asiarchs, as well as a host of attendants who saw to the sacrifices, offerings, and the like. Even within *collegia* and other social associations, people had clearly defined roles. At a temple banquet for just one such group, the food was distributed in ways that confirmed the various roles and statuses of its participants:

> And when portions are distributed, let them be taken by the priest, the vice-priest, archibakchos, treasurer, boukolikos, Dionysos, Kore, Palaimon, Aphrodite, and Proteurythmos; and let these names be apportioned by lot among the members. (Smith 1980, 16)

When we turn to the specific society described in the pages of the New Testament, we first of all learn of many social roles: scribes, fishermen, carpenters, workers of leather, sowers, fullers, merchants of fine pearls, smiths, sailors, athletes, soldiers, architects, shepherds, potters, teachers, tax collectors, and so forth. As we learn about the classificatory system of the societies around the Mediterranean (Neyrey 1986b, 95–98; 1990b, 33–42; 1991, 286–88), we discover more about the social location of these people, where they stood in relation to one another, and what they were expected to do and not do (Neyrey 1994b, 86–87). For example, the priests and Levites in Luke 10:31–32 are living up to role expectations when they pass by the presumably dead victim of robbers to keep pure (see John 18:28). Martha asks Jesus to reprimand Mary, her sister, for failing to live up to her role (Luke 10:39–40). We might be tempted to think the centurion who builds a synagogue for local Galileans is stepping out of his role as officer of a foreign military force (Luke 7:4–5). However, when we consider that Romans did not "occupy" but saw their task as "civilizing" the Mediterranean basin, then we see that the officer properly acts according to typical patron-client expectations when he calls in his favor to the villagers by asking their intercession with Jesus on his behalf.

Some Conclusions

These are some of the more obvious social niches in which group-oriented people perceive themselves and one another. Conversely it is through such niches that they inform one another of their identities. Group-oriented personalities, then, take their identity from the social groups into which they have been inserted (i.e., generation and geography): as *son* of so-and-so (as first-born, third-born, and so forth), born to such-and-such *ethnic group,* in a particular *village,* in a specific *region;* and this person may belong to a specific *craft* or *party,* which is more often than not that of the father. Family, kin, and neighbors would feed back these clues to the group-oriented members of their circle, who in turn take from these clues a sense of identity and social worth, along with the particular roles and expected behaviors based on these positive stereotypes.

Consequently, group-oriented persons perceive themselves in terms of qualities specific to their ascribed status. They tend to presume that human character, as specified in unique groups and their individual components, is fixed and unchanging. Every social entity such as family, village, or polis would be quite predictable and so would the individuals embedded in and sharing the qualities of that family, village, or polis. For unpredictability derives from something or someone beyond the control of the predictable and unchanging human beings they know. Hence, people need not look within individuals for the sources of unpredictability. In other words, there was no reason to ascribe anything to personal and unique individual, psychological motives or introspectively generated reasons and motivations.

Moreover, because human beings have no control over their gender, geography, or generation, group-oriented persons tend to perceive existing roles and statuses within clans and families, as well as of individual members within them, as ordained by God or gods. It is important for U.S. readers to realize that the person responsible for the insertion of individuals into their specific family, ethnicity, village, region, craft, or party is the divinity. Just as a person's insertion into a marriage relation, based on parental selection of marriage partners, is due to God ("What God has joined together . . ." [Matt. 19:6]), so too all other dimensions of human social existence into which individuals are inserted are by no choice of their own. Paul, for example, intimates a similar social perspective when he asserts that the body has many parts; it is not all head or eye or hand. But its specific ordering is done by God, for "God arranged the organs in the body, each one of them, as he chose" (1 Cor. 12:18; see Neyrey 1986a). The social body is quite similar, "for there is no authority except from God, and those that exist have been instituted by God" (Rom. 13:1). Not a few modern historians speak of social mobility in the ancient world. Both the reality and possible extent of such mobility are highly questionable. Social mobility, as a rule, replicates physical mobility, and there was little of that in antiquity.

> In pre-modern populations, migration over long distances (between countries, or, in historical empires, between provinces) usually had slight impact since populations were largely sedentary. But internal migration over shorter distances, for instance between an urban center and the surrounding countryside, could play a major role in shaping the demographic characteristics of a population. (Bagnall and Frier 1994, 160)

People were tied to the place they were born by means of ties with people who actually "formed" those places. Territorial borders consisted of groups of people who populated a region. Physical location and social order were two sides of one coin. And because the social order, both theoretically and actually, is God's doing, it follows that there will be a built-in resistance to social mobility and to status and role changing. For if it pleased God to create so-and-so as third son of a farmer in such-and-such a place, this identity then becomes legitimated as the order of nature: "Only let everyone lead the life which the Lord has assigned to him and in which God has called him" (1 Cor. 7:17).

HONOR AND
SHAME—MALE AND FEMALE

In our estimation, first-century Mediterranean personality cannot be understood without a detailed consideration of the prevailing social sanctions used to gain compliance with social norms. All societies require a degree of conformity, if only to maintain minimal social order. Cross-culturally, the prevailing, internalized sanctions include anxiety, shame, and guilt. The fact is that all human beings are capable of experiencing anxiety, shame, and guilt. Social approval, equally available to all human beings, is experienced in the positive correlatives of this trio: a sense of security, a grant of honor, and a sense of innocence (see Augsburger 1986, 111–35). As a rule, internalized assessments of guilt and innocence are to be found in societies marked by individualist cultures. Mediterranean society has traditionally employed the experience of shame deriving from public disapproval as social sanction. Alternately it awards public praise as reward for laudable behavior. This reward of positive public acknowledgment constitutes a grant of honor. Honor and shame are the anthropological terms used to express the core native values of praise and blame; they mark the general pathways of praiseworthy and censurable behavior. We consider it essential to understand the pivotal role of honor and shame as they relate to one of the most important stereotypes in antiquity, namely, gender and cultural definitions of male and female (see Malina and Neyrey 1991a). Here we expand on the notions of gender discussed in regard to physiognomic literature in the previous chapter and mentioned in passing in this general view of a group-oriented person.

Cultural anthropologists regularly distinguish between sex (biological inheritance) and gender (cultural norms). Put simply, the individual human being learns how to be a gender-specific person, either a male or a female, from the family into which the individual is born and by whom she or he is socialized. To be a fair and considerate reader of the New Testament, one must necessarily discover and utilize the male and female stereotypes current in the cultural world of the first-century Mediterranean. These are the gender stereotypes into which men and women were socialized as boys and girls. For this purpose, we begin by citing remarks from several ancient Mediterranean informants, who consciously articulate culturally specific understandings of gender.

> Market-places and council-halls and law-courts and gatherings and meetings where a large number of people are assembled, and open-air life with full scope for discussion and action—all these are suitable to men both in war and peace. The women are best suited to the indoor life which never strays from the house, within which the middle door is taken by the maidens as their boundary, and the outer door by those who have reached full womanhood. (Philo, *Spec. leg.* 3.169, Loeb)

Modern anthropologists usually discuss this somewhat intricate division of the world into male/female and public/private in terms of "the moral division of labor." Modern theory in this case follows and illustrates quite closely ancient discussions of the same phenomenon. The following quotation from Xenophon elaborates on the cultural definition of male/public and female/private.

> Human beings live not in the open air, like beasts, but obviously need shelter. Nevertheless, those who mean to win store to fill the covered place, have need of someone to work at the open-air occupations; since ploughing, sowing, planting and grazing are all such open-air employments; and these supply the needful food. Then again, as soon as this is stored in the covered place, then there is need for someone to keep it and to work at the things that must be done under cover. Cover is needed for the nursing of the infants; cover is needed for the making of corn into bread, and likewise for the manufacture of clothing from the wool. And since both the indoor and the outdoor tasks demand labor and attention, God from the first adapted the woman's nature, I think, to the indoor and man's to the outdoor tasks and cares. (Xenophon, *Oeconomicus* 7.19–22, Loeb)

Native Mediterranean informants from Theophrastus (Ps.-Aristotle, *Oeconomica* 1.3.4) to Hierocles (*On Duties* 4.28.21) keep repeating the same stereotype, thus giving us important clues about the general and constant expectations of gender in antiquity.

Females/Private

We have already seen in the physiognomic literature certain stereotypical understandings of "female" in antiquity. In the interest of showing how extensive the gender roles of males and females were in antiquity, we develop first the expectations of "females" (= private) and then of "males" (= public). Ancient gender division of labor rests upon an elaborate set of tasks and functions that are likewise gender specific: public, outdoor tasks for males and private, indoor tasks for females. Note that our ancient informer, who is neither Israelite nor Christian, insists that God created the nature of females for certain gender-specific tasks to be done in gender-specific places.

> For he made the man's body and mind more capable of enduring cold and heat, and journeys and campaigns; and therefore imposed on him the outdoor tasks. To the woman, since he has made her body less capable of such endurance, I take it that God has assigned the indoor tasks. And knowing that he had created in the woman and had imposed on her the nourishment of the infants, he meted out to her a larger portion of affection for new-born babes than to the man. And since he imposed on the woman the protection of stores also, knowing that for protection a fearful disposition is no disadvantage, God meted out a larger share of fear to the woman than to the man; and knowing that he who deals with the outdoor tasks will have to be their defender against any wrong-doer, he meted out to him again a larger share of courage. (Xenophon, *Oeconomicus* 7.23–25, Loeb)

The social roles of females, then, had to do with the bearing and raising of children, food preparation, and management of the household. All of these, moreover, should be done in "covered" space, that is, space appropriate to the household and its related tasks. We will treat successively each of these gender-specific tasks in an effort to show what the ancients expected of females and what therefore they awarded with praise and honor. And it is a matter of honor and praise that each gender keeps to its own gender-specific tasks. Finally, although we rely on Greco-Roman informants, we should recognize that ancient Judean informants provide the same information regarding earlier traditional viewpoints. For example, in *m. Kethub.* 5.5, we find a list of tasks appropriate to females, which focus on food production, clothing production, and child rearing: "These are works which the wife must perform for her husband: grinding flour and baking bread and washing clothing and cooking food and giving suck to her child and making ready his bed and working in wool."

Childbearing

In addition to the information gleaned from our ancient informants such as Philo, Aristotle, and Xenophon, the code of household duties in 1 Timothy instructs females that they will find their salvation in bearing children (2:15). In the same document, widows are enjoined to "marry, bear children, and rule their households" (5:14). Conversely it is a great shame to be barren, the relief of which means social salvation and restoration of honor (Gen. 16:1; 30:1; 1 Sam. 1:5–6; Luke 1:7; Malina and

Rohrbaugh 1992, 287; Demand 1994, 121–40). Honor and shame, then, are apportioned to the gender-specific role of childbearing.

Food Preparation

Females attend the family hearth, see to the grinding of grain and the baking of bread (1 Kings 17:8–15). Hence, females are mentioned in association with leaven and bread baking (Luke 13:21). They are, of course, frequently recorded drawing water from the village well, always in the company of other women (Gen. 24:15–21; 29:9–12; Exod. 2:15–22; John 4:6–15), as well as foraging for the fuel needed to cook the family meal. Females herded goats for their milk; males shepherded sheep. Goats may forage close to home in a yard and around a house, whereas sheep require pasturage far removed from the home (Blok 1984, 51–70). Praise and blame, then, accord with the fulfillment of the gender-specific role of food preparation (see Demand 1994, 1–32).

Household Management

Females are to "rule their households" (1 Tim. 5:14), which involves not only food storage and preparation, but clothing production, supervision of slaves, and the like. Proverbs 30:10–28, from which we offer an excerpt providing a sense of the duties of a household-managing female, rewards this gender-specific role with public praise.

> 31:13 *She seeks wood and flax,*
> *and works with willing hands. . . .*
> *15 She rises while it is yet night*
> *and provides food for her household*
> *and tasks for her maidens. . . .*
> *19 She puts her hand to the distaff,*
> *and her fingers touch the spindle. . . .*
> *22 She makes herself coverings;*
> *her clothing is fine linen and purple. . . .*
> *24 She makes garments and sells them;*
> *she delivers girdles to the merchant.*

Males/Public

If females are socialized to the indoors and the private space of the family, males are expected to be outdoors and involved in public activity in public spaces. It is hardly surprising, then, that the Gospels so frequently describe Jesus as "out of doors" and in public, in particular in the marketplace (Mark 6:56) and talking about what occurs in the marketplace (Matt. 11:16; 20:3; 23:7; see also Acts 16:19; 17:17). He publicly visits John the Baptizer, calls fishermen beside the sea, enters public buildings such as market stoas and synagogues. Seldom if ever does Jesus perform a healing within a house, except when he specifically enters the women's quarters of a house (Mark 1:30–31; 5:40–41). Male roles, which were also scripted according to cultural expectations, centered around food production, commerce, soldiering, and other public activities. We briefly consider the expectations concerning male roles and behavior mentioned by our ancient Mediterranean informants, as we previously did with female roles.

Food Production

Males lead the household's flocks of sheep, donkeys, and the like out to pasture away from villages or settlements (Gen. 37:12; 1 Sam. 16:11; Luke 15:3–5; John 10:1–5). They are the plowmen (1 Kings 19:19; Luke 9:62) and sowers of the grain, which females then grind to make bread. Where hunting is possible, they hunt (Gen. 10:9; 25:27; 27:2); when fish is available, they fish (Mark 1:16–20; John 21:3–8). Males probably attend to the making of wine.

Trades and Commerce

The merchant of Matt. 13:45–46 is surely a male who leaves home to search for fine pearls. The silversmiths of Acts 18 are likewise males, as are sailors, traders, scribes, teachers, tax collectors, and soldiers.

Public Activities

Males read the Scriptures at synagogue meetings (Luke 4:15–19), which are by and large gatherings of males; they might speak, when invited (Acts 13:14–41). They sit and judge in the gate and participate in forensic trials. Outside of the immediate family, public meals are attended by males; the only women who might be present are courtesans or prostitutes (Corley 1993, 25–31). Although males and females may make the pilgrimage to Jerusalem, they travel in gender-specific groups (Luke 2:43–44). Ordinarily such mobility is acceptable for males only.

Furthermore, we can easily illustrate these gender stereotypes in the way the Gospels respect such gender definitions by presenting pairs of activities and places that are specifically male or female. For example, Jesus says, "Do not be anxious about your life, what you are to eat or what you shall drink, nor about your body, what you shall put on" (Matt. 6:35). He tells one part of his audience to look at the birds of the air. We argue that the birds correspond to the males in the audience, for what is said about them reflects male concerns: "They neither sow nor reap nor gather into barns" (6:26). This relates to agriculture and food production ("what to eat, what to drink"). Balancing this is the remark about the lilies of the field who "neither toil nor spin" (6:28–29), which pertains to female activity such as clothing production. The same gender sensitivity occurs in the remarks about those snatched to heaven. "Two men will be in the field; one is taken and one is left" (Matt 24:40); again males are found in public space tending to male-specific tasks, such as agriculture. "Two women will be grinding at the mill; one is taken and one is left" (24:41); females are again associated with the private world of the house, the hearth, and food. Similarly, two parables of mercy are told in Luke 15, one about a shepherd searching for a lost sheep (15:3–7) and another about a woman who sweeps her home to find a lost coin (15:8–10); again, males are about in the countryside pasturing animals, and females are found in houses. Comparably, parables about the kingdom balance similes about males, who either travel as merchants, fish, or dig in fields (Matt. 13:44–50, with those about females, who put leaven into flour (13:33). A parable about maidservants in charge of lamps for the household (Matt. 25:1–13) balances one about male servants entrusted with the master's property (25:14–30). These patterns are further illustrated in the way Jesus' healing of a man in public (Mark 1:21–28) is balanced with a healing of a woman in private (1:29–31; see Mark 5:1–20 and 35–43).

Gender-Specific
Honor and Shame

Socialization into these gender-specific conceptions of male and female activity was strengthened by public praise and blame. Public acknowledgment resulted in honor, while public criticism produced shame. The following summary observation by Xenophon illustrates this clearly:

> Now since we know, dear, what duties have been assigned to each of us by God, we must endeavor, each of us, to do the duties allotted to us as well as possible. . . . And besides, the law declares those tasks to be honorable for each of them wherein God has made the one to excel the other. Thus, to the woman it is more honorable to stay indoors than to abide in the fields, but to the man it is unseemly rather to stay indoors than to attend to the work outside. If a man acts contrary to the nature God has given him, possibly his defiance is detected by the gods and he is punished for neglecting his own work, or meddling with his wife's. (*Oeconomicus* 7.30–31, Loeb)

A male's honor rating requires that he be a public person, doing public actions and avoiding the world of women. Conversely, female honor requires women to be private persons, doing home-related activities in that sphere, and avoiding the world of men.

Males, then, are public persons, with a practical sense for maintaining honor, confident in behavior, in risk taking on behalf of their family, in search of honor. At home, males embody the family's authority and receive the obedience and respect of their children and wives. Females, on the other hand, are private persons, passive, defensive of family honor and fortunes. Except for the males in their husbands' family, they shun male company, so much so that Plutarch records a saying that the honorable female is she who is unknown to any but her husband: "There ought to be no random talk about fair and noble women, and their characters ought to be totally unknown save only to their consorts" (Plutarch, *Sayings of the Spartans* 217F, Loeb). Thucydides, remarking on the "glory" (i.e., honor) of females, observed: "Great is your glory if you do not fall below the standard which nature has set for your sex, and great also is hers of whom there is least talk among men whether in praise or blame" (*History* 2.45, Loeb). Thus rewards of praise and sanctions of blame attend these widely accepted cultural notions of gender roles.

It is impossible to underestimate the importance of honor and shame in the socialization of males and females in the ancient Mediterranean world. The manner in which these pivotal values were imparted to family members formed the way people understood themselves, perceived others, and developed moral judgments about proper behavior. To know the gender of someone was already to know a whole set of norms to which they must conform if they were to be honorable in that society. Such expectations formed clear cultural norms about what clothes (Deut. 22:5), hairdos (1 Cor. 11:4–14), and sexual partners (Rom. 1:26–27) are appropriate to males and females. We conclude this section with a summary statement by Philo on the honor and shame appropriate to males and females, a remark that will have considerable importance in our investigation of Paul's self-understanding and his expectations of community behavior:

> (God) counsels man figuratively to take care of woman as of a daughter, and woman to honor man as a father. And this is proper; a woman changes her habitation from her family to her husband. Wherefore it is fitting and proper that one who receives something should in return show good will to those who have given it, but one (i.e. woman) who has made a change should give to him who has taken her the honor which she showed those who begot her. For a man has a wife entrusted to him as a deposit from her parents. But woman takes a husband by law. (Philo, *Q. Gen* 1.27, about Gen. 2:21, Loeb)

In conclusion, males and females in the ancient Mediterranean learned about the cultural meanings of male and female from birth on. These notions underpinned a more broadly gender-divided society that classified certain places, times, and things as either male or female. Thus, group-oriented persons were quickly and thoroughly socialized to these gender roles and stereotypes. Moreover, gender stereotypes were backed with rewards of praise and sanctions of blame. On this point, our ancient Mediterranean informers were generally unanimous.

MORALITY AND DEVIANCE

For group-oriented persons, morality too was a matter of stereotypical thinking deriving from group-supported values. In their world, meaningful human existence depended on a person's full awareness of what others thought and felt about them, along with their living up to that awareness. Literally this awareness means "conscience." The Latin word *conscientia* and the Greek word *syn-eidesis* mean "with-knowledge," that is, knowledge shared with others, internalized common knowledge, commonly shared meaning, and common sense (Malina 1993b, 63–65; Malina and Neyrey 1991a, 76–80). Conscience for group-oriented persons is not so much an internal voice as an external prod deriving from what others say and do. Conscience for group-oriented persons is sensitive attention to one's publicly assessed ego-image, along with one's striving to align one's own personal behavior and self-assessment with that publicly assessed ego-image. It is the group that keeps a person within moral bounds. In such a context, conscience is an awareness of what others say, do, and think about oneself, because these others play the role of witness and judge. Their verdicts supply the person with grants of honor necessary for meaningful human existence.

How Conscience Works

To understand how conscience works in group-oriented cultures such as the ancient Mediterranean, we must remember that people continually mind each other's business. Two New Testament documents censure such behavior, actually using a common Greek word for the term "busybody" (*periergos;* 2 Thess. 3:11; 1 Tim. 5:3), but by mentioning this phenomenon, even negatively, they attest to its presence. Privacy is a relatively unknown and unexpected experience for the ancients. Because of the constant vigilance of people over their neighbors, along with constant concern for rewards of honor and sanctions of shame, social situations have to be controlled. And that control comes from group members minding each others' business, not from an individual person exercising self-control and following internalized norms. Anyone who closes house doors to snooping children in the village or anyone who does something in secret (see John 18:20) is considered up to no good. In such cultural contexts, people do not expect others to control their behavior by following internalized norms. Rather, people control others by watching over them, threatening them with shaming gossip, loss of reputation, and public dishonor. We need only open the Gospels to notice how the Pharisees seem to mind Jesus' business all the time.

Group-oriented individuals are embedded in, and thus represent, some group. From this perspective, the responsibility for morality and deviance lies not with individuals alone but rather with the social body in which they are embedded. Deviance springs up because something is amiss in the functioning of the social body; the body fails to keep watch over its members. Thus Paul stigmatizes whole groups, all Judeans and Greeks (Romans 1—3) or all Galatians (Gal. 3:1), because he sees some socially infecting *hamartia* or sin behind individual sinful actions.

The moral norms we find in the New Testament have relevance for individual behavior. But all such moral listings and descriptions do not focus primarily on individuals. Commonplace moral norms were written from the point of view of the individual-as-embedded-in-something-bigger, namely, the family, fictive family, polis, or tribe. Examples of such moral descriptions would include the various lists of sins (Mark 7:21–22), the lists of virtues and vices (Gal. 5:16–24), and the codes of household duties (Col. 3:18–4:1 and 1 Tim. 2:8–3:15). In this context, we might recall the list of the four cardinal virtues and their varying parts discussed in the previous chapters of this study.

As most New Testament scholars indicate, such norms represent what is generally known and accepted by the culture at large. They aim to keep the family, the group, the village, and the people sound, both corporately and socially. Among the followers of Jesus, the main problem was to keep the Christian group, the individual church, in harmony and unity, that is, in a sound state (e.g., 1 Corinthians 12; Rom. 12:3–21; see Titus 2:2, 8). In such a group, the individual as such was expendable: "It is expedient for you that one man die for the people, and that the whole people not perish" (John 11:50). For the sake of the group, individuals might be rather ruthlessly ejected from the group as in the expulsion procedures described in 1 Cor. 5:5, 13 and Rom. 16:17 (see Matt. 18:15–18). The soundness of the group, like the behavior of a group-oriented individual, is heavily determined by its impact on surrounding groups and by the expectations of outsiders (e.g. 1 Cor. 6:6; 10:32–33; 14:23–25; 1 Thess. 4:12; 1 Tim. 3:7). Christians had to be at least as good as outsiders. In a group-oriented society, then, conscience represents the advice, customs, norms, praise, and censure of the fellow human beings with whom one lives.

Deviance

Within this framework we now look at how morality for group-oriented persons relates to deviance. Deviance refers to behavior that violates the sense of order or classification that social groups construct and maintain to make a predictable and intelligible society. Deviance thus represents a socially construed label that group members attempt to apply to a person who commits an infraction against socially required norms and the order those norms support. People are "deviants" when they are caught and labeled by persons representing the dominant culture for breaking laws or causing social disorder. Now let us see how this might help us understand morality among first-century Mediterranean people.

To clarify how deviance expresses the social norms of groups, once more let us contrast how an American individualist and a group-oriented person such as Paul attempt to explain why they regard someone as abnormal or as a deviant. To explain the behavior of persons who breach the social order, Americans look to psychology, to childhood experiences, personality type, or to some significant event in the past that affects an adult's interaction with other members of society. Biography in the United States currently favors a description of psychological development that identifies singular events in the career of an individualist person passing through the psychological stages of life. We assess someone as abnormal who is psychologically "retarded," aberrant, "neurotic," or "psychotic" because he or she was "an abused child," and the like. In contrast, Mediterranean persons past and present are anti-introspective and simply not psychologically minded at all. Consequently, disturbing or abnormal internal states are blamed on personal causes outside the deviant, either human causes ("you made me angry") or nonhuman ones (". . .for he has a dumb spirit and wherever it seizes him it dashes him down," Mark 9:18). If no external personal cause is at hand, because persons are understood in terms of their embeddedness in others, deviance is attributed to deviant ancestors, parents, and teachers. Moreover, among the grounds for praise we noted a person's fortune, which included benevolent (but possibly malevolent) influence on a person by demons and spirits, *tychê,* Fortune, gods, and God. Thus biography in antiquity consists of a description of the influences on a person due to generation and geography, and the fulfillment of gender and role expectations that derive from the culture.

By way of illustration, when Roman elites described their lives, they catalogued the series of responsible offices they held. They called this their *cursus honorum,* a sequence of honors bestowed on them. As we noted previously, Mediterraneans paid scant attention to developmental stages apart from raw biology (especially the onset of menarche in girls). Ptolemy summarizes the stereotypical perception of "development" in individuals:

> In all creatures the earliest ages, like the spring, have a larger share of moisture and are tender and still delicate. The second age, up to the prime of life, exceeds in heat, like summer; the third, which is now past the prime and on the verge of decline, has an excess of dryness, like autumn; and the last which approaches dissolution, exceeds in its coldness, like winter. (*Tetrabiblos* 1.10.20, Loeb)

A Mediterranean such as Paul, for example, would describe abnormal persons by saying: "Who has bewitched you?" (Gal. 3:1; Neyrey 1990b, 181–86, 196–97); "Death was reigning" over them (Rom. 5:14); "When you were a heathen, you were led astray to dumb idols" (1 Cor. 12:2); sinners are subject to "the law of sin and death" (Rom. 8:2); and "sin reigns in your mortal bodies to make you obey their passions" (Rom. 6:12). Paul regularly perceives himself and others as attacked by celestial powers and spirits (Neyrey 1990b, 161–65). As one anthropologist expressed it: "the person is in an abnormal position because the matrix of relationships in which he is embedded is abnormal" (Selby 1974, 15).

For group-oriented persons, then, deviance lies not within persons but outside them, in faulty interpersonal relations over which they inevitably have no control. While deviance refers to the evaluation of one's fellow human beings concerning failure to measure up to social expectations, norms, and customs, the causes of this deviance are inevitably external and caused by persons.

Social Awareness

Expanding on notions of conscience as knowledge shared with one's social group and of deviance as actions performed under the influence of powers external to the individual, we can further clarify the social controls over the behavior of group-oriented individuals by attending to the type of social awareness characteristic of such persons. In this aspect of behavior, as well, group-oriented persons stand thoroughly outside our experience of being psychologically minded and using introspection for self-assessment. Instead, group-oriented persons rely on institutional arrangements that serve as external social controls to back up social norms. For example, the eastern Mediterranean practices of keeping females away from males by means of women's quarters, chaperoning unattached females, and various gender-based space prohibitions (no males at the common outdoor oven or common water supply) indicate strong behavioral controls in specific social situations. Such institutional arrangements are rooted in the common belief that a male could not possibly suppress the strong urges that surely take possession of him every time he is alone with any woman. And all women are considered even more unable to resist males. Hence, both sexes then expect their "will power" to be provided by other people, rather than by personal inhibition (Hall 1959, 66–67). Collectivist cultures generally presume their members to lack personal inhibition and consequently develop strong social inhibition. Emphatically, behavioral controls lie outside the person. Such controls are not "psychological," inwardly assimilated, and overseen by the individual's "conscience." Rather, controls consist of situations that are socially controlled, and control of situations rests not with individual persons following internalized norms but with others in the group enforcing group norms in various ways. Onlookers control behavior with full force of custom, which grants honor (praise) or withholds it (blame). Little concern is given, then, to controlling persons with the full force of individualistically assimilated internalized norms (Hall 1959, 114). No one in a group-oriented context would understand something as culturally nonsensical as "Let your conscience be your guide."

If certain situations are highly controlled, there are others in which a person is expected to lose control, while group members are expected to provide due restraint. For example, close women relations are expected to attempt to jump into the grave (or pyre) of their deceased, but also to be held back by others; males ready to square off in a fight expect those around them to hold them back; feuds go on escalating yet mediators are to intervene to restrain the feuding parties (see Boehm 1984).

These social-minded, group-oriented, anti-introspective and nonindividualist perspectives have been duly codified in the stories and ethical systems of Israel, Christianity, and Islam. Paul, for example, acts as the jealous father of his family groups and so informs the people at Corinth of what a proper "conscience" is. He acts with knowledge of what is socially appropriate in regard to women's behavior and attire and so acts to control behavior (1 Cor. 11:3–16; 14:33–35); he controls what people eat (1 Cor. 8:10–13; 10:14–21, 23–29) and when they eat it (1 Cor. 11:33–34). He controls who may marry and who may divorce (1 Cor. 5:1; 7:8–15). In fact, 1 Corinthians 5—15 may be profitably read as a study in "social awareness" in which Paul articulates common notions of bodily control and so acts to control the social behavior of his family (Neyrey 1990b, 107–40). Note also Paul's emphasis on having his representative (Timothy) as an on-site overseer and, further, that he gets reports and will himself show up to see what is going on (1 Cor. 4:14–21).

Those values and lines of behavior that tend to strengthen group cohesion are considered positive values and virtues. On the other hand, those values and lines of behavior that can in any way be detrimental to group cohesion are considered negative values, vices, or sins. Such codification points to the powerful group quality of such ethical systems, to their sanctions in community control rather than in individual responsibility.

VALUES AND VIRTUES

A final way of articulating what a group-oriented person is like can be found in the study of cultural or social values. By *value,* we mean the general directionality of behavior, that is, how a given instance of behavior is supposed to go (Pilch and Malina 1993, xiii–xxii). As we noted earlier, when we compare the culture of the United States and the Mediterranean region, it becomes immediately clear that a constitutive part of the differences between the two can be identified by the values proper to each group. We may safely say that a paramount value in the United States culture is democracy, which is expressed by the unique individual's right to vote, to own property, to make individual decisions binding oneself alone, to choose a career that satisfies individual aspirations, to marry whomsoever one pleases, and to be included in Gallup polls. What, then, were the social values of ancient Mediterraneans, who were group oriented and not individualists? (For a more complete sense of contrast between modern Western and ancient Mediterranean values and behavior, see the chart in Appendix 2.)

Differing Cultural Values

Persons, whether individualists or collectivists, follow the pathways marked by values in their choice of behavior. To better imagine the sorts of behaviors urged upon first-century, group-oriented persons, we need to introduce a model developed precisely for discovering diverse values among different ethnic groups. Anthropologists F. R. Kluckhohn and F. L. Strodtbeck (1961) originally constructed this model, and John Papajohn and John Spiegel (1975) subsequently adapted it to identify comparative variations in values between ethnic groups. The model enjoys wide currency today and has proved quite insightful and useful to a variety of people who wish to make comparisons across cultures.

The Kluckhohn-Strodtbeck model describes the fundamental values people prefer because of the way they were enculturated and socialized. The model operates on the basis of the following questions: When a crisis or problem arises, how are people expected to react? How are they supposed to behave? To what resource are they expected to turn? Five areas are considered: (a) activity, (b) relations, (c) time orientation, (d) relation of human beings to nature, and (e) the evaluation of human nature. Our purpose for introducing this value-preference orientation model at this point is to supply a somewhat broader canvas on which to depict the behavioral scenarios of our Mediterranean group-oriented persons. The model more than amply indicates that the values of ancient Mediterranean people, Paul and his churches to be specific, are certainly different from the values of most EuroAmericans. Any consideration of first-century persons must be acutely aware of these differences. And this model affords us a reliable means of uncovering those differences.

In the interest of brevity, we suggest that the differences between the people of Paul's world and that of the contemporary United States be identified as follows (see Pilch and Malina 1993, xxii–xxxviii). Given the question, "What line of behavior are human beings expected to pick as first choice option to face basic human problems?" we get this sort of breakdown:

Behavior Area	Paul's World	United States Today
Activity	being	doing
Relations	collateral	individual
Time	present; past	future; present
Humans-Nature	subordinate to	mastery over
Human Nature	mixed; evil	neutral

If this model indeed indicates different value orientations, then truly U.S. people will think and act quite differently from those in Paul's society. To be considerate readers of Paul's letters, we will have to strive to know as accurately as possible the different social values that function in a group-oriented society.

Activity

When faced with a crisis or significant problem, U.S. persons are expected "to do something about it." Problem solvers regularly ask, "What can we do?" in response to a crisis or calamity. And they do not feel good about the problem unless they start doing something. Not so the ancient Mediterraneans. As we have seen in the previous chapters, ancient Mediterraneans are products of generation and geography, and they perceive themselves controlled by other persons, by sky beings of various sorts, and ultimately by God. Their roles and statuses are ascribed to them by God (1 Cor. 7:17; 12:18) and so belong to the order of creation and cannot be "uncreated." Thus, they tend to face crises and calamities somewhat passively, expressing their understanding of events in terms of a doctrine of divine providence, fortune, or fate controlling all existence. Given this view of reality, we should ascribe to ancient Mediterraneans the major activity of "being" and surviving, not solving problems or achieving. Endurance in the face of opposition and conflict is the proper, honorable choice. It is not by accident that Job became the model of "being" in crisis to ancient Israelites and Christians (see James 5:7–11).

Relations

In the United States, relations tend to be individualist, with a view to status based on success in competition; after all, that is what capitalism is all about: maximizing individual benefit (Bellah et al. 1985). The relations of ancient Mediterraneans were basically collateral, that is group-oriented and nonindividualist. We recall how in the forensic defense speech and the encomium, identity derived from generation, that is, embeddedness in family, clan, and tribe. Not only did people take their basic identity from such collateral relations, but praiseworthy deeds were those done for others in the group. People were strongly embedded in a group whose goals and wishes prevailed over those of individual members of that group. Group well-being always came first. Group integrity was the priority.

In regard to Paul, we note that he has two sets of relations in view: (1) vertical (Neyrey 1990b, 33–41, 134) and (2) horizontal. As to the latter, he regularly addresses the members of his churches in kinship terms, "brothers and sisters." He boasts, moreover, of his accommodation of his own desires for the good of the group and even the expectations of those outside his group: "Give no offense to Judeans or to Greeks, or to the church of God, just as I try to please all people in everything I do, not seeking my own advantage, but that of many" (1 Cor. 10:32–33). Indeed, it was Paul's strategy to be "all things to everyone" (1 Cor. 9:19–23), which was, on occasion, interpreted as shameful flattery or "pleasing people" (Gal. 1:10; see Marshall 1987, 70–90). Finally, one need only recall all of the special compound words Paul creates to indicate his relationship with certain people: Paul labels quite a few individuals as his "fellow workers" (*synergoi*): Ephaphroditus (Phil. 2:25), Clement (Phil. 4:3), Aquila and Prisca (Rom. 16:3), Urbanus (Rom. 16:8), and even Apollos (1 Cor. 3:9). Ephaphroditus is not only "fellow worker" (*synergos*) but "brother" and "fellow soldier" (Phil. 2:25). Thus Paul particularly strives in Philippians to maintain "fellowship" (*koinônia*) with that church (Sampley 1980, 51–77). We are reminded, moreover, of how Paul expresses collateral relationships as he attempts to form the group conscience of the Corinthians concerning marriage, diet, and public behavior. Furthermore, he instructs members of his churches *not* to please themselves, but others in the in-group: "We who are strong ought to bear with the failings of the weak, and not to please ourselves; let each of us please his neighbor for his good, to edify him" (Rom. 15:1). After all, Jesus did not "please himself" (15:3) but obediently served his God. Hence, a great value lies in being unmarried, for such persons may "please the Lord," rather than please their spouses (1 Cor. 7:32–34).

Time Orientation

Most persons in the United States are quite aware of their future orientation. From childhood on, people constantly live in a state of "preparation" for the immediate future: schooling is for a job, the job enables marriage, while marriage and children require life insurance and plans for college education for those children. Throughout their adult lives, people save for a rainy day, contributing to their Social Security and retirement funds. The worst disaster, we are told, is to be underinsured. On the other hand, ancient Mediterranean people shared a time orientation focused primarily on the present and the past, not the future (Malina 1989:1–31). They were interested in today's bread (Luke 11:3) and today's problems (Matt. 6:34). They sought examples for imitation from the legendary heroes of the past, as their use of sacred writings indicates.

Paul, for example, often makes travel plans, but this is hardly a sign of his future orientation, as he rarely seems to have followed through with them (2 Cor. 1:15–17; 1 Thess. 2:17–18; 1 Cor. 4:18). Although he occasionally bemoans how frail he is and how likely to die, he invariably indicates that his main concern lies in his present service of the churches: "To remain in the flesh is more necessary on your account. Convinced of this, I know that I shall remain and continue with you all, for your progress and joy in the faith" (Phil. 1:24–25; see 2 Cor. 5:6–10). Even when he seems to discourse on the future, he disclaims all knowledge of when the forthcoming events will occur: "As to the times and seasons, you have no need to have anything written to you. For you yourselves know well that the day of the Lord will come like a thief in the night" (1 Thess. 5:1–2). Paul urges vigilance, watchfulness, and constancy—all present time indicators. Moral exhortation in the New Testament, which we label as group-oriented norms and values, focuses on hearing God's voice "today" to enter into God's rest (Heb. 3:7).

Indeed, after concern about the present, Paul places far more interest on the past than on any abstract future. The past contains the great exemplars of faith (Romans 4; Gal. 3:6–9), patterns of God's consistent actions (Rom. 9:7–13), and warning figures (1 Cor. 10:6–11). The past yields the Scriptures, with all of their prophecies of the Christ, which have come true in the present time (Rom. 1:3–4; 16:25–26). The past yields the great tradition, which must be upheld in the present time in all its purity and wholeness (Neyrey 1993, 53–54).

Humans vis-à-vis Nature

Given the general "doing" orientation in the United States, people think that they can control nature and use it for their own success, even at the cost of environmental destruction. People in the United States believe that they should control nature so that the individual may succeed (i.e., that they should reroute rivers, seed clouds for rain, manufacture prostheses, promote immunizations, and the like). Ancient Mediterraneans, on the other hand, understood humankind as helpless in the face of nature. To master or subdue nature belonged to God alone. In the same

way that they envisioned individuals as passive before God's providence,
Fate, or Fortune, as determined by generation and geography, so they
saw themselves as subject to nature and natural forces. Therefore,
they tended not to be technologically progressive or ecologically aware.
They were a people used to being put upon by famine, floods, storms, and
locusts, and they understood endurance to be the proper response (see
1 Cor. 4:9–13; 2 Cor. 5:3–10).

Human Nature

Finally, as we saw above, most Westerners believe that human deviance derives from faulty childhood socialization or deficient education.
Ancient Mediterraneans, on the other hand, viewed human nature as a
mixture of good and evil, not neutral or therapeutically remediable. For
example, New Testament writers—who understood persons in terms of
geography and generation—viewed people from Crete as "always liars,
evil beasts, lazy gluttons" (Titus 1:12) and believed "nothing good can
come from Nazareth" (John 1:46). Similarly, regarding generation, all inherit the faults and sins of their ancestor Adam (Rom. 5:12–14), just as all
of Abraham's offspring inherit his promise. Education consisted of "beat-
ing the ribs" of one's children on the supposition that they were fundamentally selfish and inclined to evil (Prov. 13:24; 22:15; 23:13–14; 29:15;
Sir. 30:12; see especially Pilch 1993a,101–7).

When Paul takes up the issue of human nature, he views it entirely
through a dualistic group perspective, which contrasts social life before
Christ and social life after Christ. "Then" is always the time of the former
in-group, a time of unremitting evil and sin, which is absent "now" in the
present in-group (Dahl 1976, 33–34):

1. *"Then" versus "now"*: "Formerly you did not know God, you
   were in bondage to beings that by nature are no gods; but
   now that you have come to know God . . ." (Gal. 4:8–9; see
   Gal. 3:23–27; Rom. 6:17–22; Eph. 2:11–22; 5:8).
2. *"Once" but "now"*: "When we were children, we were slaves
   to the elemental spirits of the universe. But when the time
   had fully come, God sent forth his Son . . ." (Gal. 4:3–7; see
   Rom. 1:18–3:30; 3:21–8:39). Furthermore, Paul perceives
   all non-Christians through a comparable dualistic lens, contrasting their vice and uncleanness with virtue and purity in
   Christ (Neyrey 1990b, 159–61). Because acceptance into
   the Christian in-group involved entry into fictive kinship,
   and one became kin only by birth, baptism is likened to a
   new birth, which indicates a transition from an utterly negative past into a positive present:

"before"	vs.	"after"
darkness	vs.	light
ignorance	vs.	knowledge
passion/flesh	vs.	spirit
deceit	vs.	truth
drunk/asleep	vs.	sober/awake
blindness	vs.	sight

These sorts of dualistic perceptions clearly indicate that Paul considered human nature as evil and sorely in need of restoration. Indeed, Christ gave himself to redeem us from "the present evil age" (Gal. 1:4). For Paul and his contemporaries, it was easy to see the world in dualistic terms, as an arena where evil, Satan, and demons attacked God's holy people. This was a world of dishonoring sin and pervasive evil, to which a savior was sent to rescue those whom God chose (Ephesians 1).

At the very least, modern readers of Paul should be acutely aware that Paul and the people of his world shared value orientations that differed radically from those generally in vogue in the United States. Paul and his fellow Christians surely would appear quite different from contemporary Euro-Americans, as one would expect when comparing and contrasting individualist and group-oriented societies. The Kluckhohn-Strodtbeck model of cross-cultural values preferences, then, can be an initial, important step in clarifying the differences that marked a person's behavior preferences, and an especially important step in gaining insight into that other world.

Resulting Cultural Virtues

The foregoing model of values might seem quite abstract. When, however, we put it in conversation with other elements of this study of person in the first-century Mediterranean, we can begin to see specific values and virtues pertinent to the people of Paul's world.

"Being":
Endurance and Obedience

For example, "being" as a value correlates with what we described above as a collectivist or group-oriented person. In such collectivist culture, individuals are basically given their identity from their family and embedded in a specific primary in-group (generation). One's character is considered to be determined by geography. Moreover, role and status are understood in terms of group expectations and legitimated in the order of creation (1 Cor. 12:18). The consequent moral norm, then, is clear: Be what you are! Born a slave, remain a slave (1 Cor. 7:17). One would assume that where the value of "being" is strong, one will find corresponding importance given to obedience, acceptance of suffering, endurance, maintaining the status quo, and contentment. The same norms apply to gender identity and roles.

From Paul's letters we glean the following remarks indicative of two important values that reinforce the dominant value of "being," namely, endurance and obedience. Concerning endurance, we present but a sample of his remarks, with special note about the variety of linguistic expressions for "being" (or enduring, practicing patience, remaining, and the like).

1. *Endure, put up with (pherô)*: "God will not let you be tempted beyond your strength, but with temptation will also provide the way of escape, that you may be able to endure it" (1 Cor. 10:13; see 2 Tim. 3:11).
2. *Keep on (kartereô)*: "Keep on praying" (Rom. 12:12; see Acts 1:14; 2:42; 6:4).
3. *Remain (menô)*: "God's kindness to you, provided you remain in his kindness" (Rom. 11:22); "To the unmarried and the widows . . . it is well for them to remain single as I do" (1 Cor. 7:8; see Gal. 3:10).
4. *Bear, put up with (stegô)*: "We put up with anything rather than put an obstacle in the way of the gospel of Christ" (1 Cor. 9:12; see 13:7).
5. *Endure, tolerate (anechomai)*: "When persecuted, we endure" (1 Cor. 4:12; 2 Cor. 11:1, 4, 19–20).
6. *Persevere (hypomoneô)*: "Love bears all things, believes all things, hopes all things, endures all things" (1 Cor. 13:7; see 2 Cor. 1:6; 6:4; 1 Thess. 1:4).
7. *Patience (makrothymia)*: "Encourage the fainthearted, help the weak, be patient with them all" (1 Thess. 5:14; see Gal. 5:22).

The catalogues of suffering and affliction that we have commented on repeatedly in this study offer further evidence of Paul's passive stance of "being," not "doing," in the face of ever-present adversity. Endurance, of course, belongs to the virtue of "courage" (*andreia*), and so Paul's description of himself as well as his appeal to others for endurance would be readily perceived to reflect one of the culturally important virtues of antiquity.

Concerning obedience, we noted that in all his letters, Paul constantly expresses his sense of his God-given role, the will of God for him, the necessity laid upon him, and the consequent duty to obey and submit to his celestial patron. For example, Paul begins his Corinthian letters by indicating that his role and status were not of his doing; rather, he was "called by the will of God" (1 Cor. 1:1; 2 Cor. 1:1). He readily acknowledges that "God's will" directs his career (Rom. 1:10; 15:32) and urges all people to learn that will (Rom. 2:18) to "prove what is the will of God, what is good and acceptable and perfect" (Rom 12:2). "The will of God is your sanctification" (1 Thess. 4:3), which includes constant thanksgiving to the celestial patron (1 Thess. 5:18). Paul likewise understands the figure of Jesus as one who gave himself completely to the will of God (Gal. 1:4) and was obedient even unto death (Phil. 2:8; Rom. 5:18).

Often Paul describes his role in terms of a "commission" from his heavenly patron (1 Cor. 3:10; 15:10; Rom. 15:15; for *charis* or "grace" as a patronage word, see Malina 1988b, 5–6). He speaks of a cosmic "necessity" (*anagkê*) that compels him in his work (1 Cor. 9:16), comparable to the "necessity" whereby Christians must be subject to civil authorities (Rom. 13:5). Even his trials are a form of "necessity" from God (1 Thess. 3:7). Another form of obligation is expressed by the term *dei,* which is generally translated as "must" or "ought" or "should," implying that the obligation comes from God: " . . . as you have learned from us how you ought to live and so to please God, you do so more and more" (1 Thess. 4:1; see Rom. 12:3; 1 Cor. 8:2; 15:25). In light of this, it is hardly surprising to find a rich variety of exhortations to submission and obedience in Paul's letters.

1. *Obey (hypakouô, hypakoê):* "We have received grace and apostleship to bring about the obedience of faith" (Rom. 1:5; 6:16–17; 2 Cor. 2:9).
2. *Obey (peithô):* "For those who are factious and do not obey the truth, there will be wrath and fury" (Rom. 2:8; see Rom. 1:30; 10:21; 11:30–32).
3. *Be subject to, submit (hypotassô):* "The spirits of prophets are subject to the prophets" (1 Cor. 14:32; see Rom. 13:1, 5; 1 Cor. 15:27–28).
4. *Submit to (enechô):* "Do not submit again to a yoke of slavery" (Gal. 5:1).
5. *Under (hypo):* "To those under the law I became as one under the law . . . that I might win those under the law" (1 Cor. 9:20).

Obedience, moreover, belongs to the cardinal virtue of justice (*dikaiosynê*), which would likewise be readily perceived by Paul's audience as implying other consequent values such as faithfulness and loyalty.

"Collateral Relations":
Common Good, Love, Self-sacrifice

The value preference for "collateral relations" suggests that individuals understand society as readily divided into in-groups and out-groups. To survive, persons belong to various groups, primarily to kin groups, but also to fictive kin groups (such as work groups, various clubs or collegia, Paul's fictive kin groups or churches), fictive political factions (like John the Baptist's reform group, Jesus' revitalizing group), and political types of parties (Sadducees, Pharisees, Essenes, Herodians). The importance given here to horizontal relationships will express itself in concern for kinship relations, knowing who is one's neighbor, the common good of the in-group, and love for that in-group neighbor.

In the world of Paul, we find many values consequent to the primary value of collateral relations. Things are valued by Paul precisely insofar as they "build up" the group rather than the individual at the group's expense. Hence, he prefers the gift of prophecy over that of tongues because it strengthens group relationships and benefits the many rather than the few: "They who speak in a tongue edify themselves, but they who prophesy edify the church" (1 Cor. 14:4; see 14:5, 12, 17, 26). Hence, "love" (self-giving solidarity) is preferable to "knowledge," for love "builds up," whereas the latter "puffs up" (1 Cor. 8:1). The group and group integrity, then, come first (see 1 Thess. 5:11; 1 Cor. 10:23).

This leads us inevitably to Paul's exhortation to "love." Given the nonpsychological quality of group-oriented society, love will have little to do with feelings of affection, sentiments of fondness, and warm, glowing affinity. Rather, as has been argued, "love" is "the value of group attachment and group bonding" (Malina 1993c, 47–70). Unlike other spiritual gifts, which can tend to exalt the individual, this greatest gift strives precisely to put the group first, with maximum effort given to maintaining group integrity:

> Love is patient and kind; love is not jealous or boastful; it is not arrogant or rude. Love does not insist on its own way; it is not irritable or resentful. (1 Cor. 13:4–5)

Besides highlighting "God's love," an attachment that benefits others (Rom. 5:5, 8; 8:39), Paul regularly exhorts members of his churches to look to their collateral relationships to benefit those relationships. Such concern is transformed into bonds of kinship: "Love one another with brotherly affection; outdo one another in showing honor" (Rom. 12:10). The only duty owed is "love" (Rom. 13:8); the worst evil is to harm another, which is to lack love (Rom. 14:15). This, too, would be readily recognized by Paul's audience as one of the major virtues of antiquity, *philadelphia,* or "kinship bonding": "Concerning love of the brethren [*philadelphia*] . . . you yourselves have been taught by God to love [*agapan*] one another" (1 Thess. 4:9).

Finally, the value of constantly attending to collateral relations leads inevitably to the consequent value of "self-sacrifice." Paul presents himself as the chief example of this, as he emphasizes how he is "poured as a libation upon the sacrifical offering of your faith" (Phil. 2:17). He praises the collection for the poor saints of Jerusalem as "a service" (*leitourgia,* 2 Cor. 9:12; Rom. 15:27). Christ, of course, is the exalted model of this value and behavior, for he "emptied himself" and "gave himself up" for the church. Thus it comes as no surprise to hear Paul praise various types of gifts and roles as "service" toward others (1 Cor. 4:1; 12:4–6). Alternately, Paul expresses this in terms of "harmony and relinquishing of one's own way" (Osiek 1993, 157). How praiseworthy are those who "do nothing from selfishness or conceit, but in humility count others better than themselves" (Phil. 2:3); they "look to the interests of others" (v. 4). "Let no one seek his own good, but the good of his neighbor" (1 Cor. 10:24). "Through love be servants of one another" (Gal. 5:13).

Present-Time Orientation:
Constancy, Loyalty, and Tradition

Present-time orientation is the usual value preference of groups and societies in which present survival needs cannot be taken for granted. As such, present-time orientation is typical of traditional peasant societies whose proverbs instruct: "Do not be anxious about tomorrow for tomorrow will be anxious for itself," or "Let the day's own trouble be sufficient for the day" (Matt. 6:34). People with this value orientation are not interested in promises about a remote future, whether it be a utopian transformation of the world or a delayed messiah. What is important is *today.* If today offers little, then it is to the past that one must look, for as we saw in the previous chapters, individuals are shaped by generation as well as geography. We are who we are today thanks to our ancestors, as our genealogies indicate (Luke 3:23–38). Tradition, custom, and ancient writings point to elements from the past that are still present, not unlike one's inherited status, craft, house, and land. Values attendant to a present-time orientation tend to be loyalty and constancy, obedience to tradition, and endurance.

Paul's exhortations to his churches focus on the duties of today, namely, "Live a life worthy of your calling" (1 Thess. 2:12; Phil. 1:27; Eph. 4:1). As we saw, such duties would include the present values of "love" and "service." Even when disclaiming knowledge of the time of Jesus' coming, Paul's orientation is squarely on the present time, which he characterizes as a time of "soberness" and "vigilance" (1 Thess. 5:6, 8).

Moreover, if individuals are shaped by generation and geography,

their time orientation will tend to suggest that today's advice and principles can be found in the past. Hence, we find constant value placed on
knowing and observing "traditions." Not only do the Gospels reflect how
individuals cling to the "traditions of their elders" (Matt. 15:2, 3, 6), but
Paul also was "zealous for the traditions of my fathers" (Gal. 1:14). As "father" to the Corinthians, he likewise insists that they follow his traditions:
"I commend you because you remember me in everything and maintain
the traditions even as I have delivered them to you" (1 Cor. 11:2). So many
of Paul's exhortations consist of bringing past traditions into the present,
as in the case of the Eucharist (1 Cor. 11:23) and the resurrection (1 Cor.
15:3).

Another aspect clustering with the value of present-time orientation
can be seen in the attention given to constancy and fidelity to past traditions. Paul's "handing on" of what "he received" matters in the way his
churches continue to "stand" in those traditions: "Now I remind you in
what terms I preached to you the gospel, which you received, in which
you stand, by which you are saved" (1 Cor. 15:1). Similarly, whatever instruction Paul gave in the past should be followed in the present: "We be-
seech and exhort you, that as you have learned from us how you ought to
live and to please God, just as you are doing, you do so more and more"
(1 Thess. 4:1). Just as God who has called the churches is "faithful"
(1 Tim. 5:24; 1 Cor. 1:9), so disciples must likewise maintain an abiding
loyalty and constancy in their beliefs and behaviors.

COLLECTIVIST SELVES:
A CONCLUDING PORTRAIT

All the persons we read about in the ancient progymnasmata, rhetorical handbooks, physiognomic writings, as well as the New Testament
documents, are group-oriented persons from collectivist cultures. By way
of conclusion, we present here a summary description of the group-
oriented person whom we have encountered throughout this book (for
more details, see Malina 1986c). Admittedly, as a conclusion to a detailed
study, this composite portrait of a collectivist self will be abstract and generalized, and so lacking in illustration and detail. But we believe that we
have amply provided such detail in our exposition of the kind of person
described in the encomium, the forensic defense speech, and physiognomic literature.

First of all, collectivism, as opposed to individualism, may be described
as the belief that the groups in which a person is embedded are each and
singly an end in themselves. As such these groups ought to realize distinctive group values, notwithstanding the weight of individuals' personal

drive toward self-satisfaction. In collectivist cultures, most people's social behavior is largely determined by group goals that require the pursuit of achievements that improve the position of the group, that is, "the common good." The defining attributes of collectivist cultures are family integrity, solidarity, and keeping the primary in-group in "good health." The salient features of collectivist cultures include the following:

In-group. The groups in which a person is embedded form "in-groups" in comparison with other groups, "out-groups," that do not command a person's allegiance and commitment. In-groups consist of persons who share a common fate because they have been generally rooted in similar circumstances of birth and place of origin (generation and geography). While individualists may belong to many in-groups— yet have shallow attachment to all of them—collectivists are embedded in few in-groups. Moreover, collectivists are strongly attached to these few in-groups, and the in-groups in turn dictate a wide range of behaviors. A person's behavior toward the in-group is consistent with what the in-group expects. This feature is the root of an honor-based society: sensitivity to the expectations of others in the in-group. In contrast, behavior toward everyone else (for example, strangers) tends to be characterized by defiance of authority, competition, resentment of control, formality, and dogmatism.

Virtue and Value. The cardinal virtues of antiquity are collectivist virtues. They direct persons to emphasize the views, needs, and goals of the in-group rather than those of individual group members. These virtues encompass values such as: generalized reciprocity, obligation, duty, security, traditionalism, harmony, obedience to authority, in-group equilibrium, concern for what is proper, cooperation, fatalism, family centeredness, high need for affiliation, succor, abasement, nurturance, acquiescence, dependency, and strong superordination and subordination.

Social Virtue. As we have noted in the course of this chapter, collectivist cultures include a whole range of shared values, such as those mentioned in the progymnasmata and physiognomics, directed to bolstering group integrity. For example, ideally sexual relations exist exclusively for procreation, which is a fulfillment of social duty. The virtues extolled by collectivist cultures are social virtues, attitudes that look to the benefits of the group, rather than individualist virtues. Thus we find the following: a sense of shame, filial piety, respect for the social order, self-discipline, concern for social recognition, humility, respect for parents and elders, acceptance of one's position in life, and preserving one's public image. Anything that cements and supports interpersonal relationships will be valued.

Social Norms and Obligations. These are defined by the in-group rather than by behavior oriented toward personal satisfaction. Persons harbor

beliefs shared with the rest of the in-group members rather than beliefs
that distinguish them from the in-group. And group members put great
stock on readiness to cooperate with other in-group members. In the case
of extreme collectivism, individuals do not have personal goals, attitudes,
beliefs, or values but only reflect those of the in-group. As a matter of fact
persons enjoy doing what the in-group expects.

Socialization and Duty. Socialization patterns are keyed to developing
habits of obedience, duty, sacrifice for the group, group-oriented tasks,
cooperation, favoritism toward in-group members, acceptance of in-group
authorities, nurturing, sociability, and interdependence. Such socialization produces persons with strong emotional attachment to others, broad
concerns for family and in-group cooperation, and group protectiveness.
Thus persons in such collectivist cultures will do what they must as dictated by groups, authorities, and parents, rather than what brings personal satisfaction. The great temptation is to pursue some self-centered
enjoyable activity. Should persons yield to such temptation and be found
out, in-group sanctions run from shaming to expulsion. In conflict,
collectivists side with vertical relationships (parents, authorities) over
against horizontal ones (spouses, siblings, friends).

Nonindividualist Self. The collectivist person is a group-oriented self as
opposed to an individualist self. A group-oriented self constantly requires
another person to know who one is. Collectivist selves are group-oriented
persons who tend to internalize group expectations and ideals to such an
extent that they automatically respond as in-group norms specify without
any sort of utilitarian calculation. This is a sort of unquestioned attachment to the in-group. It includes the perception that in-group norms are
universally valid (a form of ethnocentrism), along with automatic obedience to in-group authorities, and willingness to fight and die for the in-
group. These characteristics are usually associated with distrust of and
unwillingness to cooperate with out-groups. As a matter of fact, out-
groups are often considered a different species, to be evaluated and
treated like a different species of animate being.

Collectivist persons define the self to outsiders, as we have seen, by
generation, geography, and gender. Hence we find descriptions of persons largely circumscribed by generation and geography: family, gender,
age, ethnicity, along with place of origin and residence. To out-groups, the
self is always an aspect or a representative of the in-group that consists of
related, gendered persons who come from and live in a certain place. To
in-group members, however, the self is a bundle of roles that are likewise
rooted in generation and geography. One does not readily distinguish self
from social role(s). The performance of duties associated with roles is the
path to social respect.

Effects on Others. Collectivist persons are concerned about the results of their actions on others in the in-group. They readily share material and nonmaterial sources with group members. They are concerned about how their behavior appears to others because they believe the outcomes of their behavior should correspond with in-group values. All in-group members feel involved in the contributions of their fellows and share in their lives. Thus individuals feel strong emotional attachment to the in-group, perceiving all group members as relatively homogeneous.

Shared Affect. Collectivism is associated with homogeneity of affect; if in-group members are sad, one is sad; if joyful, one is joyful (see 1 Cor. 12:26). Moreover, those in authority expect unquestioned acceptance of in-group norms as well as homogeneity of attitudes and values. Interpersonal relations within the in-group are seen as an end in themselves. There is a perception of limited good, according to which something good that happens to an in-group member is bad for the in-group because "good" is finite and thus resources are always in a zero-sum distribution pattern (John 3:26). Finally, the in-group is responsible for the actions of its members. This has implications for intergroup relations. Specifically, in collectivism one expects solidarity in action toward other groups, and joint action is the norm. Each individual is responsible for the actions of all other in-group members, and the in-group is responsible for the actions of each individual member.

At this point we have finished sketching a complicated model of the first-century Mediterranean person. If we have been successful, typical modern Western readers must feel perplexed. For if the model is accurate, contemporary U.S. Bible readers will find persons such as Paul and those who joined his churches quite strange, even bizarre by U.S. standards. Such a feeling at this point would be quite appropriate. And that points up the very value of this model. For if Paul and the persons with whom he interacts are so radically different from us, then an adequate scenario of person is absolutely essential if we are to understand them at all. How else can we escape imposing our notions of individualist personality on them?

6

Paul:
Apostle and Prophet

Paul insisted that he was an apostle, an apostle with the added credentials of a prophet. In this final chapter, our first concern is to present a summary overview of the information we have been given about Paul of Tarsus. It was this information that contributed to the formulation of his culturally sensitive self-conception. Subsequently, we shall consider how Paul's self-conscious role of prophet impacted on his self-conception. To begin with, the directives provided by authors of the progymnasmata, forensic defense speeches, and physiognomic treatises instruct us in the categories deemed by the ancients to be essential and significant for knowing a person. Paul himself used common first-century Mediterranean stereotypes to present himself, and Luke employed these as well in his descriptions of the apostle. Throughout, Paul was a group-oriented person, deeply and permanently embedded in significant others.

PAUL, THE FIRST-CENTURY
MEDITERRANEAN PERSON

From all that we have considered, it seems rather obvious that Paul and his contemporaries did not understand themselves as individualist persons. They did know one another, although not very well *by our standards*. For they did not know one another psychologically, as unique, idiosyncratic, singular persons. Rather, according to our native Mediterranean informants, a person's social standing, social identification, and social worth derived from one's group orientation in terms of generation, geography, and gender. Virtues are not acquired behavior but indicative of one's group heritage. Bravery, devotion to literature, skill in law, and the like, are all group features—acquired, innate, inherited (hence the outcome of family lines). A person's biography was expected to reflect lifelong constancy, with childhood and youth a retrojection of adult attainments.

In the ancient world, one's role and status were tied to what we consider circumstances essentially external to the person. All persons were basically group-made persons, never self-made persons. While one had little if any control over one's fortune, yet one was responsible for how events turned out in life. Generation, geography, and gender, with positively valued origins, formation, accomplishments—all in comparative presentation—duly described the praiseworthy person. The encomium, forensic defense speech, and physiognomic descriptions all underscored such group-contributed, externally derived features that enabled the first-century Mediterranean to know another very, very well.

The encomium encoded a set of expectations and values derived from the social system shared by both Paul and his audience. In that social system, persons were publicly praised and thus accrued honor. It was the culturally valued, praiseworthy features that the encomium expressed. These features both constrained and liberated. They constrained because they forced persons to see themselves and others only in limited, stereotyped terms. But they liberated because they set forth quite clearly and unequivocally what was required of a person to be a decent human being in that society.

By following this genre in his letters, Paul obviously set out all the information of social relevance that he could: birth, manner of life, education, and the like. "Relevance" here refers to the code of honor into which all males were socialized in Paul's society (see Malina 1993b, 28–62). In this perspective, Paul presented himself as the quintessential group-oriented person, controlled by forces greater than he: God ascribes his role, status, and honor at birth. Paul is duly group affiliated, a Pharisee, a member of a specific group. He insists that he learned nothing on his own but received everything from God. He is totally group oriented: loyal, faithful and obedient, seeking God's honor and group benefits. And finally, he is ever sensitive to the opinion of others: his detractors, his Galatian audience, or the Jerusalem "pillars." For this group-oriented person, the acknowledgment by the Jerusalem "pillars" was a matter of the highest significance.

Then, in the formal defense speeches of Acts 22—26, Luke presents all of the vital information about Paul that would portray him most favorably. In this depiction, Paul comes across as an outstanding person, with all proper, group-based credentials. By setting forth Paul's education, piety, and authorization, Luke shows him to be a witness of reputable social standing—upright, stable, and pious—whose testimony deserves a fair hearing in court.

Finally, in the physiognomic presentation of Paul in *The Acts of Paul,* the apostle is clearly depicted as an ideal male figure. The composite of his various physical features suggests a certain kind of person: benevolent and good (eyes); sincere, kind, truthful (voice); an active person who accomplishes much (stature); an excellent person ("balanced" humors); pious (shaved head); fearless and unyielding (crooked legs); of high social status (healthy); manly (meeting eyebrows); virtuous and handsome (longish nose); suitable for leadership (full of grace). The description fills out Paul's "character" by indicating what he must have looked like as a good Roman citizen (Acts 16:37; 22:25–28).

The encomium, forensic defense speech, and physiognomic descriptions essentially underscored culturally relevant traits. And significantly, these culturally relevant traits all derive from outside a person. They are qualities a person receives from others or that befall a person. All of these attributes describe persons as not in control of life at all. Thus, what counted in knowing a person were those consistent, stable, "natural" features that lay beyond the control of the individual. The fact is, the person described in progymnasmata, rhetorical manuals, physiognomics, or by Luke and Paul was simply not in control of life at all. The deeds of body and soul further underscored inherited qualities that a person might develop should the person seize the responsibility. And a person is praised for taking responsibility—yet in a situation totally controlled by other persons, human or divine.

PAUL'S SELF-PRESENTATION

Consider the salient and consistent highlights of Paul's self-presentation as they have emerged from our study.

Pedigree

Paul himself tells us in his own letters about his honorable origins: "Of the people of Israel, of the tribe of Benjamin, a Hebrew born of Hebrews" (Phil. 3:5) and "Hebrew . . . Israelite . . . descendant of Abraham" (2 Cor. 11:22). Luke records similar information: "a Judean, born at Tarsus in Cilicia (no low-status polis!) brought up in this polis [Jerusalem]" (Acts 22:3). By knowing his gender, geography, and generation, we are directed to identify Paul as an honorable and full member of an ancient, honorable ethnic group, as well as a person rooted in noble poleis, Tarsus and Jerusalem. In their respective contexts, both sets of remarks function precisely as honor claims, that is, claims to the honor that resides in others, either ethnic or geographical groups. Moreover, Paul boasts of these claims to excellence and thus affirms that he too accepts them as indicators of his basic personhood.

Education and Training

In his own letters Paul speaks only obliquely of his formation when he states that "as to the law a Pharisee" (Phil. 3:5, see Gal. 2:14). By his own admission, he is a Pharisee's Pharisee: "as to righteousness under the law blameless" (Phil. 3:6). He boldly admits, then, that he accepted his socialization into the Pharisaic way of life; by this he attests his embeddedness in group values and traditions, even to the point of being "blameless." But because his career depended on changing the focus of his formation from being zealous for God's law to being zealous for God's Christ, it is not surprising that Paul speaks so infrequently of his primary formation except to say that it now counts as rubbish for the sake of Christ (Phil. 3:7–8). Yet in Acts, Luke makes much of Paul's formation: "Brought up in this polis at the feet of Gamaliel, educated according to the strict manner of our fathers" (22:3; see 26:4). In the elite Jerusalem Temple setting, this is vital information about the person on trial, precisely because it indicates that Paul was not a boor or rustic, an 'am ha'aretz, a maverick individualist, but an educated person of considerable standing who embodies one of the great and honorable ways of being a servant of God. We know him to be quite knowledgeable in the traditions of his ethnic group, obedient to these traditions, and embedded in the group's values and structures. He is, in short, a decidedly group-embedded person.

Accomplishments/Moral Decisions

Paul's earliest life choice was to be zealous for God as a strict Pharisee: "As to the law a Pharisee, as to zeal a persecutor of the church, as to righteousness under the law blameless" (Phil. 3:6). This zeal manifests itself in his lifelong dedication to purity and perfection (Neyrey 1990a), which represent the con-scientia or "shared knowledge" Paul derived from his Pharisaic father and from membership in the Pharisaic group: "I am a Pharisee, the son of a Pharisee" (Acts 23:6). Note that Paul has sufficiently identified himself by proclaiming himself a member of a group, which both he and Luke presume is understood in terms of some stereotype (see Acts 23:7–8; Neyrey 1990a, 129–33). Paul's life is characterized, then, by a formation in and dedication to a disciplined way of living as a follower of God's will. He boasts only of his excellence in assimilating the education and discipline into which he was socialized. For he is at core a group-oriented person, not an inidividualist.

Most important, his Pharisaic dedication led him into conflict with the followers of the Jesus movement, whom he perceived as deviant (1 Cor. 15:9; Gal. 1:13, 23; Phil. 3:6; Acts 9:4–5; 22:4, 7–8; 26:11,14–15). Of course, the praiseworthy significance of his zeal will be assessed differently, depending on whether his audience consists of followers of the Way or its Judean opponents. Yet he is fully and adequately identified as a thoroughgoing party member, whether as a Pharisee persecuting or preaching the Way: ". . . the churches in Judea . . . only heard it said, 'He who once persecuted us is now preaching the faith he once tried to destroy'" (Gal. 1:23).

What is the origin of the obvious change in Paul's behavior from persecutor to preacher? It was not the result of individual investigation or study. It did not derive from his individual and personal anguish, anxiety, uncertainty, distress, or any other psychological state that we normally associate with soul-searching decision making or "conversion." Paul simply had no individualist "soul" to search. Rather, the change in his life was mandated to him from the outside, by God who revealed new information to him (Gal. 1:15–16), or by God's Messiah, Jesus, who commanded Paul to alter the thrust of his dedication to God and to change the way he lived his life (Acts 22:7–10; 26:14–18). In Damascus, God's prophet, Ananias, served as his new mentor, as Paul had been told: "There you will be told all that is appointed for you to do" (Acts 22:10). Paul's zeal, then, is always directed by others to new tasks. Paul is essentially obedient to group norms and group-sanctioned persons. He accepts the directives given to him, and thus manifests himself once more as a group-oriented person, a loyal "party member." He was transformed from being a figure who defended God's honor by applying sanctions to those deviants whom he believed challenged God's honor, to one who defended that same honor by proclaiming a gospel given him directly by God. God's patronage and favor are subsequently made known to Paul in manifestations of great favor: (1) revealing Israel's Messiah to him (Gal. 1:16) and (2) ascribing the role and status of prophet to him (Gal. 1:15; Acts 26:16–18). Basically, then, Paul's style is to concur with the decisions of others, either Pharisees (against the Way) or God (on behalf of the Way). It would be quite difficult to call Paul's transformation a "conversion" in any modern sense of the term. It really was God who changed matters by raising Jesus from the dead, not Paul!

Yet even prior to his experiencing God's greater patronage, divine providence placed Paul on an honorable life course. It associated him with honorable people: Israel, its Temple authorities, the Pharisees. Paul was a loyal son of the covenant and obedient to its values and structures. His divinely directed course of life led him to be associated with elites in Jerusalem because it was the high priest and the whole council of elders who commissioned Paul to persecute the Way in Damascus (Acts 22:5;

26:10). Had Paul remained a Pharisee and become a Jerusalem resident, he would have been praised in Israel for his purity and his zeal. But God had other plans, not Paul!

Deeds of the Body

In this regard, Paul tells us not of deeds of the body that bring him honor but of his shameful physical condition. Instead of strength, Paul acknowledges only weakness to the church at Corinth. He tells them, "I was with you in weakness and in much fear and trembling" (1 Cor. 2:3). And in later communications, he notes:

> Who is weak, and I am not weak? Who is made to fall, and I am not indignant? If I must boast, I will boast of the things that show my weakness. (2 Cor. 11:29–30)
> On behalf of this man I will boast, but on my own behalf I will not boast, except of my weakness. . . . he [God] said to me, "My grace is sufficient for you, for my power is made perfect in weakness." I will all the more gladly boast of my weaknesses, that the power of Christ may rest upon me. For the sake of Christ, then I am content with weaknesses, insults, hardships, persecutions, and calamities; for when I am weak, then I am strong. (2 Cor. 12:5, 9–10)

Instead of being credited with beauty as defined by the canons of his culture, he is stigmatized as a person with weak bodily presence: "His letters are weighty and strong, but his bodily presence is weak and his speech of no account" (2 Cor. 10:10). Instead of health, he admits to bodily ailments, but these work quite providentially: "You know it was because of a bodily ailment that I preached the gospel to you at first" (Gal. 4:13). And it seems that Paul is continually afflicted with illness: "We are . . . always carrying in the body the death of Jesus" (2 Cor. 4:10), presumably a bodily ailment of some sort. In short, Paul had no deeds of the body to recommend him, just the opposite.

Cultural conventions in the Greco-Roman world would interpret such phenomena negatively. Without strength, a man would be hard-pressed to claim or defend honor. In comparison to others, especially the elite ecstatics at Corinth, Paul is faulted for notably lacking the valued bodily skill of public speaking. While he preaches the power of God's spirit, he himself is weak and so calls into question either the message (which shames God) or his suitability for his role (which shames himself). Elliott has underscored Paul's bodily ailment in Gal. 4:12–16 from the perspective of the evil eye (1990; see Neyrey 1988a). He notes how Paul might have been feared and avoided because of his physical failings, thus highlighting the potential shame in his bodily ailment. In short, the radical absence of deeds of the body would normally betoken a lack of honor. Yet Paul turns dishonor into honor by using his weakness as his boast. Nevertheless, Paul's physical body is socially perceived and described; it is classified in terms of group meanings that Paul accepts.

Deeds of the Soul

The category of deeds of soul entails the four cardinal virtues as indices of a person's behavior. The traditional quartet bears the labels "prudence, justice, temperance, fortitude." What these refer to are practical know-how, fairness, a sense of shame, and courage—cultural categories that express group values and ideals. All through his letters, Paul sprinkles his claims to these; here we offer a sampling. Of the four, Paul makes the strongest claim for courage.

> So we are always of good courage [*tharrountes*]; we know that while we are at home in the body we are away from the Lord, for we walk by faith, not by sight. We are of good courage, and we would rather be away from the body and at home with the Lord. (2 Cor. 5:6–8)

He couples courage with the concern for honor that a sense of shame entails. For as a group-oriented person bent on the main collectivist goal of group integrity, Paul rests assured "that I shall not be at all ashamed, but that with full courage (*parrêsia*) now as always Christ will be honored in my body, whether by life or by death" (Phil. 1:20). We recall from chapter 2 how Paul showed courage in defending God's honor before Cephas at Antioch and the enemies of the gospel at Jerusalem (Gal. 2:12–14 and 2:4–5). As we noted, John Fitzgerald labeled Paul's repeated endurance of hardships in 2 Corinthians as examples of courage (1988, 87–91).

Paul surely considers himself endowed with wisdom, as is apparent from his sarcastic remarks to Corinthians who claim superior wisdom: "We are fools for Christ's sake, but you are wise in Christ. We are weak, but you are strong. You are held in honor, but we in disrepute" (1 Cor. 4:10). Paul is wise, indeed, but not by Corinthian norms:

> When I came to you, brethren, I did not come proclaiming to you the testimony of God in lofty words or wisdom . . . and my speech and my message were not in plausible words of wisdom, but in demonstration of the Spirit and of power, that your faith might not rest in the wisdom of men but in the power of God. Yet among the mature we do impart wisdom, although it is not a wisdom of this age or of the rulers of this age, who are doomed to pass away. But we impart a secret and hidden wisdom of God, which God decreed before the ages for our glorification. (1 Cor. 2:1–7)

Nevertheless, he claims to be a "wise" master builder (1 Cor. 3:10).

Furthermore, Paul knows and insists on justice. Since justice pertains to what is owed God, one's ancestors, and one's parents, Paul can claim in all candor to be a just person. In his incessant repetition of his divine commission, Paul presents himself as a person of exceptional *dikaiosynê:* he demonstrates faithfulness (*pistis*) to his celestial Patron and constant reverence (*eusebeia*), both elements of justice. He likewise celebrates the faithfulness of that Patron: "God is faithful, by whom you were called into fellowship" (1 Cor. 1:9; see 1 Thess. 5:24). He credits to God "everything laid down in the law and written in the prophets" (Acts 24:15). In regard to his ancestors, Paul followed their traditions with blamelessness: "Circumcised on the eighth day. . ." (Phil. 3:5; see Acts 22:3). Although Paul never speaks of his own parents, he presents himself as "father" and defends the rights and duties of a father, thus illustrating his appreciation of this cultural aspect of justice: "For though you have many guides in Christ, you do not have many fathers. For I became your father in Christ Jesus through the gospel" (1 Cor. 4:15). As a father, he jealously guards the church at Corinth as a father protects his daughter from evil suitors (2 Cor. 11:2). Beyond the classical three loci of justice, Paul also acknowledges justice toward those who have legitimate authority, even local magistrates. "Pay all of them their due, taxes to whom taxes are due, revenue to whom revenue is due, respect to whom respect is due, honor to whom honor is due" (Rom. 13:7).

Deeds of Fortune

As regards the deeds of fortune listed in the encomia and forensic defense speeches, Paul not only claims few but acknowledges what might be called "deeds of ill fortune." For example, regarding reputation, fame, and honor, Paul calls attention to his shame. In what follows, we include parallel references from Acts. Even though these pieces of information are not formally contained in the forensic defense speeches, notice of the lack of deeds of fortune is a major element in Luke's presentation of Paul.

Dishonor, not fame or reputation
a spectacle (1 Cor. 4:9)
a fool (1 Cor. 4:10)
in disrepute and dishonor (1 Cor. 4:10; 2 Cor. 6:8)
slandered (1 Cor. 4:13; Acts 17:4–5; 18:12–16; 21:21–29)
refuse of the world, offscouring of all things (1 Cor. 4:13)
treated as an imposter (2 Cor. 6:8)
unknown (2 Cor. 6:9)
mocked, reviled (Acts 17:32; 18:6)

Regarding wealth, Paul knows of its persistent lack.

Absence of wealth and riches

hungry and thirsty (1 Cor. 4:11; 2 Cor. 6:5; 11:27)

ill clad, homeless (1 Cor. 4:11; 2 Cor. 11:27)

enduring toil, labors (2 Cor. 6:5; 11:27)

suffering hardships (2 Cor. 11:27)

But especially in regard to power, Paul tells us of his afflictions at the hands of others and his shameful physical treatment.

Physical affronts, not power

persecution (1 Cor. 4:12; 2 Cor. 4:9; Acts 13:50; 20:3)

buffeting (1 Cor. 4:11)

affliction (2 Cor. 4:8; 6:4)

beatings (2 Cor. 6:5; 11:23–25; 12:7)

imprisonment (2 Cor. 11:25; Phil. 1:12–14, 17; Philemon; Acts 16:19–24; 22:22–26:31)

dangers (2 Cor. 11:26)

death threats (1 Cor. 4:9; 2 Cor. 11:32; Acts 9:23–25, 29; 14:5; 19:21–41; 21:31; 23:12–22; 25:3)

shipwrecks (2 Cor. 11:25; Acts 27:9–44)

Regarding patrons and "friendship," Paul boasts that while in residence, he does not allow the local church to support him and thus act as "friends" to him (1 Cor. 9:4–12; 2 Cor. 11:7–9). Marshall has argued that part of Paul's crisis at Corinth is precisely his refusal to accept local patronage and thus lower status there (1987, 101–5 and 165–77). To accept patronage from persons at Corinth would make Paul beholden to another. While Paul positively resists "friends," at least at Corinth, Philippi "entered into partnership with him" (Phil. 4:15–19). But Paul himself prefers to act as the broker of God's patronage and as the dispenser of God's favor. His exclusive claims to be God's broker have put him at odds with various church members.

Yet should we consider the flip side of "friendship," we find very little evidence that Paul made clients of people in his churches. Paul, like Jesus, acted like a broker. Brokers connect prospective clients with sought-after patrons. And brokers do not have clients; only patrons do. Stephanus, Paul's first adherent in Achaia, is described by Paul as a leader of the Corinthian church (1 Cor. 16:15–16), perhaps for his personal loyalty to Paul (vv. 17–18). Philemon is a special case, for Paul requires the assistance of his slave, and this would balance Philemon's debt to Paul (v. 19); but it does not entirely sound as though Paul was formally a patron to Philemon. Otherwise, we know very little of Paul's "friendship" relationships with members of his churches, at least in ways that might be cited as marks of honor.

Relative to another feature of fortune, marriage, Paul tells us that he was not married, at least at the time he wrote his first letter to the Corinthians (1 Cor. 7:7–8). And he tells us nothing of his children, whether numerous, accomplished, or well married themselves. Finally, Paul's letters obviously do not tell us of his death, yet neither does Luke in Acts. We know only of a persistent wish on his part to die as a transforming experience (2 Cor. 5:1–5; Phil. 1:19–26); and we are alerted to numerous death threats and plots. Thus Paul is singularly lacking in the honorable marks of divine favor, as these were conventionally understood.

In spite of his specific lists of deeds of ill fortune, Paul nevertheless claims God's singular favor and thus the honor of God's patronage. How frequently he celebrates the "gift" or "grace" given him by God (Malina 1988b, 3–11)! First, he never tires of proclaiming and defending the role and status God has ascribed to him—as apostle, prophet, master builder, father, and the like. Although acknowledging his ill fortune, Paul maintains that God defended his honor in these challenges and repeatedly vindicated him. He was *not* crushed, *not* driven to despair, *not* forsaken, *nor* destroyed (2 Cor. 6:8–9). Even his most shameful list of ill fortunes (2 Cor. 11:23–33) is cited as the boast of a "madman," in that such shameful events are actually his "boast" (v. 30). For in weakness he is "strong" (12:10), and through weakness he is made "perfect" (v. 9). As we previously noted, these catalogues of ill fortune resemble the lists of trials philosophers overcame and are mentioned as proof of the excellence of their teaching (Fitzgerald 1988, 114–16). Although philosophers underscored their courage and discipline in overcoming such hardships, Paul attributes his victories to divine favor as well. Hence, his deeds of ill fortune actually serve as proof of his ultimate good fortune and favor from God.

PAUL THE PROPHET

At one time Paul was a devoted adherent of Pharisaic ideology with its program of Israelite in-group exclusivity (motto: "no mixtures," Acts 8:3; 9:1). Yet he ended up as equally devoted to the advancement of a Messianic ideology focused on the inclusivity of all "in Messiah Jesus" (motto: "mixtures do not count"—"there is neither Judean nor Greek, there is neither slave nor free, there is neither male nor female; for you are all one in Christ Jesus," Gal. 3:28). Paul ascribes his acceptance of and dedication to the latter program to a personal experience of Jesus as raised by God (Gal. 1:15–16). Now what can be more individualistic than a divinely ordained, direct, personal experience of Jesus as raised Lord (as in Acts 9:2–22)? After that experience, the apostle portrays himself as a prophet, called from his mother's womb like the prophets of old, to make known God's will. Again, what can be more individualistic than consciousness of a divinely ordained birth of a single individual for a unique task at the divine direction? Do not the biblical writings clearly indicate that all of Israel's prophets were individualists? Does not prophetic awareness trace back to a singular, idiosyncratic, and unique person fully conscious of his uniqueness? Do not these events point to Paul as a true individualist, with Jesus as his "personal Lord and Savior," as a result of truly individualist, divinely ordained ecstatic experiences? And would not Paul's self-understanding as divinely called prophet and divinely directed "convert" simply nullify all that we have said about Paul as a collectivist, group-oriented person?

Of all persons depicted in the New Testament, prophets seem to speak most like U.S. individualist persons. First John the Baptist, then Jesus, then Paul (and others in Acts)—all these prophets seem to be speaking their individual minds regardless of consequences to their groups or to themselves. They are forthright, sincere, honest, just like North Americans are supposed to be. They "tell it like it is!" They rely on their individual, personal experience and express their individual, singular convictions thanks to their personal devotedness to God. If all that we have said in the foregoing pages is true, then how do such prophets take on such individualist traits in a collectivist culture like that of the ancient Mediterranean? How can group-oriented persons end up sounding so individualistic?

The purpose of what follows is to explain why these persons sound like individualists to us. They have a feature about their manner of speaking that definitely sounds individualist and resonates with our own individualism. To discern this feature, we rely on the work of the social psychologist Harry Triandis (1990).

Self-Defined Persons:
Private, Public, In-Group

There is an aspect of the social self that specifically looks to the mesh between individual person and the general culture type. In the framework of the model of individualist and collectivist cultures, Triandis notes that the various ways persons deal with their distinctive selves are specifically defined in the process of socialization and in later social experience. For a person's self is in fact defined by a range of sources. We ourselves define ourselves to ourselves—who we think we are. But a range of other persons do the same by the titles they give us, the way they treat us, the expectations they set for us, and the like. In other words, apart from who we think we are, there are a number of persons who tell us who we are, and we—even individualists—more often than not take these other persons quite seriously. Triandis distinguishes three distinctive selves: the privately defined self, the publicly defined self, and the collectively, or better, in-group-defined, self. The outcomes of the various processes of defining the self are as follows.

1. First, there is a *private self* deriving from what I myself say about my own traits, states, behaviors. Who is it I think I really am in my heart of hearts?
2. Then there is a *public self* that refers to what the general group says about me. Who does that range of people with whom I regularly come in contact think I am? What do neighbors, merchants, teachers, and the like say about me? Do I live up to their expectations when I interact with them? And what do I think of all that these people think of me?
3. Finally there is a *collective or in-group self* referring to what the in-group says about me. Who do my parents say I am? What are their expectations for me? Did my family give me a nickname? What does it say about me? What are the expectations of my grandparents, aunts and uncles, cousins, and brothers and sisters in regard to who I am, how I should behave, what I will be? And what do I think of what these people think of me? What do my friends want me to do, over against what my parents want me to do?

Socially Defined Self
in Collectivist Cultures

To understand the self in terms of social psychology, we need to know the way the defined self emerges in the contrasting cultural types. Thus people from collectivist cultures sample and take stock of in-group self-assessments far more than people in individualist cultures. In collectivist cultures, there is a general conformity between private self and in-group self. What this means is that people are expected to tell others in the in-group what they believe those others want to hear, rather than what they really think. Matthew's Gospel tells a relevant parable: "What do you think? A man had two sons; and he went to the first and said, 'Son, go and work in the vineyard today.' And he answered, 'I will not'; but afterward he repented and went. And he went to the second and said the same; and he answered, 'I go, sir,' but did not go" (Matt. 21:28–30). Of course, in collectivist cultures, the better son is the second since he does not embarrass his father. The privately defined self and its concerns are to stay submerged in the self defined by the in-group, here defined by the father.

Similarly, note how in the Gospel narratives, whole groups speak at one time. Of course this never happens in real life. Yet by ascribing a statement to a group, the authors witness to the perspective that the individual's viewpoint is that of the group: private and in-group selves coincide. In this way, no individual is agent alone, rather the whole group is. For example, consider these few passages from Matthew's Gospel: "And they went and woke him, saying, 'Save, Lord; we are perishing'" (Matt. 8:25); "And the men marveled, saying, 'What sort of man is this, that even winds and sea obey him?'" (Matt. 8:27); "Then the disciples of John came to him, saying, 'Why do we and the Pharisees fast, but your disciples do not fast?'" (Matt. 9:14; see also Matt. 13:36; 14:2, 33; 16:7; 18:1; 19:25; 21:10, 20; 22:16; 24:3; 25:11; 26:8, 17; 27:29, 41–43).

In collectivist cultures, individuals are enculturated not to express what they personally think but to say what their conversation partner or audience needs or wants to hear from their in-group. This split between the private and in-group self is required by politeness and a sense of shame. Thus, when it comes to dealing with in-group others, individuals are expected to think one way and speak another. For the most part, harmony or getting along with in-group neighbors is valued above all sorts of other concerns. Saying the right thing to maintain harmony is far more important than telling what seems to be the truth to the private self. In fact, truth might be defined here as conformity between what the in-group thinks about some person, event, or thing, and what the private self believes and knows. We see this sort of truth emerging when at Jesus' degradation before Pilate, all involved agree that Jesus should be crucified since the in-group core, the chief priests, "accused him of many things" (Mark 15:3). The crowd verdict, "Crucify him," is quick to follow (Mark 15:13–14). Collectivist persons are not expected to have personal opinions, much less to voice their own opinions. It is sufficient and required to hold only those opinions that derive from social consensus. Social behavior derives from relative status where hierarchy is the essence of social order. (For an example from an earlier period, yet with similar social structure, see Jeremiah 26, where groups speak to one another and arrive at a decision based upon tradition and the leadership of the village elders.)

Socially Defined Self
and Individualist Cultures

In individualist cultures, the in-group self recedes while the public and private selves converge to form a single "objectively" defined private self. This is because two inconsistent selves cause the individual to experience dissonance as well as to undergo a sort of information overload. Furthermore, in individualist cultures, the public and private selves are influenced by the same factors. People, like their publicly defined selves, are expected to be "honest" even if ignorant, "frank" even if brutal, and "sincere" even if stupid. Here one must think and say the same thing. Honesty, frankness, sincerity are more abstract and less interpersonal for individualists. Everyone is expected to have an opinion on everything. Others are supposed to act as though everyone's opinion counted for something. Social behavior derives from individualist choices based on one's publicly defined class affiliation.

Comparative Conclusions

Relative to behavior springing from the ways in which the self is defined, the collectivist individual represents the in-group and is presumed to always speak in its name. It is shameful to tell the truth if it dishonors one's in-group or one's serious conversation partner or causes them discomfort. It is equally shameful to expect to be told the truth if one is not an in-group member. Out-group persons have no right to in-group truth (notice how Jesus explains the real meaning of his teaching only to the in-group, in private: Mark 4:2–20; 7:14–23; 10:2–12; Matt. 13:3–23; 15:10–20; 19:3–12). In nonchallenging situations, out-group persons are almost always told what makes for harmony and what is to be expected. An individual is not expected to have his or her own, personal opinion on anything. Making a friend feel good by what one has to say is a way of honoring the other, and that is far more important than "telling the truth." Thus, in collectivist cultures, the privately defined self and the in-group self tend to coincide. The person speaks in the group's name in public.

On the other hand, individualists as a rule fuse the privately and publicly defined selves. The private self is in fact the acting public self. This is called "objectivity," and individualists value being objective in speech. To lie is to say one thing publicly while thinking another privately. Thus, in individualist cultures, the privately defined self and the publicly defined self tend to coincide. I speak in my own name in public.

Consider the following diagram in which the enclosed, boxed-in defined selves are expected to match to produce 'truth."

Collectivist Culture	Individualist Culture
privately defined self in-group defined self	privately defined self publicly defined self
publicly defined self	in-group defined self

In each type of culture a lie consists in splitting the selves included in the boxes. Thus, an individualistic lie is to think one thing and say another. That involves splitting what one privately knows from what one publicly says. To a collectivist, a lie involves splitting private and in-group "truth." As for outsiders, the individual is always to give the public what the in-group expects and holds. (For examples, look at statements coming from hierarchical and collectivist U.S. government spokespersons, for whom statements are not true or false, but operative or inoperative, with or without plausible deniability!) In a collectivist culture, one's private knowledge has nothing to do with truth. Deviations from such general orientations readily stand out. This is especially notable in the case of the prophet in collectivist cultures.

PROPHETS

The biblical record is peopled by collectivist personages. Bible readers, therefore, must learn to appreciate the prophetic role as a collectivist cultural role. Now from the point of view of defined selves, what is distinctive about prophets is their willingness to have their private self dissociated from their in-group self. That means they will readily blurt out both to the in-group and in public what they really think, just as a child does. When a child loudly exclaims how fat his or her mother's friend is, that might be embarrassing to the mother and the mother's friend. But for a child to speak "the truth" is considered both childish and childlike. This holds in collectivist cultures as well.

But in collectivist cultures, as we have noted, adults tend to conform their private self and its judgments with the in-group self. While people in these societies are socialized to suppress their private self in favor of an in-group-shaped self presented to the public, the prophet allows private and public self controlling position. For the prophet does not submerge his privately defined self and its private experiences in favor of telling others what they want to hear. He does not conform his privately defined self with his in-group-defined self. Rather, the prophet publicly tells a message derived from private experience, thus conforming the private with the in-group.

What the prophet's privately defined self has to say is ascribed to personal, individual, ecstatic experience, but it is the private self nonetheless. Prophets can always behave like adults and keep their private thoughts to themselves. But their experience of God, their prophetic experience, takes place in an altered state of consciousness, an experience that socially entitles and impels them to speak freely and publicly. Hence, prophets must make their private self coincide with the public prophetic self because they believe that the burden of their message is rooted in a divinely caused private experience with a public objective, the experience of "revelation." The same is true of experiences involving dreams, visions, and stars, for example. In collectivist contexts, prophets (and magi and astrologers), thanks to their altered states of consciousness, seem to fall into individualist interludes in their normally collectivist lives, interludes characterized by altered states of consciousness (see Pilch 1993b; 1995).

Thus to Euro-American individualist Bible readers, prophets sound honest, frank, sincere, and direct. They "tell it like it is" or ought to be. This feature of a prophet's behavior, therefore, is not surprising to individualist persons because this is normal individualist behavior. But such is not the case in collectivist cultures. Hence, when Paul speaks like a prophet, with authority based on his experiences in an altered state of consciousness, he only sounds like an individualist. In fact, he is speaking as a prophet, quite aware of the collectivist dimensions of his culture, as noted throughout this book. He continues to be a collectivist or group-oriented person but acts in an individualist mode, joining private and public self in the process of delivering a divine message.

CONCLUSION

For all of the "independence" claimed for Paul by modern Western readers, he presents himself as utterly dependent on group expectations and the controlling hand of forces greater than he: ancestors, groups, God. He was a typically group-oriented person. In fact, "independence" of any group authorization would have been a major liability to him. From the viewpoint of modern biography, we must admit that we know nothing of his character, personality, idiosyncrasies, likes and dislikes, and other vast dimensions of his life. The most we can say is that he was a group-oriented person, not at all an individualist. But in terms of ancient Mediterranean concerns, we do not need to know any more than we do, for from what he tells us, we can fill in all that is necessary to know the man in his society.

All in all, the most significant determinants of who or what a person is is derived from outside the individual person. It is these determinants that the ancients believed were worth knowing and noting. Everyone was an "other-made" man or woman. "Self-made" persons simply did not exist at all. And even if they did exist, given cultural norms, they would either not be noticed at all, or they would be branded as deviants and degenerates. We have continually mentioned the various levels of embeddedness all persons experience (generation, geography, and gender; and the fictive generation of patron-client relations). Moreover, one is not permitted to forget that everything in life that counts has been received from others. Hence, one actually has no control over anything of importance. Persons surely have no control over generation, geography, and gender. They have no control over who forms them, over the stages of growth they undergo, over the events and persons they encounter. For the most part, what situates a person socially befalls or just happens to the person. Significant achievements derive from ascribed status and are not produced by the individual achiever as we understand "self-made" persons. Instead of a "vanity wall" with plaques marking personal accomplishments such as we might see in a friend's office or home, the first-century Mediterranean would feature masks, busts, and memorials of ancestors who made them to be who they were, thanks, of course, to the God(s) of these ancestors. Romans actually set out these representations on the walls of their houses. Israelites did much the same in the cadences of their genealogies. We conclude, then, with the cultural truism noted by Paul: "What have you that you did not receive? If then you received it, why do you boast as if it were not a gift?" (1 Cor. 4:7).

Appendix 1

Progymnasmata and Rhetorical Treatises

In this appendix, we present a listing of the progymnasmata and rhetorical treatises used in this book, followed by a sampling of encomia from progymnasmata. For an assessment of these ancient works (author, dating, historical significance, and the like), see the excellent study of George A. Kennedy (1994).

Progymnasmata

Aelius Theon of Alexandria, cited from Leonard Spengel, ed. *Rhetores Graeci*. 3 vols. Leipzig: Teubner, 1853–56. Reprint, Frankfurt: Minerva, 1966. II.112.20–115.10. See Butts (1986).

Aphthonius of Ephesus, cited from Spengel, *Rhetores Graeci,* II.42.20–44.19. An English translation was done by Nadeau (1952).

Hermogenes of Tarsus, cited from Spengel, *Rhetores Graeci,* II.14.8–15.5. An English translation was done by Baldwin (1928, 23–38); see also Wooten (1987).

Menander Rhetor, cited from Russell and Wilson (1981).

Rhetorical Treatises

Aristotle. *Rhetorica.* Trans. J. H. Freese. Loeb Classical Library. Cambridge, Mass.: Harvard University Press, 1926.

Aristotle. *Rhetorica ad Alexandrum.* Trans. H. Rackham. Loeb Classical Library. Cambridge, Mass.: Harvard University Press, 1957.

Cicero. *De Inventione.* Trans. H. M. Hubbell. Loeb Classical Library. Cambridge, Mass.: Harvard University Press, 1949.

Quintilian, *Institutio Oratoria*. 4 Vols. Trans. H. E. Butler. Loeb Classical Library. Cambridge, Mass.: Harvard University Press, 1920–22.

Rhetorica ad Herennium. Trans. Harry Caplan. Loeb Classical Library. Cambridge, Mass.: Harvard University Press, 1954.

Sample Texts of the Encomium in the Progymnasmata

I.   Quintilian (*Inst. Orat.* 2.4.1–42)

   A.   First subjects of rhetoric (to teach to youths)

      1.   Narratio (2.4.2)

      2.   Refutation/Confirmation (2.4.18)

      3.   Praise/Blame (2.4.20)

      4.   Commonplaces (2.4.22)

      5.   Theses (2.4.24)

      6.   Chreia (or Moral Essay) (2.4.26)

      7.   Laws (2.4.33)

II. Quintilian (*Inst. Orat.* 3.7.10–18)

> In the Praise of Men. In the first place there is a distinction to be made as regards time between the period in which the objects of our praise lived and the time preceding their birth; and further, in the case of the dead we must also distinguish the period following their death. With regard to things preceding a man's birth, there are his country, his parents and ancestors, a theme which may be handled in two ways. For either it will be creditable to the objects of our praise not to have fallen short of the fair fame of their country and of their sires or to have ennobled a humble origin by the glory of their achievements. Other topics to be drawn from the period preceding their birth will have reference to omens or prophecies foretelling their future greatness, such as the oracle which is said to have foretold that the son of Thetis would be greater than his father. The praise of the individual will be based on his character, his physical endowments and external circumstances. Physical and accidental advantages provide a comparatively unimportant theme, which requires variety of treatment. Homer does in the case of Agamemnon and Achilles; at times again weakness may contribute largely to our admiration, as when Homer says that Tydeus was small of stature but a good fighter. Fortune too may confer dignity as in the case of kings and princes (for they have a fairer field for the display of their excellences) but on the other hand the glory of good deeds may be enhanced

by the smallness of the resources. Moreover the praise awarded to external and accidental advantages is given, not to their possession, but to their honourable employment. For wealth and power and influence, since they are the sources of strength, make the surest test of character for good or evil; they make us better or they make us worse. Praise awarded to character is always just, but may be given in various ways. It has sometimes proved the more effective to trace a man's life and deeds in due chronological order, praising his natural gifts as a child, then his progress at school, and finally the whole course of his life, including words as well as deeds. At times on the other hand it is well to divide our praises, dealing separately with the various virtues, fortitude, justice, self-control and the rest of them and to assign to each virtue the deeds performed under its influence. We shall have to decide which of these two methods will be the more serviceable, according to the nature of the subject; but we must bear in mind the fact that what most pleases an audience is the celebration of deeds which our hero was the first or only man or at any rate one of the very few to perform: and to these we must add any other achievements which surpassed hope or expectation, emphasizing what was done for the sake of others rather than what he performed on his own behalf. It is not always possible to deal with the time subsequent to our hero's death: this is due not merely to the fact that we sometimes praise him, while still alive, but also that there are but few occasions when we have a chance to celebrate the award of divine honours, posthumous votes of thanks, or statues erected at the public expense. Among such themes of panegyric [praise] I would mention monuments of genius that have stood the test of time. For some great men like Menander have received ampler justice from the verdict of posterity than from their own age. Children reflect glory on their parents, cities on their founders, laws on those who made them, arts on their inventors and institutions on those that first introduced them; for instance Numa first laid down rules for the worship of the gods, and Publicola first ordered that the lictor's rods should be lowered in salutation to the people.

III. Theon of Alexandria (List of topics found in Marrou 1964; a schematic translation of Spengel, II.109.28–110)

    A. External excellences

        1. Noble birth (eugeneia)

        2. Environment

           a) Native polis

           b) Fellow politai

        c) Excellence of polis's political regime

        d) Parents and family

    3. Personal advantages

        a) Education

        b) Friends

        c) Fame

        d) Public service

        e) Wealth

        f) Children, number and beauty of

        g) Happy death (euthanasia)

B. Bodily excellences

    1. Health

    2. Strength

    3. Beauty

    4. Bubbling vitality and capacity for deep feeling

C. Spiritual excellences

    1. Virtues

        a) Wisdom

        b) Temperance

        c) Courage

        d) Justice

        e) Piety

        f) Nobility

        g) Sense of greatness

    2. Resultant actions

        a) As to their objectives

            (i) Altruistic and disinterested

            (ii) Good, not utilitarian or pleasant

            (iii) In the public interest

            (iv) Braving risks and dangers

        b) As to their circumstances

            (i) Timely

            (ii) Original

            (iii) Performed alone

      (iv) More than anyone else
      (v) Few to help him
      (vi) Old head on young shoulders
      (vii) Against all odds
      (viii) At great cost to himself
      (ix) Prompt and efficient

IV.   Hermogenes (Translated by C. S. Baldwin 1928, 31–32)

Subjects for encomia are: a race, as the Greek, a city, as Athens, a family, as the Alcmaeonidae. You will say what marvelous things befell at the birth, as dreams or signs or the like. Next, the nurture, as, in the case of Achilles, that he was reared on lion's marrow and by Chiron. Then the training, how he was trained and how educated. Not only so, but the nature of soul and body will be set forth, and of each under heads: for the body, beauty, stature, agility, might; for the soul, justice, self-control, wisdom, manliness. Next his pursuits, what sort of life he pursued, that of philosopher, orator, or soldier, and most properly his deeds, for deeds come under the head of pursuits. For example, if he chose the life of a soldier, what in this did he achieve? Then external resources, such as kin, friends, possessions, household, fortune, etc. Then from the (topic) time, how long he lived, much or little; for either gives rise to encomia. A long-lived man you will praise on this score; a short-lived, on the score of his not sharing those diseases which come from age. Then, too, from the manner of his end, as that he died fighting for his fatherland, and, if there were anything extraordinary under that head, as in the case of Callimachus that even in death he stood. You will draw praise also from the one who slew him, as that Achilles died at the hands of the god Apollo. You will describe also what was done after his end, whether funeral games were ordained in his honor, as in the case of Patroclus, whether there was an oracle concerning his bones; as in the case of Orestes, whether his children were famous, as Neoptolemus. But the greatest opportunity in encomia is through comparisons, which you will draw as the occasion may suggest.

V.   Aphthonius (Translated by Nadeau 1952, 260)

Now this is the exact division of the encomium, and you should work it out under these topics: You will make the exordium according to the subject at hand; next, you will place genus, which you will divide into race, fatherland, forebears, and fathers; then, you will take up education, which you will divide into inclination to study, talent, and rules; then, you will bring out the most important topic of the encomium, the achievements, which you will divide into the spirit, the body, and fortune—the spirit like courage or prudence, the body like beauty, swiftness, or strength, and fortune like power, wealth, and friends. To these you will add comparison, in order to infer a greater position for the one being praised through the process of placing side by side; finally, the epilogue more in the style of a solemn prayer.

VI.   Scolion on Aphthonius (Translated from Walz, *Rhetores Graeci,* II.617.18–27)

The five divisions of an egkômion are: birth, education, actions, comparison, and epilogue. Into how many parts is "birth" divided? into four: race/tribe, country, ancestors, and elders/ fathers. Into how many parts is "education" divided? into three: pursuit in life, manner-craft, customs. Into how many parts is "action" divided? in what pertains to the soul, the body and fortune. The virtues of the soul are: prudence, courage, temperance and justice. Of the body: stature, strength, beauty and health. In addition to these [of fortune]: wealth, good fortune, friendship.

Appendix 2

Individualists and Collectivists:
A Comparative Table

To make it easier for the reader to grasp the differences between a person from modern Western society and an ancient Mediterranean, we present a comparative table of salient features that summarizes most of the themes presented in the course of this book. However, before setting out that table, we believe it might be profitable to offer a brief consideration of self-centeredness and other-centeredness as these relate to individualist and collectivist cultures.

SELF-CENTERED AND OTHER-CENTERED PERSONS

Triandis and his associates have pointed out (1990, 1993) that along with the cultural setting of human socialization along the axes of individualist and collectivist cultures, it is important to note direction of individual behavior within both individualist and collectivist cultures. For persons, whether individualists or collectivists by enculturation, direct their activities toward other persons with a quality that can be styled self-centered or other-centered. From the viewpoint of who is to benefit, the personal orientation of behavior runs along a scale from self-centered activity (also called idiocentric behavior) on the one end, to other-centered activity (also called allocentric behavior) on the other. With this perspective, we can say that just as in our individualist society, we have narcissistic, self-centered individualists as well as supportive, other-centered individualists, so in antiquity, there were self-centered collectivists and other-centered collectivists.

This, of course, means that individualism need not be, and—as most United States persons know—most often is not selfish! Individualist Christians today can and very frequently do work for the good of others. But this also means that collectivists are not altruistic and other-centered just because they are collectivist. Given their in-group orientation, chances are high that collectivist cultures produce self-centered families far more than individualist cultures produce self-centered individuals! The Gospel tradition, of course, says little about self-centered individuals apart from the "rich" (that is, the "greedy rich") who wield the household's wealth. But it does note self-centered families (e.g., the brothers John and James seeking precedence over the others, Mark 10:37—at the instigation of their mother, in Matt. 20:21). The Gospel tradition also insists on a person's need to "leave" or "hate" family! In collectivist society, to "deny one-self" essentially means to reject one's family, the roots and support of the self (see Malina 1994a, 106–119).

The reason we consider a person's self-centered or other-centered orientation is that this dimension adds a further nuance to the fundamental way in which persons are socialized in line with cultural cues, as individualist and collectivist. For both individualists as well as collectivists may be oriented to the self or to others in interpersonal relations. In the case of Paul, note that his enculturation into the Pharisaic "no mixture" ideology would tend to focus on collectivist self-centeredness. After all, one must be constantly centered on the collectivist self to be sure nothing untoward—such as a foreigner or a foreign substance—mixes in and infects the group. Pharisaic concern in this regard is indicated by the effort to "strain out the gnat" so as not to ingest an "unclean" entity, "to wash the outside of the cup" lest anything adhere to it, or "to whitewash tombs" lest persons step on them (Matt. 23:24–26). This sort of social narcissism, best summed up in the motto "no mixtures," is an excellent instance of collectivistic self-centeredness. Of course, the "mixtures do not matter" perspective of Paul's Messianic movement groups stands somewhat opposed to his previous ideology.

COMPARATIVE TABLE
OF SALIENT FEATURES

The following table lists those features of individualist Western cultures next to comparable features in collectivist ancient Mediterranean cultures. The listing should contribute to building better scenarios for fairer Bible reading.

Western Cultures	Ancient Mediterranean Cultures
Individualist: people are socialized to think of themselves as individualists and to relate to others as individuals.	Collectivist: people are socialized to think of themselves as dyadic group members and to relate to others stereotypically.
Individual persons are to think psychologically and individualistically, and to avoid stereotypes.	Group-oriented persons are to think "socially," in group terms, and to employ inherited stereotypes.
Individuals represent themselves and their own opinions alone.	Individuals always represent their groups and the views of their groups.
Individuals and groups are unpredictable and always changing.	Individuals and groups are quite predictable, stable, and unchanging.
Individuals, singly and corporately, are responsible for social choices: marriage, economy, political decisions.	God (fate, fortune, providence) alone ordains all social arrangements and outcomes.
Social authority is from the populace.	Social authority is from above (divine controlling force, God).
Individuals are expected to experience a great deal of geographical and social mobility and status change.	Individuals and groups are expected to experience little if any geographical and social mobility or status change over many generations.
Individuals constantly probe themselves about their true identity. "Know thyself" is an introvert, psychological maxim.	Individuals and groups are endowed with clear and certain social identity. "Know thyself" is an extravert, social maxim for probing whether others still think the same of our group.
Individually internalized norms (conscience) are the main behavioral control.	Socially supervised social situations are the main behavioral control.
There is an unwillingness to enter the private lives of others or to have others enter one's own private life.	There is an unwillingness to leave the lives of others or to have others leave one's own life.
People have to freely join communities; they tend to have broad, shallow relationships rather than deep, long-term ones.	People have no choice but to fit into inherited communities; they have extremely few but deep relationships within those communities.
Basic belief: individualist realism. The individual is believed to be the primary reality, with society as a second-order, artificial or derived construct.	Basic belief: group realism. Society (groups) is believed to be the primary reality, while the individual is a second-order, artificial or derived construct.

(TABLE CONTINUES)

TABLE (CONTINUED)

Western Cultures	Ancient Mediterranean Cultures
Focus in childhood: psychological development is on separation, individuation, and leaving home in late adolescence (a sort of second birth). The prospect of the child never leaving home is a discomforting option for both parent and child.	Focus in childhood: psychological development is on codependence, on group embeddedness, "dyadization," and the son's and wife's fitting into the paternal home upon marriage rather early in adolescence. The prospect of a (male) child ever leaving home is a frightening thing for both parent and (male) child.
Moral imperative: be good because it makes sense, it is right, it works, it leads to competitive success.	Moral imperative: be good to those in the group so that people in the group would continue to love/like/help you. The outside is important only insofar as it impacts the group.
One discovers one's personal beliefs in the isolation of one's private self. The self is seen as autonomous, imagined as existing independently, entirely outside any controlling tradition and community; individuals see themselves as actually free to choose their tradition and community.	One discovers one's deepest beliefs in and through the group, the community, and its traditions. There is rarely if ever an experience of an autonomous self; it is rather impossible to imagine a self acting independently, outside the inherited tradition and the community that upholds it.
Life is like a game in which one joins teams for sociable problem solving, requiring respect for rules as much as love of competition. The good life offers achievement-oriented security within a fixed social order.	When social life is stable, life is like a pilgrimage or quest, with a story line or narrative that links present to past, the individual to society, and both to a meaningful, ever-unfolding cosmos. When social life is unstable, life is a skirmish of ongoing conflicts in defense of the scarce acquisitions amassed by one's group and always desired by others. In these conflicts it seems that the immoral are ever victorious.
Salient features: self-reliance, individual happiness and success, self-realization, psychological gratification.	Salient features: group well-being, prudence (being controlled by in-group advice), justice (performing in-group obligations), temperance (sense of shame, concern for status), fortitude (endurance, courage, strength of character).
United States focus is on efficient cause (on how to produce effects, on know-how, pragmatism). The focus is on future-oriented po-	Mediterranean focus is on final cause (for what purpose, on knowing why, purposiveness). The focus is on purpose for pursuing

(TABLE CONTINUES)

TABLE (CONTINUED)

tential (but without asking, For what purpose? Why?). Achievement orientation is assessed by quantity (and often regardless of the quality of the achievement). In popular morality, the core problem lies in the goodness or badness of strategies, means, or techniques, hence on utilitarian concerns.

present-oriented selection of tasks (but without a thought to how these goals might in fact be realized; good facade, good show, and good intention suffice). In popular morality, the core problem always lies in the goodness or badness of principles concerning the ends pursued, hence on the nature of principles as guiding the intentions of agents.

Concern is with a freer, more autonomous self; to be free of obstacles is a good in itself, with little concern about asking, Free for what?

Concern is with the primary goal of group integrity while maintaining the status quo; to be free of constraints is a precarious position, hence little concern about asking, How do I get free of the in-group?

Constant attentiveness to what one does as individual agent. Total inattentiveness to what one has received from others or to one's obligations to those from whom one has received.

Constant attentiveness to what one has received from others and one's duties to those from whom one has received. Total inattentiveness to what one in fact has individually contributed to the realization of goals.

An individualist-oriented society based on individual achievement orientation. Tenancy is temporary; no hereditary dependency. Obligation derives from individuals contracting to their own self-interest.

A kinship-oriented society; lineage, inherited status are decisive. Tenancy is permanent, the basis of hereditary dependency. Obligation derives from group membership and serves the survival of the group.

Because kinship relations are independent of individual choice and will, they can be dismissed to a considerable extent (unless elaborated on another basis, e.g. economic dependency, friendship).

Because kinship relations are independent of individual choice and will, they are perceived as God-given, sacred. They couple with other imposed relations such as civic friendship in public solidarity (when society is stable) or in contending groups or factions (when society is unstable).

Anything that creates more sensitive, more open, more intense, more allocentric relationships points to achievements of which group members may be proud.

But anything that renders those same relationships fragile and vulnerable is seen to undermine those achievements (although free individual choice requires fragile and vulnerable relationships).

Anything that creates more obedient, more in-group-oriented, more compliant, more group-centered relationships points to achievements of which group members may be proud.

And anything that renders those same relationships permanent and unwaveringly impermeable is seen to further support those achievements.

Because the only measure of the good is what is good for the self, something that is really a burden to the self cannot be good.

Because the only measure of good is what is good for the group, something that is really a burden to the group cannot be good.

(TABLE CONTINUES)

TABLE (CONTINUED)

Western Cultures	Ancient Mediterranean Cultures
The ultimate meaning of life stands quite apart from conforming to the purely procedural and institutionally variable rules and regulations that surround the individual in society; self-integration is what counts.	The ultimate meaning of life consists precisely in conforming to the purely procedural and institutionally variable rules and regulations that surround the individual in society; social integration is what counts.
It is ethically and religiously wrong to violate the individual's right to think for himself or herself, to judge for himself or herself, to make one's own decisions, to live life as one sees fit.	It is ethically and religiously wrong to violate the group's right to have its legitimate "leaders" think for its members, to judge on their behalf, to make decisions for them, to make sure that life is lived as those "leaders" see fit.
The individual is prior to society; society only comes into existence through the voluntary contract of individuals trying to maximize their own self-interests.	Society is prior to the individual; individuals come into existence as singular persons only through (1) the societal recognition and legitimation of singular individual roles and statuses exercised by persons on behalf of their group(s) and (2) by trying to maximize the group's collective interests.
Success is the outcome of free competition among individuals in an open market.	Success consists in living up to and maintaining one's inherited social status.
Achievement is deserved only to the extent that individuals can claim to have succeeded through their own efforts. While others may have contributed, a successful person denies the moral relevance of those contributions.	Achievement is deserved only to the extent that individuals can claim to have succeeded through inherited status, kinship connections, and the group support that is one's due. A successful person is aware only of the moral relevance of the contribution of others to his or her success.
Politics is viewed in terms of a consensual community of autonomous but essentially similar individuals.	When social life is stable, politics is viewed in terms of the ethnic group in which concerns of ethnic interest and the best families that embody and represent those concerns transcend particular interests. When social life is unstable, politics is viewed in terms of conflict among contending groups with differing utilitarian and expressive interests.
Nonautonomous individuals are illegitimate and anomalous.	When social life is stable, families that represent nonelite and nonethnic interests are illegitimate and anomalous. One must respect the well-born.

(TABLE CONTINUES)

TABLE (CONTINUED)

When social life is unstable, groupless, unconnected individuals and families are illegitimate and anomalous. One must belong to some group.

Different levels and degrees of wealth and power derive from competition and achievement, which are assessed as amoral.

When social life is stable, different levels and degrees of wealth and power derive from inherited family statuses that constitute the social body and have positive moral meaning. (United States people see such wealth and power as due to exploitation and oppression, but Mediterraneans see it as deriving from some higher order norm that ennobles and obliges high-status people.)

When social life is unstable, inherited social statuses and the different levels and degrees of wealth and power are due to inequalities of moral probity, with the well-born and their greater wealth and power perceived as more corrupt.

Religion, a free-standing institution, is concerned with the moral order. Religion is an individual concern operating through voluntary associations.

Religion, embedded in kinship and/or politics, is concerned with the moral order. Political religion is a public concern, controlled by elites and operating to maintain the status quo that is public order. Domestic religion is a kinship concern, controlled by the head of the family and operating to maintain family integrity.

Emphasis is on self-control, self-respect, and ethical commitments in a competitive world.

Emphasis is on deference and obedience to public authorities, on submission toward serving the stable harmony of an organic community.

Thus individualistic, self-affirming, affective emphasis in religion is, for example, on "God's" love or equivalent, on sentiment and emotion, demonstrating one as a "good" person, on acceptance of the self.

Thus collective, group-affirming, rational emphasis in religion is, for example on God's truth and commands, on doctrine, and on objective ethical norms.

Bibliography

Anderson, Benedict. 1983. *Imagined Communities: Reflections on the Origin and Spread of Nationalism.* London: Verso.

André, Jacques, ed. and trans. 1981. *Anonyme Latin, Traité de physiognomonie.* Paris: Belles Lettres.

Augsburger, David W. 1986. *Pastoral Counseling Across Cultures.* Philadelphia: Westminster Press.

Aujac, Germaine. 1966. *Strabon et la science de son temps: Le sciences du monde.* Paris: Belle Lettres.

Aune, David. 1988. Greco-Roman Biography. Pp. 107–26 in *Greco-Roman Literature and the New Testament: Selected Forms and Genres.* Edited by David E. Aune. Sources for Biblical Study 21. Atlanta: Society of Biblical Literature.

Bagnall, Roger S., and Bruce W. Frier. 1994. *The Demography of Roman Egypt.* New York: Cambridge University Press.

Bailey, Jon Nelson. 1993. *Repentance in Luke-Acts.* Ph.D. diss., University of Notre Dame.

Baldwin, C. S. 1928. *Medieval Rhetoric and Poetic.* New York: Macmillan Publishing Co.

Barrett, C. K. 1994. *Paul: An Introduction to His Thought.* Louisville, Ky.: Westminster John Knox Press.

Becker, Jürgen. 1993. *Paul: Apostle to the Gentiles.* Translated by O. C. Dean Jr. Louisville, Ky.: Westminster/John Knox Press.

Bell, Daniel. 1976. *The Cultural Contradictions of Capitalism.* New York: Basic Books.

Bellah, Robert et al. 1985. *Habits of the Heart: Individualism and Commitment in American Life.* Berkeley, Calif.: University of California Press.

Berman, Ronald. 1987. *How Television Sees Its Audience: A Look at the Looking Glass.* Newbury Park, Calif.: Sage.

Betz, Hans Dieter. 1979. *Galatians: A Commentary on Paul's Letter to the Churches in Galatia.* Hermeneia. Philadelphia: Fortress Press.

Beutler, J. 1972. *Martyria.* Frankfurt: Josef Knecht.

Billerbeck, Paul (Strack and Billerbeck). 1922–1961. *Kommentar zum Neuen Testament aus Talmud und Midrasch.* 6 Vols. 1965. Reprint, Munich: Beck.

Black, Mark. 1981. Paul and Roman Law in Acts. *Revue de Qumran* 24:209–18.

Blok, Anton. 1981. Rams and Billy Goats: A Key to the Mediterranean Code of Honour. *Man* 16:427–40. Reprinted, pp. 51–70 in *Religion, Power and Protest in Local Communities. The Northern Shore of the Mediterranean.* Edited by Eric Wolf. New York: Mouton Publishers, 1984.

Bodson, Liliane. 1982. La notion de race animale chez les zoologistes et les agronomes dans l'antiquité. *Bulletin de la société d'ethnozootechnie* 29:7–14.

Boehm, Christopher. 1984. *Blood Revenge: The Anthropology of Feuding in Montenegro and Other Tribal Societies.* Lawrence, Kans.: University Press of Kansas.

Boman, Thorlief. 1960. *Hebrew Thought Compared with Greek.* Translated by Jules L. Moreau. Philadelphia: Westminster Press.

Bonner, Robert J. 1905. *Evidence in Athenian Courts.* Chicago: University of Chicago Press.

———. 1927. *Lawyers and Litigants in Ancient Athens.* Chicago: University of Chicago Press.

Brunt, P. A. 1976. The Romanization of the Local Ruling Classes in the Roman Empire. Pp. 161–173 in *Assimilation et Resistance a la Culture Greco-Romaine dans le Monde Ancien: Travaux du VI Congres International d'Etudes Classiques.* Paris: Editura Academiei.

Buck, Robert J. 1983. *Agriculture and Agricultural Practice in Roman Law.* Historia Einzelschriften, no. 45. Wiesbaden: Franz Steiner.

Butts, James R. 1986. *The Progymnasmata of Theon. A New Text with Translation and Commentary.* Ph.D. Diss., Claremont Graduate School.

Cadbury, H. J. 1937. Rebuttal, A Submerged Motif in the Gospels. Pp. 99–108 in *Quantulacumque.* Edited by R. P. Casey and Silva Lake. London: Christophers.

Callan, Terrence. 1987. Competition and Boasting: Toward a Psychological Portrait of Paul. *Journal of Religious Studies* 13:27–35.

———. 1990. *Psychological Perspectives on the Life of Paul: An Application of the Methodology of Gerd Theissen.* Lewiston, N.Y.: Edwin Mellen.

Collins, John N. 1990. *Diakonia. Re-interpreting the Ancient Sources.* Oxford: Oxford University Press.

Corley, Kathleen E. 1993. *Private Women. Public Meals. Social Conflict in the Synoptic Tradition.* Peabody, Mass.: Hendrickson.

Couissin, J. 1953. Suétone physiognomoniste dans les Vies des XII Césars. *Revue des Études Latins* 31:239–45.

Cox, Patricia. 1983. *Biography in Late Antiquity: A Quest for the Holy Man.* Berkeley, Calif.: University of California Press.

Dahl, Nils A. 1976. *Jesus in the Memory of the Early Church.* Minneapolis: Augsburg Publishing House.

De Fraine, Jean. 1965. *Adam and the Family of Man.* Translated by Daniel Raible. Staten Island, N.Y.: Alba House.

Demand, Nancy. 1994. *Birth, Death, and Motherhood in Classical Greece.* Baltimore: Johns Hopkins University Press.

Doohan, Helen. 1984. *Leadership in Paul.* Wilmington, Del.: Michael Glazier.

———. 1989. *Paul's Vision of Church.* Wilmington, Del.: Michael Glazier.

Duby, Georges, and Philippe Braunstein. 1988. The Emergence of the Individual. Pp. 507–630 in *A History of Private Life: II. Revelations of the Medieval World.* Edited by Georges Duby and translated by Arthur Goldhammer. Cambridge, Mass.: Belknap Press.

Dungan, David L., and David R. Cartlidge. 1974. *Sourcebook of Texts for the Comparative Study of the Gospels.* Missoula, Mont.: Scholars Press.

Dunn, James D. G. 1983. The Incident at Antioch (Gal. 2:11–14). *Journal for the Study of the New Testament* 18:3–57.

———. 1985. Once More—Gal 1:18: *Historêsai Kêphan:* In Reply to Otfried Hofius. *Zeitschrift für die Neutestamentliche Wissenschaft* 76:138–39.

Dupont, Jacques. 1967. *Etudes sur les Actes des Apotres.* Paris: Cerf.

Elliott, John H. 1986. 1 Peter, Its Situation and Strategy: A Discussion with David Balch. Pp. 61–78 in *Perspectives on First Peter.* Edited by Charles H. Talbert. Macon, Ga.: Mercer University Press.

———. 1987. Patronage and Clientilism in Early Christian Society. *Forum* 3/4:39–48.

———. 1990. Paul, Galatians and the Evil Eyes. *Currents in Theology and Mission* 17:262–73.

———. 1993. *What is Social-Science Criticism?* Guides to Biblical Scholarship. Minneapolis: Fortress Press.

———. 1994. The Evil Eye and the Sermon on the Mount: Contours of a Pervasive Belief in Social Scientific Perspective. *Biblical Interpretation* 2:51–84.

Esler, Philip. 1987. *Community and Gospel in Luke Acts. The Social and Political Motivations of Lucan Theology.* Society of New Testament Studies Monograph Series 57. Cambridge: Cambridge University Press.

Evans, Elizabeth C. 1935. Roman Descriptions of Personal Appearance in History and Biography. *Harvard Studies in Classical Philology* 46:43–84.

———. 1941. The Study of Physiognomy in the Second Century A.D. *American Philological Association Transactions and Proceedings* 72:96–108.

———. 1945. Galen the Physician as Physiognomist. *American Philological Association Transactions and Proceedings* 76:287–98.

———. 1950. Physiognomics in the Roman Empire. *Classical Journal* 45:277–82.

———. 1969. *Physiognomics in the Ancient World.* Transactions of the American Philosophical Society 59, no. 5. Philadelphia: American Philosophical Society.

Fitzgerald, John T. 1988. *Cracks in the Earthen Vessel. An Examination of the Catalogues of Hardships in the Corinthian Correspondence.* Society of Biblical Literature Dissertation Series 99. Atlanta: Scholars Press.

Fitzmyer, Joseph A. 1994. *Scripture: The Soul of Theology.* New York: Paulist Press.

Foerster, Richard. 1893. *Scriptores physiognomonici Graeci et Latini.* 2 Vols. Leipzig: Teubner.

Foerster, Werner. 1971. *Eusebês. Theological Dictionary of the New Testament* 7:175–85.

Foster, George. 1961. The Dyadic Contract: A Model for the Social Structure of a Mexican Peasant Village. *American Anthropologist* 63:1173–92.

Gamson, William A. 1992. The Social Psychology of Collective Action. Pp. 53–76 in *Frontiers in Social Movement Theory*. Edited by Aldon D. Morris and Carol McClurg Mueller, New Haven, Conn.: Yale University Press.

Geertz, Clifford. 1976. "From the Native's Point of View": On the Nature of Anthropological Understanding. Pp. 221–37 in *Meaning and Anthropology*. Edited by Keith H. Basso and Henry A. Selby. Albuquerque, N. Mex.: University of New Mexico Press.

Gigerenzer, Gerd et al. 1989. *The Empire of Change: How Probability Changed Science and Everyday Life*. Cambridge: Cambridge University Press.

Gilchrist, J. M. 1967. On What Charge Was St. Paul Brought to Rome? *Expository Times* 78:264–66.

Goitein, S. D. 1988. *A Mediterranean Society: The Jewish Communities of the Arab World as Portrayed in the Documents of the Cairo Geniza. Vol 5: The Individual*. Berkeley, Calif.: University of California Press.

Grant, Robert M. 1982. The Description of Paul in the Acts of Paul and Thecla. *Vigiliae Christianae* 36:1–4.

Greenidge, A.H.J. 1901. *The Legal Procedure of Cicero's Time*. Oxford: Clarendon Press.

Guiraud, Charles, ed. and trans. 1985. *Varron: Économie rurale*. Vol. 2. Paris: Belles Lettres.

Hall, Edward T. 1959. *The Silent Language*. Garden City, N.Y.: Doubleday & Co.

Hall, Robert C. 1987. The Rhetorical Outline for Galatians. A Reconsideration. *Journal of Biblical Literature* 106:277–87.

Hanson, K. C. 1989. The Herodians and Mediterranean Kinship. Part I: Genealogy and Descent. *Biblical Theology Bulletin* 19:75–84.

———. 1993. Progress Orientation. Pp. 142–47 in *Biblical Social Values and Their Meanings. A Handbook*. Edited by John J. Pilch and Bruce J. Malina. Peabody, Mass.: Hendrickson.

———. 1996. Transformed on the Mountain: Ritual Analysis and the Gospel of Matthew. *Semeia*. Forthcoming.

Harré, Rom. 1980. *Social Being: A Theory for Social Psychology*. Totowa, N.J.: Rowman & Littlefield.

———. 1984. *Personal Being: A Theory for Individual Psychology*. Cambridge, Mass.: Harvard University Press.

———. 1989. The "Self" as a Theoretical Concept. Pp. 387–417 in *Relativism: Interpretation and Confrontation*. Edited by Michael Krausz. Notre Dame, Ind.: University of Notre Dame Press.

Harris, Grace Gredys. 1989. Concepts of Individual, Self, and Person in Description and Analysis. *American Anthropologist* 91:599–612.

Harris, Philip, and Robert Moran. 1987. Doing Business with Middle Easterners. Pp. 466–478 in *Managing Cultural Differences*. Houston: Gulf.

Harvey, A. E. 1976. *Jesus on Trial*. Atlanta: John Knox Press.

Hester, John. 1984. The Rhetorical Structure of Galatians 1:11–2:14. *Journal of Biblical Literature* 103:223–33.

Hock, Ronald, and Edward N. O'Neil. 1986. *The Chreia in Ancient Rhetoric. Vol 1: The Progymnasmata.* Atlanta: Scholars Press.

Hofius, Otfried. 1984. Gal 1:18: *Historêsai Kêphan. Zeitschrift für die Neutestamentliche Wissenschaft* 75:73–85.

Horsley, Richard A., and John S. Hanson. 1985. *Bandits, Prophets, and Messiahs: Popular Movements at the Time of Jesus.* Minneapolis: Winston Press.

Hsu, Francis L. K. 1983. The Cultural Problem of the Cultural Anthropologist. Pp. 420–38 in *Rugged Individualism Reconsidered: Essays in Psychological Anthropology.* Knoxville, Tenn.: University of Tennessee Press.

Hubbard, Benjamin J. 1978. The Role of Commissioning Accounts in Acts. Pp. 187–98 in *Perspectives on Luke-Acts.* Edited by Charles H. Talbert. Danville, Va.: Association of Baptist Professors of Religion.

Hui, C. Harry, and Harry C. Triandis. 1986. Individualism-Collectivism. A Study of Cross-Cultural Researchers. *Journal of Cross-Cultural Psychology* 17:225–48.

Hui, C. Harry, and Marcelo J. Villareal. 1989. Individualism-Collectivism and Psychological Needs. Their Relationships in Two Cultures. *Journal of Cross-Cultural Psychology* 20:310–23.

Inkeles, Alex, and Daniel J. Levinson. 1954. National Character: The Study of Modal Personality and Sociocultural Systems. Pp. 977–1020 in *Handbook of Social Psychology. Vol. 2: Special Fields and Applications.* Edited by Gardner Lindzey. Reading, Mass.: Addison-Wesley Publishing Co.

John Paul II. 1993. Encyclical *Veritatis Splendor. Origins* 23/18:297–334.

———. 1995. Encyclical *Evangelium Vitae. Origins* 24/42:689–727.

Judge, E. A. 1980. The Social Identity of the First Christians: A Question of Method in Religious History. *Journal of Religious History* 11:201–17.

Kennedy, George A. 1972. *The Art of Rhetoric in the Roman World.* Princeton, N.J.: Princeton University Press.

———. 1994. *A New History of Classical Rhetoric.* Princeton, N.J.: Princeton University Press.

Kluckhohn, F. R., and F. L. Strodtbeck. 1961. *Variations in Value Orientation.* New York: Harper & Row.

Kurz, William S. 1980. Hellenistic Rhetoric and the Christological Proof of Luke-Acts. *Catholic Biblical Quarterly* 42:171–95.

Lévy-Bruhl, Lucien. 1923. *The Notebooks on Primitive Mentality.* Translated by Peter Riviere. Preface by Maurice Leenhardt. 1975. Reprint, New York: Harper & Row.

———. 1926. *How Natives Think.* Translated by Lilian A. Clare. 1979. Reprint, New York: Arno Press.

Liddel, Henry George, and Robert Scott. 1968. *A Greek-English Lexicon.* 9th ed. Revised and augmented by Henry Stuart Jones. Oxford: Clarendon Press.

Lloyd, G.E.R. 1964. The Hot and the Cold, The Dry and the Wet in Greek Philosophy. *Journal of Hellenic Studies* 84:92–106.

Lohfink, G. 1976. *The Conversion of St. Paul.* Translated by Bruce J. Malina. Chicago: Franciscan Herald.

Lösch, Stephan. 1931. Die Dankesrede des Tertullus: Apg 24, 1–4. *Theologische Quartalschrift* 112:295–319.

Lutz, Catherine. 1986. The Anthropology of Emotions. *Annual Review of Anthropology* 15:405–36.

Lyons, George. 1985. *Pauline Autobiography. Toward a New Understanding.* SBL Dissertation Series 73. Atlanta: Scholars Press.

Magie, David. 1950. *Roman Rule in Asia Minor, to the End of the Third Century after Christ.* 2 Vols. Princeton, N.J.: Princeton University Press.

Malherbe, Abraham J. 1986. A Physical Description of Paul. *Harvard Theological Review* 79:170–75.

Malina, Bruce J. 1978. Freedom: The Theological Dimensions of a Symbol. *Biblical Theology Bulletin* 8:62–76.

———. 1986a. *Christian Origins and Cultural Anthropology: Practical Models for Biblical Interpretation.* Atlanta: John Knox Press.

———. 1986b. The Received View and What It Cannot Do. Pp. 171–94 in *Social-Scientific Criticism of the New Testament and Its Social World.* Edited by John H. Elliott. *Semeia* 35.

———. 1986c. Religion in the World of Paul: A Preliminary Sketch. *Biblical Theology Bulletin* 16:92–101.

———. 1988a. A Conflict Approach to Mark 7. *Forum* 4/3:2–30.

———. 1988b. Patron and Client. The Analogy Behind Synoptic Theology. *Forum* 4/1:2–32.

———. 1989. Christ and Time: Swiss or Mediterranean? *Catholic Biblical Quarterly* 51:1–31.

———. 1991a. Interpretation: Reading, Abduction, Metaphor." Pp. 253–66 in *The Bible and the Politics of Exegesis: Essays in Honor of Norman K. Gottwald on His Sixty-Fifth Birthday.* Edited by David Jobling, Peggy L. Day, and Gerald T. Sheppard. Cleveland: Pilgrim Press.

———. 1991b. Reading Theory Perspective: Reading Luke-Acts. Pp. 3–23 in *The Social World of Luke-Acts: Models for Interpretation.* Edited by Jerome H. Neyrey. Peabody, Mass.: Hendrickson.

———. 1992. Is There a Circum-Mediterranean Person? Looking for Stereotypes. *Biblical Theology Bulletin* 22:66–87.

———. 1993a. Apocalyptic and Territoriality. Pp. 369–80 in *Early Christianity in Context: Monuments and Documents. Essays in Honour of Emmanuel Testa.* Edited by Frederic Manns and Eugenio Alliata. Jerusalem: Franciscan Printing.

———. 1993b. *The New Testament World: Insights from Cultural Anthropology.* Rev. ed. Louisville, Ky.: Westminster/John Knox Press.

———. 1993c. *Windows on the World of Jesus: Time Travel to Ancient Judea.* Louisville, Ky.: Westminster/John Knox Press.

———. 1994a. Establishment Violence in the New Testament World. *Scriptura* 51:51–78.

———. 1994b. "Let Him Deny Himself" (Mark 8:34//): A Social Psychological Model of Self-Denial. *Biblical Theology Bulletin* 24:106–19.

———. 1994c. Religion in the Imagined New Testament World: More Social Science Lenses. *Scriptura* 51:1–26.

———. 1995a. *On the Genre and Message of Revelation: Star Visions and Sky Journeys.* Peabody, Mass.: Hendrickson.

————. 1995b. Power, Pain and Personhood: Asceticism in the Ancient Mediterranean World. Pp. 162–77 in *Ascetism*. Edited by Vincent L. Wimbush and Richard Valantasis. New York: Oxford University Press.

Malina, Bruce J., and Jerome H. Neyrey. 1988. *Calling Jesus Names*. Sonoma, Calif.: Polebridge Press.

————. 1991a. First-Century Personality: Dyadic Not Individualistic. Pp. 67–96 in *The Social World of Luke-Acts: Models for Biblical Interpretation*. Edited by Jerome H. Neyrey. Peabody, Mass.: Hendrickson.

————. 1991b. Honor and Shame in Luke-Acts: Pivotal Values of the Mediterranean World. Pp. 25–65 in *The Social World of Luke-Acts: Models for Biblical Interpretation*. Edited by Jerome H. Neyrey. Peabody, Mass.: Hendrickson.

Malina, Bruce J., and Richard L. Rohrbaugh. 1992. *Social-Science Commentary on the Synoptic Gospels*. Minneapolis: Fortress Press.

Mann, Michael. 1986. *The Sources of Social Power: Vol. 1: A History of Power from the Beginning to A.D. 1760*. Cambridge: Cambridge University Press.

Marrou, Henri Irenee. 1964. *A History of Education in Antiquity*. Translated by George Lamb. New York: New American Library.

Marshall, Peter. 1987. *Enmity in Corinth: Social Conventions in Paul's Relations with the Corinthians*. WUNT 2.23. Tübingen: J.C.B. Mohr.

Martin, Dale B. 1990. *Slavery as Salvation. The Metaphor of Slavery in Pauline Christianity*. New Haven, Conn.: Yale University Press.

Martin, Luther H. 1994. The Anti-Individualistic Ideology of Hellenistic Culture. *Numen* 41:117–40.

Meeks, Wayne A. 1983. *The First Urban Christians: The Social World of the Apostle Paul*. New Haven, Conn.: Yale University Press.

————. 1986. *The Moral World of the First Christians*. Library of Early Christianity. Philadelphia: Westminster Press.

————. 1993. *The Origins of Christian Morality: The First Two Centuries*. New Haven, Conn.: Yale University Press.

Miller, Stephen G. 1991. *Gymnasium,* Athletics, and Education. Pp. 121–50 in *Arete: Greek Sports from Ancient Sources*. 2d and expanded edition. Berkeley, Calif.: University of California Press.

Moore, George Foot. 1927–30. *Judaism in the First Centuries of the Christian Era: The Age of the Tannaim*. 3 Vols. Cambridge, Mass.: Harvard University Press.

Moulton, James H., and George Milligan. 1930. *The Vocabulary of the Greek Testament*. 1976. Reprint, Grand Rapids, Mich.: Wm. B. Eerdmans Publishing Co.

Murphy-O'Connor, Jerome. 1984. The Corinth That Saint Paul Saw. *Biblical Archaeologist* 47:147–59.

Nadeau, Ray. 1952. The Progymnasmata of Aphthonius in Translation. *Speech Monographs* 19:264–85.

Neusner, Jacob. 1976. "First Cleanse the Inside." The "Halakhic" Background of a Controversy Saying. *New Testament Studies* 22:486–95.

————. 1990. *The Economics of the Mishnah*. Chicago: University of Chicago Press.

Neyrey, Jerome H. 1986a. Body Language in 1 Corinthians: The Use of Anthropological Models for Understanding Paul and His Opponents. Pp. 129–70 in *Social-Scientific Criticism of the New Testament and Its Social World.* Edited by John H. Elliott. *Semeia* 35.

———. 1986b. The Idea of Purity in Mark. Pp. 91–128 in *Social-Scientific Criticism of the New Testament and Its Social World.* Edited by John H. Elliott. *Semeia* 35.

———. 1986c. Witchcraft Accusations in 2 Cor. 10—13: Paul in Social-Science Perspective. *Listening* 21:160–71.

———. 1988a. Bewitched in Galatia: Paul and Cultural Anthropology. *Catholic Biblical Quarterly* 50:72–100.

———. 1988b. *An Ideology of Revolt: John's Christology in Social-Science Perspective.* Philadelphia: Fortress Press.

———. 1988c. A Symbolic Approach to Mark 7. *Forum* 4/3:63–92.

———. 1990a. Acts 17, Epicureans, and Theodicy. A Study in Stereotypes. Pp. 118–34 in *Greeks, Romans and Christians.* Edited by David Balch, Everett Ferguson, and Wayne Meeks. Minneapolis: Fortress Press.

———. 1990b. *Paul in Other Words: A Cultural Reading of His Letters.* Louisville, Ky.: Westminster/John Knox Press.

———. 1991. The Symbolic Universe of Luke-Acts: They Turn the World Upside Down. Pp. 271–304 in *The Social World of Luke-Acts: Models for Interpretation.* Edited by Jerome H. Neyrey. Peabody, Mass.: Hendrickson.

———. 1993. *2 Peter, Jude.* Anchor Bible 37C. New York: Doubleday.

———. 1994a. Josephus' *VITA* and the Encomium: A Native Model of Personality. *Journal for the Study of Judaism* 25:177–206.

———. 1994b. "What's Wrong with This Picture?" John 4, Cultural Stereotypes of Women, and Public and Private Space. *Biblical Theology Bulletin* 24: 77–91.

———. 1995. The Footwashing in John 13:6–11: Transformation Ritual or Ceremony? Pp. 178–213 in *The Social World of the First Christians.* Edited by L. Michael White and O. Larry Yarbrough. Minneapolis: Fortress Press.

Ogbu, John U. 1981. Origins of Human Competence: A Cultural-Ecological Perspective. *Child Development* 52:413–29.

Osiek, Carolyn. 1993. Self-Sacrifice. Pp. 157–58 in *Biblical Social Values and Their Meanings. A Handbook.* Edited by John J. Pilch and Bruce J. Malina. Peabody, Mass.: Hendrickson.

O'Toole, Robert J. 1978. *The Christological Climax of Paul's Defense.* Analecta Biblica 78. Rome: Pontifical Biblical Institute.

Papajohn, John, and John Spiegel. 1975. *Transactions in Families.* San Francisco: Jossey-Bass.

Patterson, Orlando. 1982. *Slavery and Social Death.* Cambridge, Mass.: Harvard University Press.

Perry, Ben E. 1964. *Secundus the Silent Philosopher.* APA Monographs, 22. Ithaca, N.Y.: The American Philological Association and Cornell University Press.

Pilch, John J. 1988. A Structural Functional Analysis of Mark 7. *Forum* 4:31–62.

———. 1992. Lying and Deceit in the Letters to the Seven Churches: Perspectives from Cultural Anthropology. *Biblical Theology Bulletin* 22:126–35.

———. 1993a. "Beat His Ribs While He Is Young" (Sir. 30:12). A Window on the Mediterranean World. *Biblical Theology Bulletin* 23:101–13.

————. 1993b. Visions in Revelation and Alternate Consciousness: A Perspective from Cultural Anthropology. *Listening* 28:231–44.

————. 1995. The Transfiguration of Jesus: An Experience of Alternate Reality. Pp. 47–64 in *Modelling Early Christianity: Social-Scientific Studies of the New Testament in Its Context.* Edited by Philip F. Esler. London: Routledge.

Pilch, John J., and Bruce J. Malina, eds. 1993. *Biblical Social Values and Their Meanings. A Handbook.* Peabody, Mass.: Hendrickson.

Prochaska, James. 1979. *Systems of Psychotherapy: A Transtheoretical Analysis.* Homewood, Ill.: Dorsey.

Räisänen, Heikki. 1986. *The Torah and Christ: Essays in German and English on the Problem of the Law in Early Christianity.* Suomen Eksegeettisen Seuran Julkaisuja 45. Helsinki: The Finnish Exegetical Society.

Ricciotti, Giuseppe. 1953. *Paul the Apostle.* Translated by Alba I. Zizzamia. Milwaukee, Wis.: Bruce.

Robinson. H. Wheeler. 1936. *Corporate Personality in Ancient Israel.* Rev. ed. with introduction by Gene M. Tucker. 1980. Reprint, Philadelphia: Fortress Press.

Rohrbaugh, Richard L. 1991a. The City in the Second Testament. *Biblical Theology Bulletin* 21:67–75.

————. 1991b. The Pre-industrial City in Luke-Acts: Urban Social Relations. Pp. 125–49 in *The Social World of Luke-Acts. Models for Interpretation.* Edited by Jerome H. Neyrey. Peabody, Mass.: Hendrickson.

Russell, D. A., and N. G. Wilson, ed. and trans. 1981. *Diairesis Ton Epideiktikon.* New York: Oxford University Press.

Sampley, J. Paul. 1977. *Societas Christis:* Roman Law and Paul's Conception of the Christian Community. Pp. 158–74 in *God's Christ and His People.* Edited by W. A. Meeks and J. Jervell. Oslo: University of Oslo.

————. 1980. *Pauline Partnership in Christ. Christian Community and Commitment in Light of Roman Law.* Philadelphia: Fortress Press.

Sattler, W. M. 1957. Conceptions of Ethos in Ancient Rhetoric. *Speech Monographs* 14:55–65.

Schlier, H. 1965. *Idiotes. Theological Dictionary of the New Testament* 3:215–16.

Schneemelcher, Wilhelm, ed. 1992. *New Testament Apocrypha.* Vol. 2. *Writings Relating to the Apostles; Apocalypses and Related Subjects.* Translated by R. McL. Wilson. Louisville, Ky.: Westminster/John Knox Press.

Schwartz, Shalom H. 1990. Individualism-Collectivism. Critique and Proposed Refinements. *Journal of Cross-Cultural Psychology* 21:139–57.

Seelye, H. Ned. 1985. *Teaching Culture: Strategies for Intercultural Communication.* Lincolnwood, Ill.: National Textbook Co.

Seland, Torrey. 1995. *Establishment Violence in Philo and Luke: Non-Conformity to the Torah and Jewish Vigilante Reactions.* Biblical Interpretation Studies 15. Leiden: Brill.

Selby, Henry. 1974. *Zapotec Deviance.* Austin, Tex. : University of Texas Press.

Sherwin-White, A. N. 1963. *Roman Society and Roman Law in the New Testament.* Oxford: Oxford University Press.

Smith, Jonathan Z. 1980. Fences and Neighbors: Some Contours of Early Judaism. Pp. 1–26 in *Approaches to Ancient Judaism: Studies in Judaism and Its Greco-Roman Context.* Vol. 2. Edited by William Green. Brown Judaic Studies 9. Chico, Calif.: Scholars Press.

Smith, M. Brewster. 1978. Perspectives on Selfhood. *American Psychologist* 33:1053–63.

Stannard, David E. 1980. *Shrinking History: On Freud and the Failure of Psychohistory.* New York: Oxford University Press.

Stendahl, Krister. 1963. The Apostle Paul and the Introspective Conscience of the West. *Harvard Theological Review* 56:199–215. 1976. Reprinted in *Paul Among Jews and Gentiles and Other Essays.* Philadelphia: Fortress Press.

Strathmann, H. 1967. *Martys. Theological Dictionary of the New Testament* 4:474–514.

Stuart, Duane R. 1928. *Epochs of Greek and Roman Biography.* Berkeley, Calif.: University of California Press.

Swarney, Paul R. 1993. Social Status and Social Behaviour as Criteria in Judicial Proceedings in the Late Republic. Pp. 137–55 in *Law, Politics and Society in the Ancient Mediterranean World.* Edited by Baruch Halpern and Deborah W. Hobson. Sheffield, Wis.: Sheffield Academic Press.

Terrien, Samuel. 1970. The Omphalos Myth and Hebrew Religion. *Vetus Testamentum* 20:315–38.

Theissen, Gerd. 1987. *Psychological Aspects of Pauline Theology.* Translated by John P. Galvin. Philadelphia: Fortress Press.

Tresmontant, Claude. 1960. *A Study of Hebrew Thought.* Translated by Michael Francis Gibson. New York: Desclee.

Triandis, Harry C. 1990. Cross-Cultural Studies of Individualism and Collectivism. Pp. 41–133 in *Nebraska Symposium on Motivation 1989: Cross-Cultural Perspectives.* Edited by John J. Berman. Lincoln, Nebr.: University of Nebraska Press.

Triandis, Harry C. *et al.* 1993. An Etic-Emic Analysis of Individualism and Collectivism. *Journal of Cross-Cultural Psychology* 24:366–83.

Trites, A. A. 1974. The Importance of Legal Scenes and Language in the Book of Acts. *Novum Testamentum* 15:278–84.

———. 1977. *The New Testament Concept of Witness.* Cambridge: Cambridge University Press.

Tuan, Yi-Fu. 1977. *Space and Place: The Perspective of Experience.* Minneapolis: University of Minnesota Press.

Ulrichs, Karl Friedrich. 1990. Grave Verbum, ut de re magna: Nochmals Gal 1:18: *Historêsai Kêphan. Zeitschrift für die Neutestamentliche Wissenschaft* 81:262–69.

Vanhoye, Albert. 1986. Personnalité de Paul et exégèse paulinienne. Pp. 3–35 in *L'apôtre Paul: Personnalité. style et Conception du ministére.* Edited by Albert Vanhoye. Leuven: Leuven University/Peeters.

Vatican II. 1966. Dei verbum. No. 12 in *Documents of Vatican II.* Edited by Walter M. Abbott. New York: Guild Press *et al.*

Veltman, Frederick. 1975. *The Defense Speeches of Paul in Acts.* Th.D. diss. Graduate Theological Union.

————. 1978. The Defense Speeches of Paul in Acts. Pp. 243–56 in *Perspectives on Luke-Acts*. Edited by Charles H. Talbert. Danville, Va.: Association of Baptist Professors of Religion.

Veyne, Paul. 1987. *A History of Private Life: From Pagan Rome to Byzantium*. Translated by Arthur Goldhammer. Cambridge, Mass.: Belknap.

————. 1989. "Humanitas": Romani e no[i]. Pp. 385–415 in *L'uomo Romano*. Edited by Andrea Giardina. Bari: Laterza.

Von Dobschütz, Ernst. 1928. *Der Apostel Paulus*. Halle (Saale): Buchhandlung des Waisenhauses.

Whiting, Robert. 1979. You've Gotta Have "Wa." *Sports Illustrated* (September 24, 1979):60–71.

Wikenhauser, A. 1948. Doppeltraume. *Biblica* 29:100–111.

Windisch, Hans. 1964. *Barbaros. Theological Dictionary of the New Testament* 1:546–53.

Winkes, Rolf. 1973a. Physiognômonia: Probleme der Charakterinterpretation Römischer Porträts. *Aufstieg und Niedergang der römischen Welt* 1.4:899–926.

————. 1973b. Physiognômonia: Probleme der Charakterinterpretation Römischer Porträts. *Aufstieg und Niedergang der römischen Welt* 1.4 (Tafeln):217–42.

Woodson, Linda. 1979. *A Handbook of Modern Rhetorical Terms*. Urbana, Ill.: National Council of Teachers of English.

Wooten, Cecil. 1987. *Hermogenes' on Types of Style*. Chapel Hill, N.C.: University of North Carolina Press.

Index of Scripture and Other Ancient Sources

OLD TESTAMENT

ANCIENT SOURCES

The standard abbreviations of works of classical authors are taken from the introduction to the *Oxford Classical Dictionary*.

Index of Authors

Index of Subjects